Literary Lives

General Editor: **Richard Dutton**, Professor of English, Lancaster University

This series offers stimulating accounts of the literary careers of the most admired and influential English-language authors. Volumes follow the outline of the writers' working lives, not in the spirit of traditional biography, but aiming to trace the professional, publishing and social contexts which shaped their writing.

Published titles include:

John Williams
MARY SHELLEY

Michael O'Neill
PERCY BYSSHE SHELLEY

Gary Waller
EDMUND SPENSER

Tony Sharpe
WALLACE STEVENS

Joseph McMinn
JONATHAN SWIFT

Leonée Ormond
ALFRED TENNYSON

Peter Shillingsburg
WILLIAM MAKEPEACE THACKERAY

David Wykes
EVELYN WAUGH

John Mepham
VIRGINIA WOOLF

John Williams
WILLIAM WORDSWORTH

Alasdair D. F. Macrae
W. B. YEATS

Literary Lives
Series Standing Order ISBN 0–333–71486–5 hardcover
Series Standing Order ISBN 0–333–80334–5 paperback
(*outside North America only*)

You can receive future titles in this series as they are published by placing a standing order. Please contact your bookseller or, in case of difficulty, write to us at the address below with your name and address, the title of the series and one of the ISBNs quoted above.

Customer Services Department, Macmillan Distribution Ltd, Houndmills, Basingstoke, Hampshire RG21 6XS, England

F. Scott Fitzgerald

A Literary Life

Andrew Hook
Emeritus Bradley Professor of English Literature
University of Glasgow

First published 2002 by
PALGRAVE MACMILLAN
Houndmills, Basingstoke, Hampshire RG21 6XS and
175 Fifth Avenue, New York, N.Y. 10010
Companies and representatives throughout the world

PALGRAVE MACMILLAN is the new global academic imprint of the Palgave Macmillan division of St. Martin's Press, LLC and of Palgrave Macmillan Ltd. Macmillan® is a registered trademark in the United States, United Kingdom and other countries. Palgrave is a registered trademark in the European Union and other countries.

ISBN 0–333–73848–9 hardback
ISBN 0–333–73849–7 paperback

This book is printed on paper suitable for recycling and made from fully managed and sustained forest sources.

A catalogue record for this book is available from the British Library.

Library of Congress Cataloging-in-Publication Data
Hook, Andrew.
   F. Scott Fitzgerald: a literary life / Andrew Hook.
      p. cm.-- (Literary lives)
   Includes bibliographical references and index.
   ISBN 0-333-73848-9
      1. Fitzgerald, F. Scott (Francis Scott), 1896-1940. 2. Authors, American--20th century--Biography. I. Title: Francis Scott Fitzgerald. II. Title. III. Literary lives (Palgrave (Firm))
   PS3511.I9 Z664 2002
   813'.52--dc21
   [B]   2002022012

10   9   8   7   6   5   4   3   2   1
11   10   09   08   07   06   05   04   03   02

Printed and bound in Great Britain by
Antony Rowe Ltd, Chippenham and Eastbourne

In memoriam

Robin Gilmour

(1943–99)

Contents

Preface

Some authors do actually lead two quite separate lives: a life as a writer on the one hand, and a life as something else – adventurer, traveller, professional person, husband, wife, mother, the possibilities are limitless – on the other. The gap between two such lives can sometimes appear unbridgeable: one thinks of Wallace Stevens, at once Vice-President of the Hartford Indemnity Insurance Company, organizing the travel insurance of herds of cattle for ranchers in Texas or Kansas, and simultaneously the poet of the incomparably unfettered imagination; or, more mundanely, of Anthony Trollope, maintaining an extraordinarily prolific output of works of fiction, while still carrying out his duties as a senior official in the British postal service. But for another category of authors, the distinction between their literary lives and the rest of their experience is much more difficult to draw. Not simply in the sense that for a full-time professional writer there is no other job to be done, though inevitably that kind of professionalism (to which Scott Fitzgerald was dedicated) does make a difference. More interesting is the case of those writers whose own everyday life and routine experience become the starting-point of all that they create. For them what they experience and what they imagine interpenetrate so far that the difference between them is sometimes scarcely distinguishable. One suspects that there have been few writers who in their creative lives never draw upon personal experience, but of course there have been many whose debt to their own lives is no more than limited, fitful, or superficial. Perhaps a kind of norm in this area is provided by Charlotte Brontë's remark that she allowed experience to suggest, never to dictate. But just as Stevens and Trollope exemplify the extreme position of writers whose literary and personal lives seem to have nothing in common, so there are writers on the other side for whom the distinction between the two lives seems to disappear completely: writers for whom the personal life is the literary life. Fitzgerald is such an author. As the years of his professional life passed, he appears to have turned more and more to every detail of his own life to find the ground material for his writing. The narrative of his life becomes increasingly the narrative of his art. If on occasion that narrative has no story to tell, then he will write about having no story to tell.

For the writer of Scott Fitzgerald's literary life there is then an obvious problem. If his life and his art so interpenetrate, is there anything at all in his life that is irrelevant? What aspect of his life can be justifiably ignored? If the autobiographical element is so central to his fiction is not his biography also his literary biography? There are no simple answers to these questions. In what follows no doubt I shall include material that some would have left out while excluding what others would have kept in. But my aim is to resolve the issue by recognizing its significance. That is, that the literary biographer's problem of deciding what does or does not belong to a study of Fitzgerald's literary life is no more than a pale reflection of Fitzgerald's own abiding problem over the relationship between his life and his art. For him the problem was not about discriminating between the two but of trying to reconcile the demands and needs of the one with the demands and needs of the other. Could the life of the writer-artist be successfully integrated with the life of the man (lover, husband, father, friend)? Or are there duties and responsibilities belonging to the one that are almost incompatible with the demands of the other? It is because Fitzgerald struggled often unsuccessfully, but more and more consciously, to find answers to such questions that an element of undecidability has to remain present in any accounting of the kinds of material relevant to his literary life.

Acknowledgements

Any book concerning the life of Scott Fitzgerald inevitably builds upon the work of his many previous biographers. This book is no exception. Like other Fitzgerald scholars, I wish in particular to acknowledge my debt to Professor M. J. Bruccoli's monumental work both as biographer and editor. I should also like to thank Princeton University, and especially Professor Michael Wood of the English Department, for enabling me to work on my book as a Visiting Fellow in Fitzgerald's own university. Don Skemer and the staff of the Special Collections department of Princeton University Library proved unfailingly helpful and supportive. Professor T. P. Roche and Professor Hans Aarsleff of the Princeton English Department sustained me both intellectually and socially, while there was no limit to the generous hospitality I received from Barrie and Dominique Royce throughout my Princeton year. Pat Devlin and David Cunningham were of invaluable help in preparing the text for publication. This book is dedicated to the memory of Dr Robin Gilmour, a fine Victorian scholar, who more than anyone encouraged me to work and write on Fitzgerald.

List of Abbreviations

L   Andrew Turnbull (ed.), *The Letters of F. Scott Fitzgerald*, Penguin Books, London, 1968.

C   Matthew J. Bruccoli, Margaret M. Duggan (eds), *Correspondence of F. Scott Fitzgerald*, Random House, New York, 1980.

LL   Matthew J. Bruccoli (ed.), *F. Scott Fitzgerald, A Life in Letters*, Simon & Schuster, New York, 1995.

FP   John Kuehl, Jackson Bryer (eds), *Dear Scott/Dear Max, The Fitzgerald–Perkins Correspondence*, Charles Scribner's Sons, New York, 1971.

FO   Matthew J. Bruccoli (ed.), *As Ever, Scott Fitzgerald, Letters Between F. Scott Fitzgerald and His Literary Agent Harold Ober 1919–1940*, Woburn Press, London, 1973.

Spelling mistakes in Fitzgerald's letters have normally been silently corrected.

The man of letters is, in truth, ever writing his own biography.

Anthony Trollope

There never was a good biography of a good novelist.
There couldn't be. He is too many people if he's any good.

Scott Fitzgerald

1
Becoming a Writer

The language of fiction engages with different kinds of reality. In the novels and stories of Fitzgerald's great contemporaries – Hemingway, Dos Passos, Faulkner – the realities of war, violence, and what Dos Passos in a letter to Fitzgerald in 1936 called 'the murderous forces of history' loom large. For Fitzgerald, however, the reality he recognized was that defined by society. In his life and in his art Fitzgerald remained focused on the social dimension of human experience, on behaviour and manners within relatively familiar social contexts. The world beyond and outside everyday society – the world that concerned writers whom he admired such as Conrad and Hemingway – interested him less than the problems and pressures experienced by individuals within a more or less conventional social world.

What distinguishes Fitzgerald's writing style at its best is an elegant fluency sometimes combining with an almost poetic intensity. Its very texture suggests an easy social grace, as if the turns of phrase and the shaping of sentences were themselves deft social statements. What is true of the style is even more true of the subject-matter. Fitzgerald's novels and stories rarely appear to grapple with the traditional 'big' subjects: philosophy, politics, religion, world-views, etc. He himself worried about this, at least until, just before beginning to write *The Great Gatsby*, he read and digested Conrad's Preface to *The Nigger of the Narcissus* and rejoiced to realize that a great writer did not have to be a profound philosopher or original thinker. Ever afterwards Fitzgerald never wavered in his allegiance to Conrad's great statement of his artistic credo. As

1

late as 1933, in an essay for the *Saturday Evening Post*, which ends with a definition of 'the serious business' of the writing profession, he wrote:

> Joseph Conrad defined it more clearly, more vividly than any man of our time: 'My task is by the power of the written word to make you hear, to make you feel – it is, before all, to make you see.'[1]

Much earlier, in April 1920, just after the publication of his first novel, *This Side of Paradise*, Fitzgerald produced a self-interview for Scribners, his New York publishers, in the course of which he touches on the issue of literature, knowledge and big subjects – but only to concede that such concerns are not for him:

> This conscious struggle to find bigness outside, to substitute bigness of theme for bigness of perception, to create an objective *Magnum Opus* such as 'The Ring and the Book' – well, all that's the antithesis of my literary aims.[2]

Exactly as he says, bigness of perception, not bigness of theme, will always be the most striking characteristic of Fitzgerald's fiction. As a result, his creative starting-point always lies deep within the subjective self; or, as he put it quite explicitly in the same 1933 article in which he cited Conrad: 'I must start out with an emotion – one that's close to me and that I can understand.'[3]

But the emotions with which Fitzgerald starts almost invariably arise within recognizable social contexts. The novels and stories return again and again to the presentation and exploration of individual emotional states – with social interactions invariably being involved. This is why questions of social values, of the nuances of manners and speech and conduct that are integral to a character's social existence, are always close to the heart of Fitzgerald's fiction. Perhaps there was a kind of inevitability about Fitzgerald's work coming to focus so strongly on the wonderfully crafted evocation of different social worlds, and the struggle of individuals to make sense of their relationship to them. Because for him it was a personal matter; the question of his own individual social positioning, from childhood on, concerned him as nothing else did.

Perhaps it was also inevitable that the only answer to his difficulties should involve above all else his literary life. Because the childhood experiences that help to clarify the problems in Fitzgerald's social life also contain elements that point to their possible solution through his literary life.

II

Fitzgerald's family background, as the briefest of sketches makes clear, provided the future writer with a social status which, while comfortable enough by most standards, was never entirely secure. Born in 1896, Fitzgerald lived initially on the edge of the most elegant and fashionable area of the Minnesotan city of St Paul. His parents, though in no sense badly off, were not rich by the standard of many of those who lived on nearby prestigious Summit Avenue. Fitzgerald's mother did in fact come from a wealthy background: she was the daughter of an Irish immigrant who had flourished in nineteenth-century America, making a fortune in the wholesale grocery business. But Mary ('Mollie') McQuillan Fitzgerald seems to have occupied a somewhat eccentric position in well-to-do St Paul society. Reminiscing in 1975, Mrs Oscar Kalman, a lifelong friend of the Fitzgeralds, insisted that 'the Fitzgeralds certainly belonged. Molly was at every debutante ball. She went everywhere'. But Mrs Kalman goes on to confirm that Molly, though intelligent and a great reader, was decidedly eccentric and absent-minded: 'We'd meet her on the street. She might have one brown shoe and one black shoe on and a perfectly goofy hat of a vintage of twenty years before.'[4] From an early age Molly's son appears to have been made less than happy by his mother's odd behaviour. Indeed Fitzgerald's earliest surviving letter is addressed to his mother from summer camp in Ontario in 1907 – and its point seems to be to dissuade her from visiting him. As an adult Fitzgerald continued as far as possible to keep his mother out of his life – he clearly always regarded her as something of an embarrassment. But if the young Fitzgerald was dismayed by his mother's eccentric manners and style, he was impressed by those of his father. Edward Fitzgerald's origins lay in an old-established and prominent Maryland family. Pursuing a career and marrying in the North, Edward Fitzgerald always preserved something of the upper-class Southerner's traditional elegance of manners. So doing, he might indeed have provided his son with a perfectly acceptable model of behaviour. Unfortunately there was a problem. His old-fashioned, courteous, Southern style did not help Edward Fitzgerald to be a success in the thrusting Northern business world in which he soon struggled to make his living. His small wicker-furniture business failed in 1897 and he had to take a job as a grocery salesman with the Procter & Gamble company, leaving St Paul first for Buffalo in New York state, then Syracuse, then back to Buffalo. In 1908, however, he lost his job – a blow from which he never fully recovered – and the Fitzgerald family had to return to St Paul and the kind of security provided by Mollie Fitzgerald's family wealth. Now eleven years old, Scott Fitzgerald seems to have understood to some degree the significance of his father's failure. Much later he wrote that on the day he lost his job, his father went out in the morning 'a comparatively young man'; he came home that evening 'an old man, a completely broken man ... He was a failure the rest of his days.'[5] This is a verdict with which Mrs Oscar Kalman agrees. Fitzgerald's father, she remembered, 'tried different things. ... He was a failure. Molly's money supported the family.'[6] In 1908 Fitzgerald could hardly have foreseen how empty of achievement the rest of his father's life would be, but what he did understand was that his father's failure, coupled with his mother's eccentricity, did not help his own position within his circle of friends in St Paul. At the age of nine he had been prepared to dream that his true parentage was much more romantic than the facts allowed; and as he grew older he seems to have increasingly distanced himself from his failed businessman father and his socially inept mother.

At first glance, Fitzgerald's life after the 1908 return to St Paul seems to reflect the pattern of insecurity suggested by the repeated moves from one city to another. Within St Paul too, the Fitzgerald family was constantly on the move – from one rented apartment to the next. But in fact after 1908 a significant change had occurred. The different Fitzgerald homes were all within the affluent Summit Avenue area, and throughout his young adolescent years Fitzgerald was a member of a definable community and enjoyed life with a more or less permanent circle of friends. While the elder Fitzgeralds hardly participated in the social life surrounding them, their son emphatically did. Scott shared fully the life-style of the young, Summit Avenue élite. He went to the right prep school and the right, very exclusive, dancing class; he was regularly invited to parties and dances at his friends' Summit Avenue homes; he had access to the new University Club; in winter he went to bobsled parties at the Town and Country Club, and in summer sailed and swam at the nearby White Bear Yacht Club. What having a good time meant for him was exactly the same as for the other boys and girls in his circle. Thus whatever the problems at home, and however far his mother and father fell short of any kind of imaginary parental ideal, as a young boy Fitzgerald moved in the world of the socially successful and the comfortably rich.

It is then not difficult to understand that from the first Fitzgerald should have wished to secure his place in the kind of world in which he enjoyed growing up. The question was exactly how he was to do it. Obviously his family background was not going to guarantee him position and status; nor was he in a position to inherit great wealth. He needed to rely almost wholly on his own resources; he had to make his own way, his own mark. As a boy he seems to have begun by trying too hard. At St Paul's Academy, for example – the private school for boys he entered in 1908 – he acquired a reputation for bossiness, boasting, and talking too much. The school magazine for 1909 referred to him thus: 'If anybody can poison Scotty or stop his mouth in some way, the school at large and myself will be obliged.'[7] And in a pattern that would be repeated throughout his school and college career, Fitzgerald failed to distinguish himself either as a scholar or a sportsman. In 1911 the family finally decided that something had to be done about Fitzgerald's poor academic record and it was decided to send him east to the (Catholic) Newman School in Hackensack, New Jersey. Fitzgerald loved the idea of going east to prep school, but once there little went well for him. He seems to have repeated the mistakes he had made at St Paul – talking too much, boasting, failing at games, and doing poorly in his academic studies. Eventually he would admit he was the most unpopular boy of his year at the school. This time though, Fitzgerald did learn from his mistakes; his second year at the Newman School was much happier. His academic performance, however, remained modest at best, and his conditional acceptance by Princeton University – to which he was deeply attracted by its glamorous reputation – for the following year, was very much a last-minute affair.

In the autumn of 1913 Fitzgerald arrived at Princeton as determined as ever to make his mark, and be a success. In fact his Princeton years would often appear simply to repeat the pattern of his schoolboy experience. At best success would coexist with failure; at worst failure would undermine and destroy success. His dream of success on the football field would fade within days of his arrival. And his level of academic performance would be consistently disappointing: he would not in fact graduate from Princeton.

There is then more than enough biographical evidence to justify the idea that Fitzgerald's early life, for whatever reasons, was often fraught and problematic. Confirmation also occurs in Fitzgerald's own subsequent comments on his early years. In July 1933, for example, he wrote to fellow novelist John O'Hara about the inferiority complex he suffered over his social background:

> I am half black Irish and half old American stock with the usual exaggerated ancestral pretensions. The black Irish half of the family had the money and looked down upon the Maryland side of the family who had, and really had, that certain series of reticences and obligations that go under the poor old shattered word 'breeding' ... (L, 522)

And in the autobiographical essays he published in *Esquire* in 1936 (which have come to be known as *The Crack-Up*), he talked openly about his failures and disappointments at Princeton: 'There were to be no badges of pride, no medals, after all ...'[8] But Fitzgerald's own account of his early life is not limited to odd remarks or comments in letters or articles. The record is in fact a great deal richer.

Given the powerful autobiographical strain in all his fiction, no doubt it was inevitable that Fitzgerald would at some point look back at his own early experiences and imaginatively transmute them into narrative art. That time came in 1928 when he was struggling to get ahead with a novel that would hopefully consolidate the critical reputation he had finally achieved with *The Great Gatsby* three years earlier. But, as we shall see, late in the 1920s Fitzgerald was finding it increasingly difficult to reconcile the demands of his purely literary life with those of the rest of his life, and as a result progress on the new novel was slow. It seems almost with relief that he turned to the writing of a group of stories exploring his own early life for the highly lucrative market provided by the *Saturday Evening Post*. (At this stage of his career – as indeed in all its stages – Fitzgerald was constantly short of money.) Of course one cannot read the 'Basil Lee' stories as simple autobiography; they are fictions, works of the imagination, offered to the reader as nothing other. But the links between them and their author's biographical record are overwhelmingly strong. And given Fitzgerald's strengths as a writer, his ability to make you see – see how the world looked to hopeful, youthful eyes – and to make you feel – feel, for example, the sense of loss at the inevitable transience of early hopes and dreams – the stories are almost certainly a truer and more vivid record of the young author's life than any documentary evidence could provide.

The Basil Lee stories may not be the best of Fitzgerald's short fiction, but they are unquestionably absorbing and entertaining. One can well understand why Maxwell Perkins, his New York editor, should have read them with enthusiasm and urged Fitzgerald to turn them into a book. Fitzgerald, in July 1928, was inclined to do so. He wrote to Perkins indicating that he was thinking in terms of 'a nice *light* novel, almost, to follow my novel in the season *immediately* after ...' (FP, 152). But of course Fitzgerald's novel – *Tender is the Night* – would not appear until 1934, and the plan to make a book out of the Basil Lee stories never materialized. From Fitzgerald's point of view the problem with the proposal is pinpointed by the italicized adjective he uses to describe the kind of novel the stories would have made. And he is absolutely right: the Basil Lee stories are exactly 'light', and that indeed is the source of their instant charm and appeal. The evocation of Fitzgerald's childhood world and youthful experiences is deft and vivid and sometimes moving; what it is not is heavy-handed or sententious. Nothing is taken too seriously, and there are sufficient touches of irony to reassure us that the author's personal backward glance, however sympathetic, is informed by a maturer understanding.

For a reader at all familiar with the basic facts of Fitzgerald's early life, the picture that emerges of Basil Lee in these stories is instantly recognizable: the Middle West city, the prep schools, the university; the dreaming, ambitious, bossy, frustrated, agonizing young man;

the succession of beautiful, selfish, frustrating young girls. All of this material, transformed and heightened by Fitzgerald's lyrical prose, can be readily related to the biographical realities. In two different stories Basil is described as 'fiercely competitive'; his earliest dream is to 'go to Yale and be a great athlete'. In 'The Freshest Boy' Basil turns down an opportunity to leave the prep school at which he has found life so difficult because he refuses to abandon his driving ambitions: 'The conquest of the successive worlds of school, college and New York – why, that was his true dream that he had carried from boyhood into adolescence ...'[9] In 'He Thinks He's Wonderful' his aim once again is 'to be a great athlete, popular, brilliant and always happy'.[10] In 'Forging Ahead' he learns that his family's financial difficulties may mean that he will not be able to attend Yale University (in all the stories Fitzgerald substitutes Yale for Princeton). He is overwhelmed by this news; he realizes 'how many friendly and familiar dreams' are being swept away:

> Yale was the far-away East, that he had loved with a vast nostalgia since he had first read books about great cities. Beyond the dreary railroad stations of Chicago and the night fires of Pittsburgh, back in the old states, something went on that made his heart beat fast with excitement. He was attuned to the vast, breathless bustle of New York, to the metropolitan days and nights that were tense as singing wires.[11]

Such a passage works by linking the intensely personal emotion, romantic as it is, to a recognizable external reality that succeeds in universalizing it. The night fires of Pittsburgh are vivid enough, but the image of the days and nights of New York tense as singing wires beautifully matches the Conradian aesthetic.

Just occasionally, in these unpretentious, popular stories, Fitzgerald places the dreams and yearnings of his young self in the context of a vaster and less privileged reality. Summit Avenue, as the name implies, looks out from its eminence over the city of St Paul where the mass of ordinary people live. In a story called 'The Scandal Detectives' Fitzgerald describes how the special qualities of the yard of a particular house had made it a favourite playground for Basil and his circle of friends:

It had many advantages. It was large, open to the yards on both sides, and it could be entered upon skates or bicycles from the street ... there were deep shadows there all day long and ever something vague in bloom, and patient dogs around, and brown spots worn bare by countless circling wheels and dragging feet.

But this particular yard had another distinctive feature:

In sordid poverty, below the bluff two hundred feet away, lived the 'micks' – they had merely inherited the name, for they were now largely of Scandinavian descent – and when other amusements palled, a few cries were enough to bring a gang of them swarming up the hill, to be faced if numbers promised well, to be fled from into convenient houses if things went the other way.[12]

In 'He Thinks He's Wonderful' that other life – life almost literally on the other side of the tracks – is allowed once more to impinge fleetingly on Basil's youthful consciousness. At his most bossily insensitive, Basil has been haranguing a friend called Joe on his disabling lack of sophistication in dress and manners: his parents should be sure to send him east to school, he should stop wearing white ties – and, warming to his subject, Basil imagines a transformed Joe 'bursting with *savoir-faire* and irresistible to girls'. Joe halts Basil's hurtful loquaciousness by stepping outside onto his house's back porch:

The house abutted on the edge of the bluff occupied by the residential section, and the two boys stood silent for a moment, gazing at the scattered lights of the lower city. Before the mystery of the unknown human life coursing through the streets below, Basil felt the purpose of his words grow thin and pale.[13]

Such moments, acknowledging the existence of a world in which being seen to date the most beautiful girl, or failing to get in to Yale, are hardly matters of consequence, threaten to undermine the significance of Basil Lee's world. (In the parallel Josephine stories, written at this time, the references to World War I do in fact make Josephine's obsessive fascination with her young men seem merely trivial.) But here Fitzgerald's inwardness with Basil's conflicting emotions allows his character to survive its encounter with a different reality. Of course the mature Fitzgerald was infinitely more aware of that ordinary, unknown human life out there than Basil is here; but he was no more prepared to be caught up or drowned in its anonymous course than Basil would have been. For Fitzgerald the only question was exactly how he was going to be able to prevent that anonymous life overtaking him.

III

The answer was by becoming a writer. Fitzgerald would succeed, make himself known, be somebody, by becoming a writer. From the beginning that was what writing meant for Fitzgerald. The literary life alone could give him what he had always desperately craved: notice, status, success. The signs had been there all along, from childhood.

Growing up in Buffalo, Syracuse and St Paul, Fitzgerald always enjoyed reading, writing and acting. He read boys' adventure stories and historical fiction, soon including the novels of G. A. Henty, as well as Scott's *Ivanhoe* and Jane Porter's romantic account of Wallace and Bruce, *The Scottish Chiefs.* He enjoyed visits to the theatre and vaudeville shows; he liked organizing performances in which he acted with his friends; he sang, recited, and took part in school debates. He contributed to school magazines, writing news articles, stories, poems and plays. His first appearance in print came in October 1909, with the appearance of 'The Mystery of the Raymond Mortgage' in a St Paul Academy magazine called *Now and Then*. (The story title may suggest a debt to the detective fiction of Edgar Allan Poe, but the Sherlock Holmes stories of Arthur Conan Doyle are the primary source.) Three more stories followed in later issues. By 1912, according to the 'Outline Chart of my Life' in the *Ledger* that Fitzgerald began to keep at the beginning of his professional writing career, he had become 'an inveterate author and a successful, not to say brilliant debater and writer'.[14]

Of course there is nothing particularly distinctive or unusual about any of this. A great many boys and girls do the kinds of thing Fitzgerald did without ever dreaming of subsequently becoming professional writers. What appears to be different about the young Fitzgerald is the degree to which his self-esteem depended on his being seen to be successful – and the way in which writing soon became the way in which that sought-after success could be attained. The context within which this proved particularly true was that of the plays he wrote for his friends and himself to perform in St Paul between 1911 and 1914. The first of these, *The Girl from Lazy J*, was written for the organizational meeting of the Elizabethan Dramatic Club (named after its founder Elizabeth Magoffin) in August 1911. A not particularly promising one-acter, it was performed in the Magoffin house; in the following three Augusts, Fitzgerald's plays would reach a substantially larger audience.

In September 1911, Fitzgerald began his first, difficult year at the Newman School in Hackensack, New Jersey, but in the course of that year he went frequently to the theatre in New York seeing performances such as *The Quaker Girl* and *The Little Millionaire*. Back in St Paul for the 1912 summer vacation, his next play for the Elizabethan Club was *The Captured Shadow*, about a gentleman burglar. A 'Melodramatic-Comedy in Two Acts', the play was performed in the Oak Hall school for girls and the audience paid to raise money for charity. The play was judged a success and gained Fitzgerald and his actor friends much favourable publicity; the society section of local newspapers applauded both the skill of the young author and the actors' performances. The 1913 production – *Coward*, a two-act play with an American Civil War setting – was even more successful. Performed before 'a large and fashionable audience' in the downtown St Paul YWCA auditorium, its reception was such that the young cast had to put on a second show a few nights later before an audience of three hundred at the fashionable White Bear Yacht Club outside St Paul. A month later Fitzgerald began his freshman year at Princeton. Failing in his attempt to make an impact at football, he did not forget his recent theatrical success. He immediately became active in the university's Triangle Club, founded by the novelist Booth Tarkington, which each year staged an original musical comedy, with an all-male cast, which after its campus performances toured in various American cities. Fitzgerald's lyrics for the 1913–14 show were not accepted, but he helped out at the club and began working on the show for the following year. (He would receive credit for writing the lyrics for the 1914–15 *Fie! Fie! Fi-Fi!*, and may well have written most of the book as well.) Back in St Paul in the summer of 1914 he staged his final work for the Elizabethan Dramatic Club: *Assorted Spirits*, a farce in two acts. Once again the play was performed with great success both at the YWCA auditorium and at the White Bear Yacht Club. The local reviews were full of praise for Scott Fitzgerald, the seventeen-year-old playwright.

Significantly, 'The Captured Shadow' reappears in Fitzgerald's literary career as a short story in the Basil Lee series. The story is of course the story of the play's production, and the reaction of the author to the success he has achieved – including his awareness of its transience:

> Even as the crowd melted away and the last few people spoke to him and went out, he felt a great vacancy come into his heart. It was over, it was done and gone – all that work, and interest and absorption. It was a hollowness like fear.[15]

But the sense of loss, so well communicated here, does not tell the whole story. The success of the Elizabethan Club plays is unquestionably a major factor in the development of Fitzgerald's literary life. The plays had shown him what he could do. They had brought him notice. As actor, but even more as author, he had made an impact. Here at the very least was a pointer towards achieving the security and success he so desired. At Princeton his commitment to writing continued to grow. Following his successful contribution to *Fie! Fie! Fi-Fi!*, in February 1915, he was elected secretary of the Triangle Club, normally a guarantee of becoming club president – and thus a Big Man on campus – the year after. Immediately afterwards he was invited to join Cottage Club, one of the top three in the social hierarchy of undergraduate eating-clubs which were a distinctive feature of student life at Princeton. Fitzgerald seemed at last to be achieving the kind of status he longed for. By now a regular contributor to *The Tiger*, Princeton's humorous undergraduate magazine – later he would claim to have written whole issues with a friend in a single night – he agreed to collaborate with his friend Edmund Wilson on the next Triangle show. Fitzgerald wrote the lyrics, Wilson the book, for the successful 1915–16 production of *The Evil Eye*. However, towards the end of this his sophomore year at Princeton, in which Fitzgerald appeared to have achieved so much, matters began to go badly wrong for him. Neglect of his academic studies meant poor exam results: even make-up exams in some subjects were failed more than once. The result was inevitable: Fitzgerald's grades were so poor that in his junior year he became ineligible for any campus office. Thus he lost his chance to become president of the Triangle Club. Fitzgerald was devastated. As he put it much later in the first of the 'Crack-Up' essays, 'to me college would never be the same'.[16] But he did not stop writing. He wrote the lyrics for *Safety First*, the Triangle Club's 1916–17 production, but was once again ineligible for the Club's Christmas tour. In the spring of 1917, however, the direction of his writing changed significantly. Rather than the Triangle Club, he focused on the *Nassau Literary Magazine* – which he later insisted was the oldest college publication in America. Edited in Fitzgerald's time by Edmund Wilson and John Peale Bishop, both destined to be important figures in America's literary culture, the *Nassau Lit* always had more serious literary pretensions than any other student publication at Princeton. Fitzgerald's earliest contributions appeared in 1915 and 1916, but it was only in 1917 that the *Nassau Lit* became the primary outlet for his writing; in that year he contributed a playlet, five short stories, three poems and five reviews. More importantly, some at least of these contributions hint for the very first time at Fitzgerald's true potential as a writer. The poems are romantic pastiche, the reviews nondescript, but the play and the stories show much more promise: they set out themes and types of character that Fitzgerald will return to in his later writing again and again; and occasionally they contain an image or term of phrase that hints at his characteristic mature style. The St Paul plays had gained some energy and vitality through their dialogue – and a kind of undergraduate slapstick humour had prevailed over romantic sentimentality. In the *Nassau Lit* pieces character and theme become much more closely focused. 'The Debutante', the short play, provides the first example in Fitzgerald's work of the cold, beautiful, self-centred young woman whose impact on the men who love her is a destructive one. (A revised version of the piece would appear in H. L. Mencken's *The Smart Set* in 1919, and Fitzgerald would also rework it in his first novel *This Side of Paradise*.) 'Babes in the Woods', again focusing on the kind of ambiguous power exercised over men by an attractive young woman, is a neatly structured story. The writing too is sometimes deftly effective. This story would become Fitzgerald's first publication in a commercial magazine when it appeared in *The Smart Set* – and it too would appear in *This Side of Paradise*. Less successful is 'Tarquin of Cheapside' which attempts to portray Shakespeare himself as guilty of the rape that he goes on to write about in 'The Rape of Lucrece'. But Fitzgerald liked it well enough to include it in his first collection of short stories, *Tales of the Jazz Age* (1920). In 'The Spire and the Gargoyle' he confronts with some success the theme of undergraduate failure at Princeton; the young protagonist's later sense of just how much he has lost by dropping out is effectively communicated. As well as a version of its title, Fitzgerald once again used some phrases from this story in *This Side of Paradise*. The last two *Nassau Lit* stories, however, which are arguably among the best of his undergraduate writings, he strangely chose not to sell or reprint. 'The Pierian Springs and the Last Straw' is about a serious novelist who writes about women who do harm, the reason being that he had loved and idealized 'about the faultiest girl I'd ever met. She was selfish, conceited and uncontrolled ...' (Fitzgerald had met and fallen in love with Ginevra King from Lake Forest, Illinois – good-looking, wealthy, much sought after – in January 1915, and remained involved with her for almost two years. For a time the relationship seemed to flourish and they went through all the socially approved motions – attending Princeton football games and proms, meeting and dining in New York, going to the theatre – but despite being bombarded with letters from Fitzgerald, which she did not preserve, Ginevra finally dropped him for other, much wealthier, suitors. Thus Ginevra is clearly the model for these early Fitzgerald portraits of beautiful but emotionally manipulative young women.) 'The Pierian Springs' is weakened by a jokey ending, but 'Sentiment – And the Use of Rouge' still reads rather well. It concerns a young conventionally minded British officer in World War I discovering how the scale of slaughter in the war is changing the attitudes and behaviour of young women of his class at home. By June 1917, when the story was published, Fitzgerald knew that fellow-Princetonians were already dying in France, but the story still displays a surprising maturity and moral sensitivity.

Looked at together, Fitzgerald's early writings in St Paul, at the Newman School, and at Princeton have one common feature: a high success rate. The Elizabethan Club plays certainly earned him status in St Paul – and that status was reinforced when he returned home on vacation from Princeton, a leading figure in the Triangle Club. At the same time his work for the *Nassau Literary Magazine* gained him attention and respect from young men whom he admired and looked up to, such as Wilson and Bishop. However many disappointments he experienced in other areas of his life – over his family, or his own failure to become a great athlete or shine at his studies – writing at least did not let him down. Looking back on his life after he had become a professional writer, he may well have been inclined to exaggerate his early commitment to writing. In 1920, emboldened perhaps by the success of his first novel, he wrote:

> The history of my life [he was twenty-four years old] is the history of the struggle between an overwhelming urge to write and a combination of circumstances bent on keeping me from it. When I lived in St Paul and was about twelve I wrote all through every class in school in the back of my geography book and first year Latin and on the margins of themes and declensions and mathematics problems. Two years later a family congress decided that the only way to force me to study was to send me to boarding school. This was a mistake. It took my mind off my writing. I decided to play football, to smoke, to go to college, to do all sorts of irrelevant things that had nothing to do with the real business of life, which, of course, was the proper mixture of description and dialogue in the short story.[17]

Such brashness is not present in a much later passage in which Fitzgerald looks back at one of his unhappiest experiences at the Newman School and suggests how it was writing alone that offered a form of redemption:

> I remember the desolate ride in the bus back to the train and the desolate ride back to school with everybody thinking I had been yellow [in a football game] on the occasion, when actually I was just distracted and sorry for that opposing end. That's the truth. I've been afraid plenty of times but that wasn't one of the times. The point is it inspired me to write a poem for the school paper which made me as big a hit with my father as if I had become a

football hero. So when I went home that Christmas vacation it was in my mind that if you weren't able to function in action you might at least be able to tell about it, because you felt the same intensity – it was a back door way out of facing reality.[18]

Writing the poem, one notices, makes him 'a hit' with his father – and to be a hit, in whatever way, was Fitzgerald's enduring ambition from the beginning. But, writing in 1936, he is perhaps being overly harsh in seeing the poem as only 'a back door way out of facing reality'. The confrontation with reality that writing about it requires may well be head-on, and for Fitzgerald most of the time at least it had nothing to do with evasion or escapism. In any event, what the passage confirms is that for Fitzgerald the way forward, the way of achieving, of making his mark, was through writing. In the first 'Crack-Up' essay he wrote that when he was young 'It seemed a romantic business to be a successful literary man – you were not ever going to be as famous as a movie star but what note you had was probably longer-lived …'[19] Leaving Princeton in 1917 to join the army, Fitzgerald was pretty sure that (were he to survive the war) the literary life was the only life that might provide him with the kind of success and fulfilment he desired.

2
Succeeding with *This Side of Paradise*

Throughout Fitzgerald's later years at Princeton World War I was pursuing its increasingly bloody course in Europe. There is nothing to suggest that he took much interest in the early progress of the war, but around 1917 – after the United States joined the Allies in April that year in order, according to President Wilson, to save the world for democracy – the situation changed. Reports of the deaths of Princetonians in France were becoming common. (By the end of the war no fewer than 152 would have been killed.) And Fitzgerald's dreams of heroic derring-do, stimulated earlier by his father's stories of the American Civil War, soon involved the contemporary battlefield as readily as the football field. More seriously, what was going on in war-torn Europe was something that a range of future American writers of Fitzgerald's generation were desperate to see and experience: Ernest Hemingway, John Dos Passos, William Faulkner, E. E. Cummings – and Fitzgerald – all strove with differing degrees of success to get over there. In Fitzgerald's case, however, the reasons behind his decision to leave Princeton in the autumn of 1917, and join the US Army, are less than clear. Even in letters to his family he has nothing to say about duty or patriotism; and nowhere is there a suggestion that Europe at war represented an ultimate reality that the potential writer could not afford to miss. The probability is that enlistment in the army struck Fitzgerald as an ideally honourable way in which to bring his Princeton career to an end.

Now twenty-one years old, Fitzgerald had learned one vital lesson from his life at university: it was through writing alone that he could hope to distinguish himself, making a mark on the world in the way he yearned to. Edmund Wilson, already established as a literary journalist in New York, recalls Fitzgerald at this time announcing that he wanted to be one of the greatest writers who ever lived. Hence it is not entirely surprising that, having arrived at Fort Leavenworth, Kansas, to begin his training as an infantry officer in November 1917 – characteristically he had acquired his uniforms from the fashionable Brooks Brothers outfitters in New York – he seems to have put more energy into his writing than his training. Like other young men in his position, Fitzgerald knew perfectly well that if he ever actually arrived as a junior officer on the Western Front his chances of long-term survival were slim. So rather than waiting for some uncertain future he decided that now was the time – perhaps the only time he had – to begin his professional literary life. He determined to write a novel. (When Shane Leslie, Irish novelist and critic, recommended the finished manuscript to Scribners, his publishers in New York, he called Fitzgerald a prose Rupert Brooke, suggested his manuscript had literary value, and added 'Of course when he is killed, it will also have a commercial value.')[1] Inevitably Fitzgerald has provided us with his own account of the writing of his first novel, initially called 'The Romantic Egotist'. In 'Who's Who – And Why,' published in the *Saturday Evening Post* in September 1920, he wrote:

> Every evening, concealing my pad behind Small Problems for Infantry, I wrote paragraph after paragraph on a somewhat edited history of me and my imagination.

When he was detected, and could no longer write during study periods, he made up for lost time by writing furiously through the weekend:

> Every Saturday at one o'clock when the week's work was over I hurried to the Officers' Club, and there, in a corner of a roomful of smoke, conversation and rattling newspapers, I wrote a one-hundred-and-twenty-thousand-word novel on the consecutive week-ends of three months.[2]

Of course this upbeat account was written only a few months after the publication of *This Side of Paradise* in March 1920, at a time when Fitzgerald was still dazzled and buoyed up by his early success. But the external evidence is broadly in line with his account. In February 1918, he had written to Shane Leslie – he had originally met the Irish writer during his years at the Newman school – warning him of the imminent arrival of the manuscript of his novel, and telling him to 'Think of a romantic egotist writing about himself in a cold barracks on Sunday afternoons ...' (L, 392).

In any event what is certain is that, from the beginning of 1918, Fitzgerald's oldest and closest literary friends were receiving chapters of 'The Romantic Egotist' almost as quickly as he was producing them. In January Edmund Wilson had received a lengthy account of the manuscript, describing its mixture of prose, poetry, and *vers libre*, its number of chapters, its plot structure, and the literary influences reflected within it. Prophetically, Fitzgerald goes on to describe his work as a modern 'Childe Harold' and continues 'if Scribners takes it I know I'll wake some morning and find that the debutantes have made me famous overnight. I really believe that no one else could have written so searchingly the story of the youth of our generation ...' (L, 343). That same January, John Peale Bishop, Fitzgerald's other contemporary friend and writer at Princeton, sent him two long letters offering perceptive criticisms of the chapters he had been sent. Yet another chapter reader was the man who up to this point had been perhaps the most influential figure in Fitzgerald's life: Monsignor Sigourney Fay whom Fitzgerald had met at the Newman school. Fay was a charismatic and socially sophisticated priest rapidly becoming an important figure in the hierarchy of the American Catholic Church. Fitzgerald had clearly been dazzled by him, with the result that for a time Fay, with his friend Shane Leslie, had certainly guided and coloured the young Fitzgerald's responses both to literature and life. Predictably Fay, who regarded Fitzgerald as a promising and talented personal protégé, was an enthusiastic reader of 'The Romantic Egotist': the more he read, he said, the 'more amazingly good I think it is'. (C, 33) And, as we have already noted, it was Shane Leslie who, having read the whole manuscript, dispatched it to Scribners, urging the firm to publish this work by an American prose Rupert Brooke.

Given such a degree of positive response from friends whose opinions he respected, Fitzgerald was understandably hopeful in the summer of 1918 that Scribners would in fact agree to publish 'The Romantic Egotist'. His only doubt seems to have been over the possibility that some of his material might appear too daringly bold and unconventional for Scribners, a publishing house with a distinctly conservative reputation. In the event his concern proved to be well-judged. Having read the manuscript, William C. Brownell, Scribner's editor-in-chief, 'could not stomach it at all', while another editor, Edward L. Burlingame, found it 'hard sledding'.[3] Scribners decided against publication. But the rejection letter Fitzgerald received in August 1918 – almost certainly written by Maxwell Perkins – was far from wholly discouraging. It praised the unusual degree of originality in the manuscript, went on to make long and detailed criticisms and suggestions for improvement, and invited resubmission. Fitzgerald plunged instantly into what he subsequently saw as ill-thought-out revisions. In October Perkins rejected the manuscript for a second time. Fitzgerald was predictably depressed and deflated; the telegram of rejection preserved in his scrapbook was headed 'the end of a dream'.

II

If October 1918 marked at least a temporary set-back in Fitzgerald's literary career, other events had occurred by then that were to have a major impact upon his writing future. After training at Fort Leavenworth, Kansas, the US Army sent Fitzgerald first to Camp Taylor, Louisville, Kentucky, then to Camp Gordon, Georgia, and finally to Camp Sheridan near Montgomery, Alabama. It was there that he met and was soon passionately involved with Zelda Sayre. The eighteen-year-old Zelda was the daughter of an Alabama Supreme Court judge and an artistically inclined mother from a distinguished Kentucky family. But despite her highly respectable and socially elevated background, Zelda was a decidedly unconventional young woman. Beautiful certainly, she may have been in a sense a Southern belle, but in no other way did she fit the mould of that stereotype. For her, Southern traditions and values, particularly in relation to the expected behaviour of eligible young women, meant only the denial of individual freedoms. She seems to have found Southern social and familial structures repressingly narrow and restrictive, wholly incompatible with the youth and energy of her own free spirit. Thus by the summer of 1918 Zelda had already acquired something of a reputation in Montgomery; her dancing and drinking, dating and smoking, suggest nothing other than the style of the Flapper girl, who is not supposed to have emerged in America until the post-Prohibition 1920s. In fact, however, life in Montgomery, Alabama, in 1918 was a world away from that of New York City in 1920. For Zelda, New York and the North were distant dreams. A powerful part of Fitzgerald's appeal for her was undoubtedly the fact that he was an exotic Northerner. Handsome, blond, elegantly uniformed, no doubt he would have made some impression; but had he been a Southern boy from Auburn or Georgia Tech, rather than a Northerner from glamorous Princeton, one wonders how long her interest would have lasted. From the first Zelda must have seen Fitzgerald as a promise of freedom, a way out of a society and culture against which she was in instinctive rebellion. Even her indulgent mother sometimes found Zelda's behaviour unacceptable: in 1919 she wrote her daughter a note which Zelda in turn passed on to Fitzgerald. 'Zelda: If you have added whiskey to your tobacco you can subtract from Mother.... If you prefer the habits of a prostitute don't try to mix them with gentility. Oil and water do not mix.'[4] Fitzgerald would never be quite as censorious as this.

But what was it about Zelda that attracted Fitzgerald? Of course she was beautiful and physically attractive, but almost certainly more important were her popularity and reputation. Like the lost Genevra King of a year or two earlier, she was the girl most in demand, most admired, most sought after. To be accepted as Zelda's partner was to be seen to be succeeding, to be coming out on top. Of course Zelda and Scott must soon have recognized their shared ambitions – their desire to be known and admired, their sense of a glamorous future that could, with the right moves, be attained. But most of all for Fitzgerald, success with Zelda would mean that he was on the winning side, taking control, dominating life rather than being dominated by it.

The affair between Fitzgerald and Zelda developed quickly in the months after their first meeting in July 1918. In October Fitzgerald was sent to Long Island to await embarkation for Europe. But with the end of the war in November he was soon back in Camp Sheridan; and in February 1919, he was discharged from the army. From the moment he realized that there was no longer any chance of his dying in France, Fitzgerald must have known that he was facing big decisions about his writing career and his personal life. 'The Romantic Egotist' had just been rejected by Scribners for a second time. So did he have a future as a writer? His affair with Zelda was arriving at a point where marriage seemed to be the necessary next step. But should he consider it? What would marriage mean in relation to his hoped-for future as a writer? Was success with Zelda compatible with success as a writer? Fitzgerald never stated his dilemma as bluntly as this, but it was certainly there at the back of his mind. In a fascinating letter to an old friend, Ruth Sturtevant, written as late as December 1918 from Camp Sheridan, when the possibility of marriage to Zelda must have been preoccupying him, he insisted that marriage would be a disaster: 'But my mind is firmly made up that I will not, shall not, can not, should not, must not marry ...' (L, 474). Of course these words can be interpreted in a host of ways: is he serious? joking? trying to convince himself? Are the repeated negatives merely an acknowledgement of the strength of the pull in the opposite direction? But it is hard not to think that behind these words lies a recognition that the possible marriage to Zelda will create problems – problems especially for the future writer.

Unquestionably, early in 1919 Fitzgerald found himself in a difficult position. He was leaving the army, was thinking about getting married, but had no job or any obvious vocational qualification. An unexpected event in January 1919, further complicated his situation: the death from pneumonia of Monsignor Fay. Fay had earlier made elaborate plans to include Fitzgerald in some kind of Roman Catholic Church mission to Europe; and writing to Shane Leslie after hearing the devastating news Fitzgerald even talks of becoming a priest. Given the ongoing affair with Zelda, this notion could hardly have been a serious one. But it is entirely possible that Fay's sudden death seemed to Fitzgerald to narrow his options still further. In the same letter to Leslie he told him he was 'coming to New York in February or March to write or something' (L, 395). That is almost exactly what happened. Considering himself engaged to Zelda, he left Alabama near the end of February 1919, and headed for New York. Finding somewhere to live near Columbia University in Manhattan, he went job-hunting. Having failed to find work as a journalist, he took a job with an advertising agency. At the same time he worked hard – presumably in the evenings and at weekends – at becoming a professional writer. Matthew J. Bruccoli tells us that in New York in the spring of 1919, he wrote nineteen short stories, and received one hundred and twenty-two rejection slips. The one glimmer of hope was the acceptance by *The Smart Set*, an up-market, sophisticated magazine edited by the increasingly powerful H. L. Mencken and George Jean Nathan, of a revised version of his *Nassau Lit* story 'Babes in the Woods' – for which Fitzgerald received 30 dollars.

If Fitzgerald's literary life appeared to be stuck in the starting-gate, he was experiencing no better fortune in his private life. Zelda Sayre, as 1919 passed, seemed less and less inclined to keep up her relationship with Fitzgerald. Zelda, as suggested above, saw marriage as her way out of the constraints of conventional Southern life and culture; Fitzgerald had seemed to promise a life of freedom and excitement in New York. But something had clearly gone wrong. Marriage to an unsuccessful writer working in advertising promised neither freedom nor excitement. In June 1919, she told Fitzgerald that she could not marry him. For Fitzgerald this was the most devastating rejection slip of them all: suddenly his life was purposeless; the romance and glamour of New York city were consumed by the shabby realities of poverty and lost love. Inevitably Fitzgerald recreated his feelings of loss and despair at this time later in his career. In 1932, in an essay entitled 'My Lost City', he graphically evoked the changing pattern of his relationship with the city from his early romantic expectations, through the months of drab despondency, to the short-lived triumph that was to follow. In that middle period of rejection and loss, he wrote, 'I was a failure – mediocre at advertising work and unable to get started as a writer.'[5] It was a moment of decision for Fitzgerald; facing up to the truth that he was getting nowhere in the New York of his dreams, he threw up his job, and returned home to St Paul.

What Fitzgerald had decided to do was to resurrect 'The Romantic Egotist' – encouraged perhaps by recollecting how positive had been the responses of his literary friends, and how close Scribners had come to accepting it. Had he been precipitate in deciding that that particular dream (of publication) was over? Working hard in his room on the top floor of the family house on Summit Avenue, Fitzgerald spent July and August 1919 producing a major revision of his manuscript. Indeed, when writing to Maxwell Perkins at Scribners at the end of July, telling him that he had given up on getting married and gone home, he went so far as to insist that his novel, now entitled 'The Education of a Personage', was 'in no sense a revision of the ill-fated *Romantic Egotist'*. That, he said, had been 'a tedious, disconnected casserole'. What he had now produced was an attempt 'at a big novel', and he really believed he had 'hit it' (FP, 17). Perkins replied by return, expressing great interest and adding 'Ever since the first reading of your first manuscript we have felt that you would succeed' (FP, 18).

The stance suggested here is one that Perkins essentially sustained throughout the period – it proved to be Fitzgerald's lifetime – that he acted as the only editor of Fitzgerald's novels. A somewhat conservative New Englander, from an old-established American family, Perkins in the 1920s and 1930s became probably the most influential editor of his time. He played a major role in publishing and supporting a significant range of American writers – Hemingway, Thomas Wolfe, Ring Lardner, J. P. Marquand, Erskine Caldwell, and Marjorie Rawlings, as well as others. His support for Fitzgerald – whether taking the form of critical advice, admiration for the outstanding quality of his writing, or money – was unstinting; and as time passed the relationship between the two became more personal than professional.

Fitzgerald's next letter, dated 16 August 1919, assured Perkins that the new manuscript would meet his expectations: 'It is a well-considered, finished *whole* this time ...' (FP, 18). Its new title, from a poem by Rupert Brooke, was *This Side of Paradise*, and Fitzgerald went on insisting that most of the material was new, and where he had used chapters from the earlier text, they had been 'completely changed and rewritten' (FP, 19). On the day that the finished manuscript was handed over to a friend for delivery to Scribners in New York, Fitzgerald wrote again to Perkins acknowledging in more detail just how much material from 'The Romantic Egotist' had been incorporated into *This Side of Paradise*. In the event Perkins proved unconcerned. The new manuscript was read by Scribners editorial board: Charles Scribner and his brother Arthur disapproved; William Brownell described it as frivolous; but Maxwell Perkins spoke strongly of the need to promote new talent – without that 'we might as well go out of business'. At the end of the discussion the board's vote was tied, but after further thought Charles Scribner changed his mind and *This Side of Paradise* was accepted for publication.[6] On 16 September 1919, Perkins wrote to Fitzgerald telling him of the decision:

> I am very glad, personally, to be able to write you that we are all for publishing your book, 'This Side of Paradise.' Viewing it as the same book that was here before, which in a sense it is, though translated into somewhat different terms and extended further, I think that you have improved it enormously. As the first manuscript did, it abounds in energy and life and it seems to me to be in much better proportion ... it is hard to prophesy how it will sell but we are all for taking a chance and supporting it with vigor. (FP, 21)

Receiving this letter a few days before his twenty-third birthday, Fitzgerald was ecstatic. On 18 September he wrote to Perkins expressing his delight and saying 'I've been in a sort of trance all day ...' Significantly he sees the publication of his book as a marker, as tangible proof of his ability to succeed: '... at last I have something to show people' he tells Perkins. In the remainder of the letter he urges Perkins to make the publication date as early as possible, because he has so much riding on the book's success – 'including of course a girl'. He accepts that he cannot expect the book to make him a fortune, but 'it will have a psychological effect on me and all my surroundings and besides open up new fields' (FP, 21). Once again, years later Fitzgerald looked back and recreated his feelings of euphoria at this wonderful moment. In 'Early Success' he describes himself running along the streets of St Paul, stopping passing cars to tell friends and acquaintances the great news, and waking up every morning 'with a world of ineffable toploftiness and promise'. But the promised publication of *This Side of Paradise* meant more than a momentary triumph, however relishable and self-satisfying. It removed all doubts about the future. His career was now determined: he would be a writer. In 'Early Success' he makes the point quite specifically:

> While I waited for the novel to appear, the metamorphosis of amateur into professional began to take place – a sort of

stitching together of your whole life into a pattern of work, so that the end of one job is automatically the beginning of another.[7]

Such a pattern of work was certainly Fitzgerald's ideal and to help it into existence one of his first steps was to acquire a literary agent. On the advice of a woman writer friend in St Paul he wrote at the end of October 1919 to the Paul Revere Reynolds agency on Fifth Avenue in New York city. At first Reynolds himself looked after Fitzgerald's interests, and began placing short stories in different magazines. However, after Fitzgerald visited the agency in New York in November, Harold Ober took over as his literary agent. Thus began the second crucial relationship in Fitzgerald's literary life – and like that with Maxwell Perkins, it was to prove an enduring one. Ober, once again like Perkins, a conservative New Englander of the highest personal integrity, would prove an invaluable support, both personally and financially, until almost the end of Fitzgerald's career. Ober worked indefatigably to place Fitzgerald's stories in a range of magazines, advised him on the serialization of his novels, discussed possible film rights – all the things that an active literary agent might be expected to do. But for most of the 1920s and 30s he was doing a great deal more – constantly responding to Fitzgerald's requests for money or advances on stories yet to be placed, and acting as a kind of personal banker every time Fitzgerald found himself in financial difficulty – which was often. In Fitzgerald's final Hollywood years, at the end of the thirties, and even after their professional relationship had come to an end because Ober had finally found himself unable to go on providing Fitzgerald with financial support, Ober and his wife would continue to act almost as foster-parents looking after the Fitzgeralds' daughter Scottie. Both Maxwell Perkins and Harold Ober remained convinced of Fitzgerald's worth as a writer; hence however uncertain his literary career might appear, and however erratic his life might become, they were prepared to stand by him. Without them, and their loyal support, it is hard to imagine how his literary life could have achieved as much as it did at the time or in the future.

Fitzgerald's reaction to the news that his novel was to be published was not to sit back and wait for the great day. Rather he plunged into a period of almost frantic literary activity. With renewed self-belief, he revised existing stories, including *Nassau Lit* material, and wrote new ones. Soon he was receiving acceptances from the editors of *The Smart Set, Scribner's Magazine*, and – most significantly in financial terms – the *Saturday Evening Post*. Thus months before the actual appearance of his first novel, Fitzgerald's work had been published in all three magazines. At the same time his letters to Perkins and Ober show him full of plans concerning future writing. Typically his letter responding to the news that *This Side of Paradise* had been accepted told Perkins that he was already working on an ambitious new novel, 'The Demon Lover'. In October 1919 he wrote to Robert Bridges, editor of *Scribner's Magazine*, asking if he would be interested in a work of novella length, the tone of which would be more like that of his forthcoming novel than the stories he'd been writing. It would be 'in turns cynical, ingenuous, life-saturated, critical and bitter'. The work is 'bound to have that streak of coarseness that both Wells and Butler have but there won't be any James Joyce flavor to it' (L, 158–9). (Fitzgerald had been much impressed by his recent reading of Samuel Butler's *Note-Books* in particular.) A few weeks later he is writing to Ober asking about writing film scenarios, and mentioning the possibility of film rights for some of his own stories. Then again he had in mind the possibility of a book of short stories. In January 1920, he wrote to Ober asking 'Is there any money in collections of short stories?' (FO, 9). But at the same time he was writing to Perkins saying he was anxious to get on with his second novel, and implying that short-story writing was getting in the way. He asks Perkins whether a second novel of the same type as his first one would have any chance of serial publication in a magazine. If it did, then he could give up writing short stories which he didn't enjoy – but continues to do because of the money such stories bring in. Here Fitzgerald is establishing a distinction between the writing of novels and the writing of short stories which he continued to make throughout his literary career. His short stories were written for the magazine market – hence they had to be tailored to meet the demands of that market. Only in his novels was he free to write as he wanted to write. The letter to Ober, asking about the money to be made from a story collection, goes on to make the same basic distinction and clarifies what was in his mind when he was quizzing Perkins about the possibility of serial publication:

Now my novels, at least my first one, are not like my short stories at all, they are rather cynical and pessimistic – and therefore I doubt if as a whole they'd stand much chance of being published serially in any of the uplift magazines at least until my first novel + these Post stories appear and I get some sort of a reputation. (FO, 9)

Ober may or may not have shared Fitzgerald's opinion of the difference between his novels and stories, but Maxwell Perkins's view was that Fitzgerald was being altogether too dismissive of his talent as a writer of short fiction. He should certainly consider publishing a collection of his stories; and such a book could well be a commercial success. Perkins's view appears to have been that *This Side of Paradise* and the early stories had something very important in common: a sharp sensitivity to the present moment, a kind of instant, recognizable, felt contemporaneity. He told Fitzgerald his stories were 'direct from life it seems to me. This is true also of the language and style: it is that of the day' (FP, 24). Such observations were certainly consonant with Fitzgerald's own sense that in *This Side of Paradise* he was writing the story of the youth of his generation. In any event, collections of his short stories would eventually become a regular feature of Fitzgerald's publishing history.

III

In the middle of January 1920, Fitzgerald left his parents' home in St Paul and went to live in New Orleans. Here was a twenty-three-year-old author who by the end of 1919, had published or had had accepted for publication, six stories, three plays, and a poem; he had already earned $879 from his writing and his first novel was about to be issued by a prestigious New York publisher. One might have thought that the trip to New Orleans would be a break, a pause, an opportunity to take stock, to take time to think about a literary career that was now clearly stretching out before him. But that is not how it was. Fitzgerald did some reading in New Orleans that would soon prove significant, but his writing and writing plans were as driven as ever. He told Maxwell Perkins he wrote the short story 'The Camel's Back' in a single day: starting at eight in the morning, finishing at seven p.m., recopying the manuscript by four-thirty a.m., and mailing it half an hour later. And he also tells Perkins he now has a plan to write three stories a month: one each for *The Smart Set, Scribner's* and the *Saturday Evening Post*. Meantime he has begun a new novel on the theme of seduction.

Rather than pausing for reflection, Fitzgerald seems if anything to be stepping up the pace of his writing. But the reason behind all this urgency is not hard to find: Fitzgerald believed that he had to secure a sizeable and regular income if the ultimate prize, and proof of success, was to be his. Fitzgerald never forgot that Zelda Sayre had given him up the previous year essentially because he was too poor to provide her with the kind of life she sought. In the 'Crack-Up' essay 'Pasting it Together' many years later, the bitterness in his comments on money and the leisured class is self-evident; someone else's money might well have bought Zelda up. But in 1920 his determination was simply to gain success and the money that went with it himself. Returning to Montgomery from New Orleans in his role as successful young author, he was able to make it happen. Zelda was sufficiently impressed; the engagement was renewed; and the couple would be married in New York as soon as *This Side of Paradise* was published. From this point on, Fitzgerald's literary life was inevitably enmeshed in his married life.

Fitzgerald and Zelda were duly married in St Patrick's Cathedral's vestry in New York on 3 April 1920. A week earlier, on 26 March 1920, *This Side of Paradise* had been published. Scribners' initial print run had been 3000 copies; these were sold out in the first three days. Just as he had predicted he would, Fitzgerald woke up, like Byron after 'Childe Harold', to find himself famous. In the following months his novel went through a series of printings, most of them amounting to 5000 copies. Abridged versions of the novel were serialized in several newspapers. By the end of 1921, sales had peaked at a little under 50,000 copies. For a first novel by an unknown author this was an amazing success. But such sales did not make *This Side of Paradise* a true best-seller; more than half-a-dozen novels, largely by now-forgotten authors, sold better in 1920. And the figure that puts Fitzgerald's achievement in true perspective is probably the near 300,000 copies that made Sinclair Lewis's *Main Street* the best-selling novel of 1921. Yet one should remember that Lewis was a well-established author, already celebrated as the author of *Babbitt*. Fitzgerald's sales were certainly fantastically better than anything his publisher had anticipated. In the circumstances it is no surprise that Maxwell Perkins's notion that a collection of short stories might be a good idea was soon being acted upon. In September 1920, *Flappers and Philosophers* duly appeared. Despite the fact that the volume included only eight stories – and none of them would subsequently be seen as among Fitzgerald's best – this volume too sold surprisingly well: over 15,000 copies in about three months. Fitzgerald's earnings from his writing in 1920 did not make him rich, but they certainly made him appear a wealthy man. The previous year he had earned $879; the 1920 figure was $18,850. *This Side of Paradise* had earned him $6200; his magazine stories, $4650; and he had received $7425 for the film rights to three stories. By the standards of most ordinary Americans at the opening of the 1920s, these were all huge sums of money. The average annual income for a worker in agriculture in 1920 was $528; for a worker in manufacturing industry $1532; for a railroad worker $1807; for a worker in all industries including farming $1407. Unsurprisingly, given these figures, from this point on in his career Fitzgerald always believed his writing could make him financially secure and independent: the next project was always going to bring in even more than the last. He was invariably wrong on both counts: he never achieved financial security and independence – even in this first year he spent more than he earned and established the pattern of obtaining advances both from Maxwell Perkins and Harold Ober – and none of his books ever matched his expectations in terms of financial returns.

As well as selling far beyond the expectations of most first novels, *This Side of Paradise* also brought Fitzgerald a degree of critical success. Most contemporary reviews were broadly favourable. Mencken in *The Smart Set* wrote that it was 'the best American novel that I have seen of late'.[8] Burton Rascoe of the *Chicago Tribune* felt the book bore the impress of genius, and announced that it was 'the only adequate study that we have had of the contemporary American in adolescence and young manhood'.[9] Such a comment reminds us of both Fitzgerald's own assertion that he was writing the story of the youth of his own generation, and Maxwell Perkins's sense of how the language and style of Fitzgerald's writing was very much 'of the day'. And the popularity of the novel at the time does seem to be best explained in terms of its success at catching the tone and mood of a new post-war American generation 'grown up to find all Gods dead, all wars fought, all faiths in man shaken ...'[10] When John O'Hara insisted that there were half a million men and women readers between the ages of fifteen and thirty who fell in love with the book, it was this aspect of its appeal that he appears to have had most in mind.

But if the popular success of *This Side of Paradise* suggests that Fitzgerald had found a way of echoing something of the contemporary public mood, the subtext of the novel hints at a quite different level of personal or private meaning. Towards the novel's end, Fitzgerald seems increasingly to be exploring, through the protagonist Amory Blaine's musings and opinions, his own uncertainties over his personal future as an artist and writer. Amory, for example, concludes that art and life are hostile, mutually exclusive spheres; he is already a tyro writer, but tells us that when he starts to write stories he is afraid he is doing it 'instead of living' – he gets to thinking 'maybe life is waiting for me in the Japanese gardens at the Ritz or at Atlantic City or on the lower East Side'.[11] Even more interestingly, in the final major scene of the novel, in which Amory argues the case for socialism with a wealthy industrialist and his secretary, Fitzgerald has him develop in the course of his argument an image of the 'spiritually married man'. Marriage here becomes a metaphor of entrapment: the married person has lost his independence – to be free is to be 'unmarried'. In terms of the argument over socialism, the entrapment in question is a kind of necessary commitment to the social status quo, to the earning of more and more money, but it is hard not to see a parallel relevance to the argument over the necessary posture of the artist. It is the artist who needs detachment and independence; it is the artist who should be uncommitted. 'Life's got him' is the text's defining comment on the married man.[12] The question for Fitzgerald the writer-artist was whether he could afford to let life get him. In this context one can hardly fail to recall the December 1919 letter to Ruth Sturtevant announcing his absolute conviction that he should not marry Zelda. A few months later, as a married man, Fitzgerald's commitment to life was complete – as complete as his parallel commitment to the profession of writing. For the rest of his life these two commitments would coexist in unsettling disharmony.

3
Locating *The Beautiful and Damned*

After their marriage in April 1920, the Fitzgeralds remained in New York partying and generally living up to their new reputation as a celebrity couple. A brief but chaotic visit to Princeton was followed by the decision to rent a house for the summer months in Westport, Connecticut, some fifty miles from New York city. Fitzgerald was becoming concerned that too much good-timing with Zelda was preventing his getting on with his writing – though such a development was one he might well have anticipated. Just a week before his wedding he had written again to Ruth Sturtevant urging her to come and meet Zelda 'because she's very beautiful and very wise and very brave as you can imagine – but she's a perfect baby and a more irresponsible pair than we'll be will be hard to imagine' (L, 479). Fitzgerald clearly hoped that life in Westport, away from the city, would be somewhat less hectic, and that he would be able to settle down to serious work. What in fact these early weeks of married life established was a pattern of existence that would remain more or less unchanged for the rest of Fitzgerald's career. The Fitzgeralds never did settle down. They never established a home, bought a house, or put down permanent roots. Their life together – and apart – would be spent in rented apartments or houses, hotels, clinics and hospitals. Even with the birth of their only child – their daughter Scottie – in October 1921, nothing changed. The Fitzgeralds remained constantly on the move: four times they would cross the Atlantic and live for longer or shorter periods in England, France, Switzerland, and Italy. Back in the US, they would move between New York, Long Island, Montgomery, St

Paul, Wilmington (Delaware) and Baltimore; and after Zelda's illness required her to be hospitalized, Fitzgerald would live in various hotels and apartments in North Carolina and Maryland before his final move to Hollywood. If in the period between the acceptance of *This Side of Paradise* for publication and its actual appearance Fitzgerald seems almost ruthlessly single-minded in pushing forward his writing career, after his marriage he would be forever juggling two lives: his life with Zelda and his life as a writer.

After an unproductive summer in Westport – the quieter life Fitzgerald had anticipated having proved largely illusory – the couple returned to New York in the autumn. *Flappers and Philosophers*, Fitzgerald's first short story collection, appeared in September, and he got down at last to serious work on his second novel. Over the winter his professional self-discipline managed to remain firm and by the early summer of 1921, the manuscript of *The Beautiful and Damned* was complete. Fitzgerald had hesitated over what the nature of his second novel should be; starts were made and quickly abandoned. Should he attempt to repeat the success of *This Side of Paradise* by writing in a similar vein, or should he move in a new direction? Writing a novel, he regarded himself as free to ignore the expectations of the mass-market uplift magazines; he could write about life and experience exactly as he saw them. In this context it is worth remembering that at this point he seems seriously to have regarded *This Side of Paradise* as reflecting quite a disillusioned, cynical point of view; in fact the popular success of the novel seems to have had much less to do with its occasional cynical moments than with the buoyancy and energy and even hope with which its protagonist confronted life and its problems. In any event by August 1920, Fitzgerald had focused what the main movement of *The Beautiful and Damned* would be. In a letter to Charles Scribner he wrote that his new novel would concern the life of Anthony Patch – 'He is one of those many with the tastes and weaknesses of an artist but with no actual creative inspiration. How he and his beautiful young wife are wrecked on the shoals of dissipation is told in the story.' Fitzgerald goes on to say that 'it's really a most sensational book' and he hopes that it 'won't disappoint the critics who liked my first one' (L, 163). The scenario described here is in fact very much the one that appears in *The Beautiful and Damned*. But Fitzgerald is quite wrong in expecting those who liked his first novel to be equally attracted to his second. The story of the slow deterioration of the outwardly glamorous couple, Gloria and Anthony Patch, is an altogether darker and more sombre affair than anything in *This Side of Paradise*. The mood and tone of the two novels could hardly have been more different, and Fitzgerald could only have convinced himself otherwise by finding in *This Side of Paradise* a much profounder strain of cynicism than anything his enthusiastic readership had actually discovered.

Later in his career, Fitzgerald remained ambivalent over the worth or value of *This Side of Paradise*. He saw its weaknesses all too clearly, but he was never prepared to dismiss it totally. In 1925 he said he liked the book 'for the enormous emotion, mostly immature and bogus, that gives every incident a sort of silly "life"'.[1] As late as 1938, he wrote of its 'utter spuriousness' but goes on 'and then, here and there, I find a page that is very real and living' (L, 297). But in trying to understand where the first novel came from, perhaps the focus should be placed on his *Notebook's* remark that *This Side of Paradise* was 'A Romance and a Reading List': scholarly investigation of the text finds references to 64 literary titles and 98 writers.[2] In other words, *This Side of Paradise* is shaped and influenced by those authors whom Fitzgerald as an undergraduate at Princeton read and admired. A look at who those writers were does produce some surprises. First of all they were overwhelmingly British rather than American. Then broadly speaking they were neither the creators of high modernism in English fiction, nor the canonical novelists of the eighteenth and nineteenth centuries (though Fitzgerald did read and admire Thackeray). Rather they were largely British authors of the Edwardian period, particularly those who seemed to explore a particular kind of individual social and spiritual questing. In February 1921, Fitzgerald wrote a letter to his friend Thomas Boyd, then literary editor of the *St Paul Daily News*, which the paper published as 'The Credo of F. Scott Fitzgerald', remarking that the art form that was currently most overworked in America was the 'history of a young man' – and his own first novel is included among the examples cited. The form, he suggests, 'consists chiefly in dumping all your youthful adventures into the reader's lap with a profound air of importance, keeping carefully within the formulas of Wells and James Joyce' (C, 79). The formulas are to be found of course in *A Portrait of the Artist as a Young Man* and a Wells novel such as *Tono-Bungay*. And however briskly dismissive he may now be of the *Bildungsroman* novel mode, in the years leading up to the writing of *This Side of Paradise*, Wells and the early Joyce were only two of a range of British authors whom Fitzgerald and his influential Princeton contemporaries read with huge enthusiasm. Wells in fact was much in favour: in September 1917, Fitzgerald wrote to Edmund Wilson saying that he regarded *The New Machiavelli* as 'the greatest English novel of the century' (L, 338). But on the whole the English realist writers such as Arnold Bennett, John Galsworthy, or Hugh Walpole do not seem to have been much admired. Apart from Wells, those who were appear to be linked by a vaguely 'Celtic' and 'Catholic' sensibility: Compton Mackenzie, G. K. Chesterton, R. H. Benson, J. M. Barrie, George Bernard Shaw. In the background, helping to explain Fitzgerald's taste for such authors, are the figures of the Irishman Shane Leslie, and the Catholic cleric Monsignor Sigourney Fay, both of whom, as we have seen, Fitzgerald had met and admired at the Newman school. Unquestionably these two figures encouraged Fitzgerald to regard his Irish antecedents, and his Catholic upbringing, with a new seriousness.[3] This perspective carried over into the Princeton years. In his 1917 letters to Wilson, Fitzgerald signs himself, no doubt jocularly, 'Celticly' or 'Gaelicly Yours'. And five years later, in a review of Leslie's novel *The Oppidan*, he recalled how his own sense of conventional, Midwestern, Irish-American Catholicism had been transformed by the vision of Leslie and Fay: they 'made of that church a dazzling, golden thing, dispelling its oppressive mugginess and giving the succession of days upon gray days, passing under its plaintive ritual, the romantic glamour of an adolescent dream' (LL, 480).

In terms of actual commitment or belief, Fitzgerald's Catholic convictions were relatively short-lived. By the middle of 1919 – only months after Monsignor Fay's death – he was telling Wilson that he had more or less abandoned his Catholicism:

> I am ashamed to say that my Catholicism is scarcely more than a memory – no, that's wrong, it's more than that; at any rate I go not to the church nor mumble stray nothings over crystalline beads. (L, 345)

Zelda was almost certainly a factor in this development. In February 1920, Fitzgerald wrote to a school friend's sister – she had almost certainly written to him advising against marriage to Zelda – saying that while he knew his future wife was not 'beyond reproach', he was in love with her. 'You're still a Catholic,' he wrote, 'but Zelda's the only God I have left now' (C, 53). However, Fitzgerald's own religious conviction – or lack of it – is not the point. Rather it is that the context out of which Fitzgerald's first novel emerged was one in which a major element was the kind of atmospheric Catholic-Celtic spirituality characteristic of Compton Mackenzie – in, say, such a novel as *Youth's Encounter* (1912) – and the other British authors mentioned above. Fitzgerald himself was quite explicit about his debt in *This Side of Paradise* to this particular group of authors. Writing to Wilson about the plot and sources of 'The Romantic Egotist' he mentions Booth Tarkington (American novelist, Princeton graduate, and founder of the Triangle Club), alongside Chesterton, Wells, Compton Mackenzie, and Rupert Brooke. (Fitzgerald had been reading the decadent Anglo-Irish poets of the 1890s, but preferred the poetry of Brooke.) Later, after the novel had appeared, he told Shane Leslie that he was 'godfather to this book' (L, 396) to which Leslie responded by insisting that the novel was 'a Catholic minded book at heart' (C, 66). In the following year, responding to a review in the *Atlanta Constitution* in February 1921, in which he was charged with plagiarizing from Compton Mackenzie in particular, Fitzgerald acknowledged his indebtedness to *Sinister Street*: 'When I was twenty-one and began *This Side of Paradise* my literary taste was so unformed that *Youth's Encounter* was still my "perfect book." My book quite naturally shows the influence to a marked degree ...' (L, 489). But he of course denies any kind of plagiarism.

When Fitzgerald began turning over in his mind possible scenarios for what would be his third novel (*The Great Gatsby*), he wrote to Maxwell Perkins telling him that the story would be set in the Middle West and New York and 'would have a catholic element' (FP, 61). The date is June 1922, however, three years after the writing of *This Side of Paradise*, and in these years Fitzgerald's worldview had moved in directions quite antithetical to the spiritual romanticism which Leslie and Fay, and his reading of the British 'Celtic' novelists had inspired. This dramatic change is more than evident in Fitzgerald's second novel *The Beautiful and Damned*.

Perhaps one should note at this point that throughout his life Fitzgerald was unusually susceptible to outside influences. At the Newman school, at Princeton, in the New York literary world in which he moved in the early 1920s, the pattern was the same: Fitzgerald's attitudes and views would be much affected by those he met and was impressed by. At Newman, Leslie and Fay; at Princeton, Edmund Wilson and John Peale Bishop; in New York, in addition to Wilson and Bishop, H. L. Mencken and George Jean Nathan. At his low point in the 1930s, writing the 'Crack-Up' essays, Fitzgerald went further and suggested that for almost twenty years he had wilfully yielded control of almost every aspect of his intellectual, artistic, moral, and social life to his friends. The source of Fitzgerald's problem was at least in part his relative failure in academic terms: he seems never to have got over the feeling that men like Wilson and Bishop were cleverer than him. (Of course there was a reverse effect as well: Wilson and Bishop found Fitzgerald's success as a writer difficult because his grades at Princeton had been so much poorer than theirs ...) The result was that Fitzgerald was always inclined to defer to his critics. He lacked the intellectual – and often the artistic – self-confidence to stand up for himself. As we shall see, not long after the publication of *The Beautiful and Damned*, this peculiar form of critical self-abnegation will appear in a particularly egregious form in relation to Edmund Wilson, but first the sources of the second novel's difference from its predecessor require clarification.

Much in question, as has been implied, is the influence of such friends as Wilson and Mencken, replacing that of Leslie and Fay. Another highly significant new element is represented by Zelda. From the time of their marriage, Zelda became much involved in her husband's writing career: hers was another opinion to attend to, perhaps to defer to. Responding to a draft of an article about his writing career which Wilson sent him in January 1922, Fitzgerald noted the absence of any reference to his wife: 'the most enormous influence on me in the four and a half years since I met her has been the complete, fine and full-hearted selfishness and chill-mindedness of Zelda' (L, 351). Again, in 1924, in a letter to Perkins setting out his aims for *The Great Gatsby*, he lists the bad writing habits he has fallen into, and these include 'Referring everything to Zelda – a terrible habit, nothing ought to be referred to anybody until it is finished' (FP, 70). But in the earlier 1920s, Zelda was clearly among those who were influential in moving Fitzgerald away from the world-view he had held while writing *This Side of Paradise*. Probably even more important in producing this change was the new direction taken by Fitzgerald's own literary tastes. Suddenly it was mainly recent American fiction that he was reading and finding impressive. During his visit to New Orleans in early 1920, while he was awaiting the publication of *This Side of Paradise*, Fitzgerald wrote to Maxwell Perkins telling him how impressed he was by the work of Frank Norris. Norris, best known now for novels such as *McTeague* (1899) and *The Octopus* (1901), wrote of an American world remote from anything to be found in Compton Mackenzie. An inheritor of the realism that William Dean Howells had struggled to make acceptable to the genteel culture of post-Civil War America, Norris had pushed Howellsian realism towards a Zolaesque naturalism. With Hamlin Garland, who wrote of the hardship and deprivation of life on the Western frontier, Stephen Crane, Theodore Dreiser and Harold Frederic, Norris came to be seen as creating a new school of American writers committed to realism or naturalism or both.

A later generation of writers, Sherwood Anderson, Sinclair Lewis, and Willa Cather, Fitzgerald's contemporaries, were in turn influenced by that school. After his discovery of Norris – earlier, in his last year at Princeton, Fitzgerald had read *Salt*, a novel by Frank Norris's brother Charles – these realists and naturalists were the American authors he was reading. Indeed so impressed was Fitzgerald by Frank Norris's work that in October 1920, he wrote to Mencken proposing that a new uniform edition of Norris be published, with each volume having an introduction by a contemporary American novelist. A few months later he told Mencken he had just finished reading Willa Cather's *My Ántonia*: 'a great book!' he wrote (C, 78). In December 1920 he told his friend Burton Rascoe, review editor of the *Chicago Tribune*, that Lewis's *Main Street* 'is rotten' (C, 73). But a few weeks later he is writing from New York to Sinclair Lewis himself telling him 'that *Main Street* has displaced *Theron Ware* in my favor as the best American novel. The amount of sheer data in it is amazing' (L, 487). The *Damnation of Theron Ware* (1896), Harold Frederic's best known work, is a powerfully realistic attack on the bigotry, anti-intellectualism, and cultural sterility of small-town American Protestantism – but for Fitzgerald to describe it as 'the best American novel' does seem a youthful extravagance. Of his own immediate contemporaries Fitzgerald appears to have admired most John Dos Passos, and, of course, Edmund Wilson. But in 1923, he wrote to Sherwood Anderson expressing admiration for *Many Marriages* (which he had reviewed) saying it was even better than *Poor White* and the books of short stories: which presumably included Anderson's best-known work *Winesburg, Ohio* (1919), which had investigated the frustrations of small-town life in middle America with a new psychological realism.

The one writer admired by Fitzgerald at this time who seems to stand apart from the realist or naturalist school of American novelists was James Branch Cabell. Around Christmas, 1920, Cabell had sent Fitzgerald an autographed first edition of his novel *Jurgen*. Fitzgerald wrote back enthusiastically thanking Cabell for such a precious gift and telling him that his own new novel (*The Beautiful and Damned*) showed touches of Cabell's influence alongside that of Mencken and Frank Norris. A few days later, having finished reading *Jurgen*, he wrote again to Cabell telling him it was a finer work than Anatole France's novel *The Revolt of the Angels*. However, how pleased Cabell was to learn from the same letter that young Fitzgerald ranked his work as a whole 'below both Conrad and Anatole France' (L, 486) is not recorded. Perhaps he was mollified by the information that Zelda regarded him as her favourite novelist. Cabell's work now seems over-mannered, particularly in terms of language and style; what Fitzgerald probably most admired was the element in his fiction – a kind of eroticized sensuality – that was responsible for his being denounced by the conservative, genteel, moralizing critics of the day.

The only non-American author whom Fitzgerald was reading with real enthusiasm in this period was Joseph Conrad. The 1920 letter to Cabell just cited mentions Conrad as a touchstone of excellence in the novel. Earlier in the year Fitzgerald had written to Maxwell Perkins telling him of his recognition of H. L. Mencken as 'a factor in present day literature', and going on 'In fact I'm not so cocksure about things as I was last summer – this fellow Conrad seems to be pretty good after all' (FP, 28). It was almost certainly

Mencken who had urged Fitzgerald to read Conrad; and it did not take long for his obvious unfamiliarity with Conrad's work to be replaced by a growing admiration. Ultimately Conrad would become a major influence on both the form and thematic content of Fitzgerald's own fiction, but initially it seems to have been the element of scepticism in Conrad's outlook that attracted him. Soon after the publication of *This Side of Paradise* Fitzgerald had received a letter from President Hibben of Princeton University which, while expressing admiration for the descriptions of the beauty and charm of the university in the novel, also deprecated the 'country club' vision of Princeton it seemed to promulgate. In his courteous reply, Fitzgerald admitted that his account of the university did reflect the specific bitterness he felt over his own inability to adapt to the curriculum, but more generally what was in question was his own cynical temperament. 'My view of life, President Hibben,' he went on, 'is the view of the Theodore Dreisers and Joseph Conrads – that life is too strong and remorseless for the sons of men' (L, 482). Whether Hibben was impressed or amused by the pretentiousness of this assertion one has no way of knowing. More to the point is that this may well have been the view of life Fitzgerald believed he had adopted by the time he was writing the letter – not to mention *The Beautiful and Damned* – but it was hardly the view of life expressed in *This Side of Paradise*.

There can be no doubt that a series of events occurring between the writing of *This Side of Paradise* and *The Beautiful and Damned* did seriously modify the way Fitzgerald looked upon life and experience: the death of Fay, his marriage to Zelda, the influence of such men as Wilson, Mencken and Nathan, and his reading of both Conrad and the entire range of first and second generation American realists and naturalists – all of these contributed to his changing world-view. And before concluding that Fitzgerald was too naively responsive to such external influences, we have to remember just how young he was in the period in question: twenty-one when he begins work on what will be *This Side of Paradise*; twenty-four when he is writing *The Beautiful and Damned*. Few people, one imagines, have a fixed philosophy of life in their early twenties.

Fitzgerald's own sense of just where America's literary culture stood in the period when he was writing *The Beautiful and Damned* is probably best indicated by the piece, referred to above, that Thomas Boyd published as 'The Credo of F. Scott Fitzgerald'. After dismissing the *Bildungsroman* type of novel, he offers this assessment of the current American literary scene:

> Up to this year the literary people of any pretensions – Mencken, Cabell, Wharton, Dreiser, Hergesheimer, Cather and Charles Norris have been more or less bonded together in the fight against intolerance and stupidity . . .

Fitzgerald has in mind here the conservative backlash, the reaffirmation of the traditional, puritanical, moral values of nineteenth-century village or small-town America, which will clash with 'Jazz Age' America throughout the 1920s, and which will encourage a whole range of expatriate American artists and writers to prefer the cultural freedom and excitement of Paris to the provincial narrow-mindedness of home. But Fitzgerald goes on to speculate that this united literary front in face of American cultural philistinism is about to break down. Those writers who tend to see something romantic in life and experience will be dissatisfied with a purely realistic perspective, while the realists themselves will see romanticism as degenerating into sentimental nostalgia:

> On the romantic side Cabell, I suppose, would maintain that life has a certain glamor that detailed reporting – especially this reporting of the small mid-western town – can not convey to paper. On the realistic side Dreiser would probably maintain that romanticism tends immediately to deteriorate to the Zane Grey – Rupert Hughes level, as it has in the case of Tarkington, fundamentally a brilliant writer. (C, 79)

But Fitzgerald takes comfort from the fact that a man such as Mencken is now at the head of American letters, and that as a result the 'so called American upper class' is more inclined to admire Sinclair Lewis and perhaps even Dreiser and the Norrises. In writing such an account, Fitzgerald must have had in mind that his own new novel – *The Beautiful and Damned* – could be seen as combining to some degree at least the two contemporary trends towards romance and realism while not falling into the excesses of either.

And there is also the fact that he was expecting the redoubtable Mencken to be supportive of his latest work. None the less, this Fitzgerald 'credo' almost certainly does reflect his sense of the contemporary literary scene.

The evidence then is strong that the creative context out of which *The Beautiful and Damned* emerged was very dissimilar to that which had produced *This Side of Paradise*. In his heart Fitzgerald must have known that if his second novel was going to be as successful as his first – and, as always, his hopes were high – it would not be because *The Beautiful and Damned* was an imitative successor to *This Side of Paradise*. Writing to his aunt and uncle McQuillan in St Paul at the end of December 1920, thanking them for a wedding present, he seems to acknowledge that preserving his artistic integrity might involve the acceptance of financial loss: 'I'd rather live on less' he wrote, 'and preserve the one duty of a sincere writer – to set down life as he sees it as gracefully as he knows how' (L, 485). One suspects that this letter is to some degree a reflection of Fitzgerald's growing recognition that the novel he was then in the middle of writing – *The Beautiful and Damned* – might not have much appeal for the uplift magazine readership which his short stories would often cater to so successfully.

In the event Fitzgerald had no need to worry. In 1921 *Metropolitan Magazine*, which had earlier contracted with him for six short stories at the generous figure of $900 each, agreed to pay $7000 for the serial rights to *The Beautiful and Damned*. Perhaps reassured by this success, in August 1921, Fitzgerald wrote to his agent Harold Ober, full of high hopes about the novel:

> I have a hunch that is going to be almost as big a success in book form as *Main Street*. If so it would be foolish to sell it now as a movie, wouldn't it? I should say that it would be scarcely worth while under $10,000 as I think the value of my stuff will increase as it grows older. (FO, 25)

Fitzgerald's hunch proved wholly misleading. The sales of *The Beautiful and Damned* in book form would never even remotely approach those of Lewis's best-seller. And the fee he would accept for the movie rights from Warner Brothers would be only $2500. Possibly partly to blame was the novel's initial appearance in serialized form. Submitted in April 1921, the *Metropolitan Magazine* version ran from September 1921 to March 1922. But the magazine editors cut some forty thousand words from Fitzgerald's text. Hence the book that was finally published on 4 March 1922, was substantially different – and in Fitzgerald's view substantially better – than the serial version. In November 1921, he told Ober that the version he had now completed for book publication was 'a rather excellent novel' (FO, 31).

The first printing of *The Beautiful and Damned* in 1922 ran to 20,600 copies – which suggests that Scribners were probably anticipating sales at least as good as those for *This Side of Paradise*. Through the year there were in fact three printings producing a total of 50,000 copies, and sales were good enough to get Fitzgerald's novel on to the bestseller lists for March, April, and May. (The bestseller of 1922 was *If Winter Comes* by A. S. M. Hutchison, which sold 350,000 copies.) Having hoped for more, Fitzgerald was disappointed. Inevitably, his earnings from the book fell below his expectations: just over $12,000 in royalties for 1922. In 1922 as a whole he earned the huge sum of just over $25,000 – but, as always, expenditure tended to keep pace with and then outstrip income, so that there was no let-up in the pressure to go on writing for the magazine mass-market.

Like its sales, the reviews of *The Beautiful and Damned* were somewhat disappointing. Fitzgerald's best friends – Wilson, Bishop, Mencken, and even Zelda – all wrote on the novel, but not always in a manner likely to increase either the author's sales or his critical standing. Zelda's comments came in a kind of joke review in the *New York Tribune* under the heading 'Friend Husband's Latest'. She did, however, object to the 'soggy moments' in the novel when Fitzgerald attempted to explore serious philosophical issues in a pretentious, name-dropping manner. She also pointed wittily to Fitzgerald's attribution of a fragment of an old diary of hers, and scraps of her letters, to Gloria, the novel's heroine: 'Mr Fitzgerald', she wrote, 'seems to believe that plagiarism begins at home.'[4] Mencken's line in *The Smart Set* was that Fitzgerald deserved praise for not having settled for simply repeating 'the charming romance of "This Side of Paradise"'; instead he had attempted 'something much more difficult', and even if the result is not wholly successful it is 'near enough to success to be worthy of respect'. *This Side of*

Paradise may have been little more than 'a fortunate accident' but *The Beautiful and Damned* proves that Fitzgerald is a serious artist: 'There are a hundred signs in it of serious purpose and unquestionable skill.'[5] Clearly Mencken wanted to admire the change of direction in Fitzgerald's literary taste which he probably knew he had helped to inspire, but the impression of only a measure of half-success is what his review leaves with the reader. Bishop had written to Fitzgerald telling him he had agreed to review the novel for the *New York Herald* and asking him how he should proceed. Fitzgerald replied urging him to comment on specific aspects of the text: characters, style, humour, ideas, etc. To a degree Bishop does what Fitzgerald asks: but the result again falls far short of critical enthusiasm. Like Mencken, Bishop sees *The Beautiful and Damned* as an advance over *This Side of Paradise*. The text has a kind of vigorous life, but its ideas, vocabulary, aesthetics, and literary taste are all extremely flawed. Overall the approval once again seems half-hearted. But it was Edmund Wilson's commentary in *The Bookman* in March 1922, which proved most damaging. Wilson's long article, which surveyed Fitzgerald's work as a whole, went a long way to establishing what became a kind of critical orthodoxy on Fitzgerald's status as an artist: he was a gifted writer who, through a lack of intellectual power and control, had nothing very interesting to say.

The tone of Wilson's piece is set by a story he tells about Fitzgerald and 'a celebrated person' who is in fact Edna St Vincent Millay. Millay is supposed to have said that to meet Fitzgerald was like meeting a stupid old woman who has been left a diamond: the woman proudly shows the diamond to everyone, but everyone is surprised that such an ignorant woman should own such a jewel. Wilson immediately allows that this is not an accurate picture of Scott Fitzgerald, but does insist that 'there is a symbolic truth in the description'. It is true in the sense that Fitzgerald 'has been given imagination without intellectual control of it; he has been given the desire for beauty without an aesthetic ideal; and he has been given a gift for expression without very many ideas to express'. After such an opening, Wilson's unenthusiastic account of *The Beautiful and Damned*, and all of Fitzgerald's earlier writing, comes as no surprise. *This Side of Paradise* is said to possess gaiety and colour and movement; but 'it has almost every fault and deficiency that a novel can

possibly have'. It is a 'preposterous farrago', and it is 'very imma-
turely imagined'. It is well-written, but 'well-written in spite of its
illiteracies'. Towards the end of the article, Wilson suggests that
Fitzgerald's 'restless imagination may yet produce something
durable' but at present his imagination 'suffers badly from lack of
discipline and poverty of aesthetic ideas' – even his stories 'have a
way of petering out'. Finally *The Beautiful and Damned*, 'imperfect
though it is' is seen as representing an advance over *This Side of
Paradise*: 'the style is more nearly mature and the subject more
solidly unified, and there are scenes that are more convincing than
any in his previous fiction.' But as throughout the entire article,
Wilson's tone remains superior and condescending.[6]

What is really astonishing is Fitzgerald's enthusiastic response to
Wilson's article. He told his friend that he took 'an extraordinary
delight' in the article's 'considered approbation' and that he
'enjoyed it enormously'. What Wilson had said was 'pretty generally true' and 'an unprejudiced diagnosis'. 'I am considerably in
your debt,' he wrote, 'for the interest which impelled you to write
it' (L, 350–2). Fitzgerald had persuaded Wilson to remove from the
original draft some references to his drinking and his personal life,
but otherwise he seems to have felt that Wilson was doing him a
favour by writing about him at such length, and even after finally
falling out with his friend over some details, he told Wilson he
remained 'immensely grateful' for his having written the article (L,
353). Only a severe case of artistic and intellectual self-doubt could
have produced such a reaction. The article did nothing in the short-
term or the long-term to help Fitzgerald's reputation. Rather it
encouraged the view that his work was immature and hardly worth
serious critical attention. More unqualified support from the friends
he respected would have gone some way towards bolstering
Fitzgerald's always fragile artistic self-confidence. After the reception of *The Beautiful and Damned*, he must have felt that rightly or
wrongly he still had much to prove.

4
Writing *The Great Gatsby*

The Fitzgeralds' first visit to Europe had occurred in the summer of 1921. The version of *The Beautiful and Damned* that would be serialized in *Metropolitan Magazine* having been sent to Harold Ober in April, and with Zelda already pregnant with their daughter Scottie, the couple sailed in the *Aquitania* from New York to Southampton in the first week of May. In the course of the next two months they visited London, Oxford and Cambridge as well as Paris, Venice, Florence and Rome. Given the future frequency and duration of their European visits, it comes as something of a surprise to recognize that this first trip was not a success. Of the cities visited, only Oxford appears to have impressed them. At least in London Shane Leslie was on hand to take them on an exciting night-time tour of the docks area – and Lady Randolph Churchill had them to lunch with Winston Churchill. But both France and Italy they disliked intensely. The problem almost certainly was their sense of isolation. Accustomed to a supportive social circle of friends and acquaintances – and indeed to their Jazz Age celebrity in America – in France and Italy they were unreceived and unknown, their isolation intensified by the fact that English was their only language. The role of anonymous tourists was clearly one not at all to their taste. In any event, his sense of frustrated rejection by Europe led Fitzgerald to write a letter to Edmund Wilson from Paris in July 1921, that one suspects he must subsequently have regretted:

> God damn the continent of Europe. It is of merely antiquarian interest. Rome is only a few years behind Tyre and Babylon. The

negroid streak creeps northward to defile the Nordic race.
Already the Italians have the souls of blackamoors. Raise the bars
of immigration and permit only Scandinavians, Teutons, Anglo-
Saxons and Celts to enter. France made me sick. Its silly pose as
the thing the world has to save. I think it's a shame that England
and America didn't let Germany conquer Europe. It's the only
thing that would have saved the fleet of tottering old wrecks. My
reactions were all philistine, anti-socialistic, provincial and
racially snobbish. I believe at last in the white man's burden. We
are as far above the modern Frenchman as he is above the
Negro.... We will be the Romans in the next generations as the
English are now. (L, 346)

There can be no excusing such outlandish ravings. Clearly
Fitzgerald is in the darkest of moods leading him to transfer the
angry discontents he is feeling onto the world around him. All one
can say is that a few years down the line he had the good sense
partially to redeem himself by reinscribing similar racist attitudes
into the language of the bullying and hypocritical Tom Buchanan
in *The Great Gatsby*.[1]

On their return from Europe, the Fitzgeralds went first to
Montgomery, Alabama – Zelda's home town – then on to St Paul,
where they intended to remain until their baby was born. (Scottie
was duly delivered in October 1921.) In Europe, and in the succeeding months, Fitzgerald had written very little. So much so that in
August 1921 he wrote to Maxwell Perkins blaming his sense of
despondency – 'I'm feeling rather tired and discouraged with life
tonight' – on his failure to get on with creative work:

> I'm having a hell of a time because I've loafed for 5 months &
> I want to get to work. Loafing puts me in this particularly
> obnoxious and abominable gloom.... I'm sick of the flabby semi-
> intellectual softness in which I flounder with my generation.
> (FP, 41)

In fact in the following months Fitzgerald produced at least three
stories. Two of these were accepted by the high-paying *Saturday
Evening Post*, but the third was rejected. That third story, 'The
Diamond as Big as the Ritz' would come to be regarded as among

Fitzgerald's finest, despite its for him somewhat unusual allegorical mode. But G. H. Lorimer, editor of the *Post*, must have felt that the story's satirical critique of American capitalism would not be to the taste of a mass readership.

Fitzgerald's next major literary undertaking may well have been suggested by his presence in St Paul and his recollecting his earliest writing successes. In December 1921 he wrote to Harold Ober telling him he was writing a play which he was sure would make him rich. In the months that followed Fitzgerald worked hard at the play that would eventually be entitled *The Vegetable*. Perhaps the surprising thing is not that he had decided to write a play, but that he had not thought of it sooner. The success of his youthful plays in St Paul had after all been the first indication to him that writing might be the way forward towards the fulfilment of his dreams. Why should not the writing of a Broadway hit be the solution to his financial problems? Back in 1919, *The Smart Set* had published his playlet 'The Debutante' (originally written for the *Nassau Lit* at Princeton), and of course both *This Side of Paradise* and *The Beautiful and Damned* contain sections of drama-style dialogue and scenes. Then again his friends and mentors had in the past praised his potential as a playwright. In November 1919, when *The Smart Set* had accepted 'Dalyrimple Goes Wrong' and 'Porcelain and Pink (A One-Act Play)' George Jean Nathan had told him: 'You have a decidedly uncommon gift for light dialogue. Keep at the dramatic form. You will do things' (C, 47).

In the early months of 1922 Fitzgerald worked hard at his play – provisionally called 'Gabriel's Trombone'. His letters in this period all indicate the high hopes he had for its success. A first version was completed by early March and in the letter to Ober accompanying the script Fitzgerald wrote: 'I feel that Acts I + III are probably the best pieces of dramatic comedy written in English in the last 5 years' (FO, 39). More significantly, Edmund Wilson at this time was enthusiastic about the play. Through the spring and summer of 1922 Wilson and Fitzgerald corresponded regularly about the work's progress, and in May Wilson's view of its worth was even higher than Fitzgerald's own:

> I think that the play as a whole is marvelous – no doubt, the best American comedy ever written. I think you have a much better

grasp on your subject than you usually have – you know what end and point you are working for, as isn't always the case with you.... I think you have a great gift for comic dialogue – even if you never can resist a stupid gag – and should go on writing plays ...[2]

It is quite difficult to understand Wilson's enthusiasm – which in fact, much later, he attempted to deny. And the phrasing of his advice to Fitzgerald to go on writing plays is surprisingly similar to that of his colleague Nathan's of a year or two earlier. Perhaps at some level Wilson was happier to think of Fitzgerald as a popular dramatist than as a serious novelist. *The Vegetable* in fact is a rather laboured skit on the American success story of the from log cabin to White House variety: it looks back as it were to Fitzgerald's contributions to the Princeton *Tiger* rather than to his work for the *Nassau Lit.* One suspects that Fitzgerald would have done better had he kept in mind that the audience for a popular and successful play was not so very different from that for the popular, uplift magazines: rather than satire or cynical humour, he should have been offering romance and emotional intensity. In his letter Wilson goes on to see a close parallel between drunken scenes in *The Vegetable* and similar scenes in *Ulysses,* and asks Fitzgerald whether he has read Joyce's novel. The answer was no; but characteristically Fitzgerald made great efforts to secure a copy and in June was able to tell Wilson that he had managed to get one from the Brick Row Bookshop. (His immediate reaction to the book was a highly personal one: 'there is something about middle-class Ireland, that depresses me inordinately ...') (L, 357).

Over the summer of 1922 Fitzgerald's hopes of a Broadway production for his play remained understandably high. Two established Broadway producers did take an interest in the script, and Wilson and Nathan even sought advice from Eugene O'Neill about production possibilities. In August Fitzgerald was telling Maxwell Perkins at Scribners that his play was 'the best American comedy to date' and 'undoubtedly the best thing I have ever written' (FP, 62). In the end, however, no production offer was made. Fitzgerald continued to tinker with his text: he had always felt that Act II – taking the form of a surreal fantasy – was problematic; but as the months passed he seemed to accept that there was little chance of an early production. Reluctant to abandon the play completely, however, he began to think in terms of publication. By the end of 1922 Perkins had read and admired the script: at the end of the year he wrote to Fitzgerald telling him the play had great potential – that the second act remained the major problem, and offering detailed advice on how to revise it. In response to this letter Fitzgerald probably revised his text yet again (eventually he would claim the play had been revised six times). But the only development was the publication by Scribners of *The Vegetable* in April 1923, in an edition of 7650 copies. By now Fitzgerald was prepared to tell Perkins: 'of course it is written to be read' (FP, 66). However, in the summer of 1923, a deal was finally done to produce *The Vegetable*. In November 1923 a trial run of the play opened in Nixon's Theatre in Atlantic City, New Jersey. It was a disaster, 'a colossal frost' as Fitzgerald afterwards put it.[3] Act I went well enough, but Act II proved impossible on the stage. Fitzgerald tried to fix things, but to no avail. The play never made it to New York. At the time Fitzgerald seemed to accept the failure of his play philosophically; but a letter written about a year later suggests the experience was more troubling. In August 1924, he told a friend: 'I feel old too, this summer – I have ever since the failure of my play a year ago' (LL, 78).

Apart from *The Vegetable* Fitzgerald's main literary undertaking in 1922 was preparing his second collection of short stories: Scribner's published *Tales of the Jazz Age* in September 1922. The collection consisted of eleven stories of which only 'May Day' and 'The Diamond as Big as the Ritz' were of high quality. Among the others was 'Tarquin of Cheapside' which Fitzgerald had written for the *Nassau Lit* in 1917. Perkins took exception to the story, arguing that readers would be offended by the notion of Shakespeare as a rapist. Fitzgerald replied that he would cut out the story if Perkins insisted, but it would be 'very much against my better judgment and Zelda's' (FP, 62). The story, he argued, had received praise on its first appearance, and again when it had been published by Mencken in *The Smart Set*. Perkins agreed to be overruled. *Tales of the Jazz Age* was widely reviewed and for a book of its type sold rather well: the first printing amounted to 8000 copies, and there were two further printings in 1922. Fitzgerald's royalties were worth $3056. In that summer Fitzgerald also agreed to a film option price for *This Side of Paradise* – but the company in question failed to come up with the money. (In 1923, however, Fitzgerald accepted an option on the novel of $10,000 – but the film was never made.) In terms of new writing, Fitzgerald's one significant achievement in this period was a short story entitled 'Winter Dreams'. Written in September and published in *Metropolitan* in December 1922, 'Winter Dreams' was later described by its author as 'A sort of 1st draft of the Gatsby idea' (LL, 121). Dexter Green, the story's protagonist, is a poor boy who loves a rich girl; he becomes rich himself, but it is too late for him to capture either the girl or the 'winter dreams' of his youthful self. Clearly some of the themes and emotions that were to surface in *The Great Gatsby* were already circulating inside Fitzgerald's creative consciousness.

II

In the autumn of 1922, when Scottie was almost exactly one year old, the Fitzgeralds left St Paul and moved back to New York. In the city they met John Dos Passos whose *Three Soldiers* Fitzgerald had recently reviewed enthusiastically, describing the author as 'the best of all the younger men on this side'.[4] (Between 1921 and 1923 Fitzgerald wrote eleven reviews including work by Mencken, Shane Leslie, Charles Norris, Booth Tarkington, and Sherwood Anderson.) Dos Passos accompanied Fitzgerald and his family on their search for a house to rent and they finally opted for a place in Great Neck, Long Island, quite close to where Ring Lardner was living. To run their new household the Fitzgeralds employed three servants full-time, with a part-time laundress in addition.

Fitzgerald knew that the year he had spent in St Paul had been largely wasted. In his personal *Ledger* the relevant entry says: 'A bad year. No work.' The move to Long Island at first made little difference. Indeed life in Great Neck in 1922–23 sounds much like life in Westport in 1920. New York city was nearby and the round of weekend parties in Long Island was rarely interrupted; visitors came and went – eventually; and in Ring Lardner Fitzgerald found a boon drinking-partner. In fact Ring Lardner was an alcoholic and at this stage in his career Fitzgerald too was well on his way to becoming one. From undergraduate days on he had always been a heavy drinker: having a good time, partying and socializing, inevitably meant generous quantities of alcohol – even though Fitzgerald himself seems to have had a less than average capacity to tolerate liquor. As the 1920s went on his dependence on alcohol certainly increased, and most of the rest of his life would be marked by frequent episodes of binge drinking, by longer or shorter periods of being on the so-called wagon – sometimes meaning drinking only wine or beer – and by times when he absolutely needed the stimulus of alcohol to be able to go on writing. Long nights of drinking with Ring Lardner in Great Neck certainly did nothing in 1922–23 to ameliorate Fitzgerald's incipient alcohol problem, but the relationship between the writers did have its positive side. Fitzgerald would be immensely helpful to Lardner, persuading Scribners to become his book publisher; meanwhile Lardner got Fitzgerald to read Dostoevsky and probably also Dickens (up to this point, Thackeray seems to have remained the only Victorian novelist whom Fitzgerald really admired.)

Inevitably, however, the constant partying and drinking in Great Neck and New York did not do much to help Fitzgerald get on with work. He did make a deal with the Hearst publishing corporation to produce six stories in 1923 at a figure of $1500 each – but in fact only two were written and published. The truth is that at this time Fitzgerald was still able to go on believing that *The Vegetable* would be a great success – and thus solve his continuing financial problems. Subsequently he admitted as much:

> My first play was to be presented in the autumn, and even if living in the East forced our expenses a little over $1,500 a month, the play would easily make up for the difference ... we asked several playwrights what was the maximum that could be earned on a year's run.... I think my figures came to about $100,000.[5]

Of course Fitzgerald is writing after the event, and being ironic at his own expense – but one cannot doubt that part at least of the rueful truth is present here. Living in Long Island had, however, brought him contacts in the New York film industry; and in the course of the year he did make some money on film-related jobs, as well as receiving the previously mentioned $10,000 for the movie rights to *This Side of Paradise*.

But the failure of *The Vegetable* in Atlantic City in November

1923, forced Fitzgerald to reassess his position. Life in Great Neck was proving immensely expensive; he was in debt to the tune of around $5000; and he was writing almost nothing. His total income for 1923 amounted to no less than $28,759.78 – which included an advance of almost $4000 on his next novel, as well as the $10,000 for the *This Side of Paradise* film rights. But his expenditure, he calculated, was a massive $36,000. In other words disaster loomed. Fitzgerald's response does have its heroic side. He gave up drinking and between the end of 1923 and March 1924, wrote ten stories and four articles. The stories alone earned him $16,450. He also wrote about writing them in an article for the *Saturday Evening Post* called 'How to Live on $36,000 a Year' – which earned him $1000. Like the references to his high expectations of royalties from *The Vegetable*, the account he gives here of how he went about writing the necessary stories has an authentic ring to it:

> Over our garage is a large bare room whither I now retired with pencil, paper and the oil stove, emerging the next afternoon at five o'clock with a 7,000 word story. That was something; it would pay the rent and last month's overdue bills. It took twelve hours a day for five weeks to rise from abject poverty back into the middle class, but within that time we had paid our debts, and the cause for immediate worry was over.[6]

In June 1924, Fitzgerald wrote to Ober listing all the articles and stories he had recently completed: 'Including the ones already published that makes exactly 19 things sold in five months. My God! Thats well over $20,000 worth of stuff' (FO, 62). Admirable as such a sustained and disciplined burst of creativity was, Fitzgerald himself knew that this kind of feverish activity was not compatible with the production of serious literature. What the entire episode did was to reinforce his sense that his work for the mass magazine market was no more than a way of buying him time to write his novels.

III

In April 1923, Fitzgerald had contributed to a newspaper feature in which various literary figures were asked to identify the '10 Best

Books I have read'. In his list Fitzgerald cited Conrad's *Nostromo* as 'the great novel of the past fifty years, as *Ulysses* is the great novel of the future'.[7] A month later he told readers of the *Chicago Daily Tribune* that he would rather have written *Nostromo* than any other novel: 'because I think it is the greatest novel since *Vanity Fair*.'[8] Thinking like this, and reading Dickens and Dostoevsky, Fitzgerald's literary horizons were clearly expanding well beyond those marked out by the American realists and naturalists who had influenced *The Beautiful and Damned* – not to mention those of H. G. Wells and Compton Mackenzie who had contributed so much to *This Side of Paradise*.

In fact, since the summer of 1922 – indeed almost from the moment of the book publication of *The Beautiful and Damned* – Fitzgerald had been thinking about what exactly his third novel should be. In July of that year he told Perkins of his intention 'to write something *new* – something extraordinary and beautiful and simple + intricately patterned'.[9] The month before he had written Perkins a kind of thinking-aloud letter:

> I may start my novel and I may not. Its locale will be the middle west and New York of 1885 I think.... It will have a catholic element. I'm not quite sure whether I'm ready to start it quite yet or not. (FP, 61)

In the following months, *The Vegetable*, preparing *Tales of the Jazz Age*, and writing a movie synopsis for David Selznick, seem to have absorbed most of Fitzgerald's work time, but the novel was never entirely out of mind. In December 1922 he told Harold Ober that his new novel would not be suitable for serialization – even if he decided serial publication were desirable. At this point the move to Great Neck, Long Island, had already taken place, and as we have already noted, Great Neck did not turn out to be a location which favoured serious writing. However, despite the endless round of trips to New York, parties, and entertaining week-end guests, Fitzgerald did attempt, alongside his other writing tasks, to get his new novel under way. That much is proved by the existence of 'Absolution', a story published in the *American Mercury* in June 1924. In April of that year Fitzgerald wrote to Perkins of, among other things, his hopes and intentions concerning his next novel, saying that much of what he had written the previous summer (that is, in 1923) 'was good but it was so interrupted that it was ragged ...' He had decided to discard much of this material but some of it would be appearing in a story for the *Mercury*: that of course was 'Absolution' (FP, 69). Years later, in 1934, Fitzgerald said that 'Absolution' was intended to be a picture of Gatsby's early life, but he chose to cut it because he 'preferred to preserve the sense of mystery' (L, 528). Just how close in fact the link is between Rudolph Miller, the story's protagonist, and James Gatz, is a debatable question, but the existence of the story at least indicates that the summer of 1923 did see Fitzgerald beginning to get to work on what would eventually be *The Great Gatsby*.

What the long, April 1924, letter to Perkins, mentioned above, also shows is that Fitzgerald was beginning to feel a degree of reassurance about his potential as a writer. And this is despite the fact that the letter is enormously self-critical, even confessional, in tone. Fitzgerald begins by expressing the hope that the new novel will be finished by June, but insists that he intends to take whatever time is necessary to ensure that 'it has the very best I'm capable of in it or even as I feel sometimes, something better than I'm capable of'. He knows that what he has achieved in the last few years has been a long way short of his capabilities:

> It is only in the last four months [he means the months in which he has been churning out a mass of less than first-rate material to pay off his debts] that I've realized how much I've – well, almost *deteriorated* in the three years since I finished the Beautiful and Damned. The last four months of course I've worked but in the two years – over two years – before that, I produced exactly *one* play, *half a dozen* short stories and three or four articles.... If I'd spent this time reading or travelling or doing anything – even staying healthy – it'd be different but I spent it uselessly, neither in study nor in contemplation but only in drinking and raising hell generally.

He goes on to list the bad habits he has developed – laziness, self-doubt, and the constant reference of everything he writes to Zelda – but insists that he feels 'an enormous power in me now'. It is this creative power that will inform his new book: 'not trashy imaginings as in my stories but the sustained imagination of a sincere and yet radiant world.... This book will be a consciously artistic achievement & must depend on that as the 1st books did not' (FP, 69–70). Writing to his friend Thomas Boyd a week or two later, Fitzgerald makes an equally lofty statement of intent, but in a more wryly ironical vein: 'Well, I shall write a novel better than any novel ever written in America and become par excellence the best second-rater in the world' (LL, 69).

Only a year before, during a brief visit to Zelda's home in Montgomery, Alabama, Fitzgerald had written to Perkins in a very different frame of mind: 'Being in this town where the emotions of my youth culminated in one emotion makes me feel old and tired. I doubt if, after all, I'll ever write anything again worth putting in print' (FP, 67). The despondency here probably hints at Fitzgerald's growing awareness that his commitment to Zelda was putting tremendous pressure on his commitment to his art. The failure of *The Vegetable* a few months later, coupled with the endless extravagance of their Long Island life-style, could hardly have given Fitzgerald much confidence in his future as a writer. How then is the note of recovered creative confidence so powerfully present in the letters to Perkins and Boyd, to be explained? His having (temporarily) given up drinking? The successful production of the body of commercial writing needed to pay off his debts? His belief in the quality of the initial writing for what would eventually be *Gatsby* that he had somehow managed to get done in Great Neck? All these are no doubt factors; but I believe that rather than something he had done, it was something he had read or reread which best explains Fitzgerald's rediscovered artistic self-belief and aesthetic self-confidence. At Princeton Fitzgerald appears not to have come across Conrad. In the 1920 letter to Perkins, already alluded to, he refers to 'this fellow Conrad' as seeming to be 'pretty good after all' (FP, 28). In the next year or two he clearly became an Conrad enthusiast. As we have seen, in April 1923, when the earliest version of what was to become *Gatsby* was beginning to shape itself in Fitzgerald's consciousness, he cited Conrad's *Nostromo* as 'the great novel of the past fifty years'; inevitably, then, as he approached the writing of his third novel, fully aware of its immense importance in relation to his ambition to be recognized as a serious American contributor to the art of fiction, Conrad was the writer most in his mind. After *Gatsby* was published Fitzgerald was more than willing to acknowledge Conrad's influence on it: in the middle of 1925 he wrote to Mencken (another Conrad admirer who had certainly been among those urging Fitzgerald to read him) arguing that more authors had been influenced by Conrad than Mencken had allowed in a review. Included in Fitzgerald's list of such authors is 'Me in Gatsby', and alongside, 'God! I've learned a lot from him' (L, 501).

What exactly had Fitzgerald learned from Conrad that is apparent in *The Great Gatsby*? One assumes aspects of both the novel's form and content: the use of Nick Carraway as a character–narrator, and the central theme of dream/illusion and reality. But still more significantly what Fitzgerald learned from Conrad, as he approached the writing of *Gatsby*, was that he could after all go on to become the great writer that he desperately aspired to be. Fitzgerald's major handicap as a writer and artist was the intellectual inferiority complex from which he suffered. Despite what he had achieved in *This Side of Paradise* and *The Beautiful and Damned* – and possibly *because* he could get popular magazine editors to pay him huge sums of money for his short stories – Fitzgerald remained intimidated by the Wilsons, Bishops and Menckens of his world. They were his intellectual superiors – he had struggled even to pass his Princeton courses. This is why he was so meek in face of the recurring charges that his work, however popular and successful, was immature, lacking in profundity, insufficiently serious. In 1934, writing an Introduction to a new Modern Library edition of *Gatsby*, he for once attempted to fight back:

> I had recently been kidded half haywire by critics who felt that my material was such as to preclude all dealing with mature persons in a mature world. But, my God! it was my material, and it was all I had to deal with.[10]

But such a riposte was unfortunately atypical: most of the time Fitzgerald was all too ready to assent to the view that there was a superficiality about his work, and even that his supposed intellectual shortcomings were a disabling characteristic of his art. In fact he would never free himself entirely of such a confidence-draining notion. Almost a year after the publication of *Gatsby*, he wrote with

unusual bitterness to Perkins about his lack of any kind of intellectual inheritance from his family:

> My father is a moron and my mother is a neurotic, half insane
> with pathological nervous worry. Between them they haven't
> and never have had the brains of Calvin Coolidge.
>   If I knew anything I'd be the best writer in America. (FP, 134–5)

Happily this was not the mood in which he approached the writing
of *Gatsby*. Reading or rereading in this period the Preface to
Conrad's *Nigger of the Narcissus* Fitzgerald encountered a perspective
on the art of fiction which, as I suggested at the very beginning of
this book, clearly filled him with a new, exhilarating, and releasing
sense of power. Conrad's Preface is a major statement of his
aesthetic credo as a novelist, and that credo is one that has never
lost its power to persuade and instruct. How could Fitzgerald have
done other than 'learn a lot' from it? As we have seen, all his uncertainties and self-doubt were attributable to his sense, as he put it to
Edmund Wilson as late as 1939, that he was 'still the ignoramus
that you and John Bishop wrote about at Princeton' (L, 368). But
Conrad told him that it didn't matter, it wasn't relevant. The power
of the artist, Conrad insisted, has nothing to do with brilliance of
mind, or depth of thought. The artist is not like the thinker or
scientist; the sources of aesthetic power lie deep within the individual self; the appeal of the artist is not to our wisdom or ideas, but to
our enduring 'capacity for delight and wonder, to the sense of
mystery surrounding our lives; to our sense of pity, and beauty, and
pain …'. 'All art', Conrad argues, 'appeals primarily to the senses,
and the artistic aim when expressing itself in written words must
also make its appeal through the senses, if its high desire is to reach
the secret opening of responsive emotions.' Thus the writer must
aim at 'the perfect blending of form and substance', must show 'an
unremitting never-discouraged care for the shape and ring of
sentences' and allow 'the light of magic suggestiveness' to 'play for
an evanescent instant over the commonplace surface of words'. All
of this must have sparked instant recognition on Fitzgerald's part.
Not just the insistence that the novelist was not in competition
with the philosopher – welcome as that insistence must have been
– but the emphasis on exactly the qualities of writing that Fitzgerald

knew he could command. 'Delight and wonder'; 'pity, and beauty, and pain'; the reaching to 'the secret spring of responsive emotions'; 'the perfect blending of form and substance'; 'the shape and ring of sentences' – were not these precisely the qualities and characteristics which his narrative prose embodied and celebrated? His reading of Conrad's Preface could only have resulted in an enormous renewal of Fitzgerald's artistic self-confidence; he could after all go forward, building on and refining his strengths, and thus produce an enduring work of art that would, as Conrad required, 'carry its justification in every line'.

IV

In the early summer of 1924 the Fitzgeralds decided to leave Great Neck and return to Europe. Behind this decision lay no notion of the irresistible pull of European high modernism. The Fitzgeralds had no idea even of sampling again the European culture which they had found so distasteful in 1921. Nor were they fleeing from the puritanical restrictiveness of conventional American morality in search of the freedom and excitement of post-war Paris. The decision was a purely financial one. Unable to begin to live within their income in America, they hoped and believed that their dollars would stretch a great deal further in France or Italy. And in a general sense they were right. Their house in Long Island had rented at $300 a month; the equivalent figure for the Villa Marie they eventually rented in the south of France was $79.

With money in hand from the burst of story-writing that had cleared off his debts earlier in the year, Fitzgerald at last felt able to get down to serious work on his novel. After a week in Paris – interviewing nannies for Scottie – the Fitzgeralds left for the French Riviera, finally settling in a house a mile or two above St Raphael. Fitzgerald was in a mood of high creative excitement. In May 1924, he wrote to Thomas Boyd insisting that his current isolation in the south of France was exactly what he needed: 'I hope to God I don't see a soul for six months. My novel grows more + more extraordinary; I feel absolutely self-sufficient ...' (LL, 68). The 'enormous power' in himself he had described to Maxwell Perkins a few months earlier was clearly still driving him forward. For perhaps the only time in his life, in these weeks and months in the south of

France, Fitzgerald let nothing, absolutely nothing, stop him from allowing a work of sustained creative power steadily and consistently to take shape under his hand. For once Fitzgerald's commitment to his art proved stronger than his commitment to anything else; in this one period not even Zelda could break the spell. Significantly, however, it was in these weeks that the Fitzgeralds' marriage faced its most serious threat. While Fitzgerald worked steadily at his novel, Zelda became romantically involved with a young French military aviator, Edouard Jozan. At first Fitzgerald seems not even to have noticed what was going on; his writing alone had his full attention. It is almost as though at some level he needed and wanted Zelda out of his way; getting on with his novel undisturbed was the only thing that mattered. Did he perhaps for a time choose to ignore Zelda and Jozan? Did the demands of his art for once shut out what was happening in his life? If so, the situation was one that could not last. The end came in mid-July. Fitzgerald's *Ledger* entry reads: 'The Big crisis – 13th of July.' Briefly there was talk of divorce, but in a week or two the whole matter seemed to blow over. The Fitzgerald marriage – and the writing of *Gatsby* – went on. Later, however, in his *Notebooks* Fitzgerald recorded: 'That September 1924, I knew something had happened that could never be repaired.'[11] How far Fitzgerald had got with the writing of *Gatsby* when this episode occurred is not clear; in any event such interruption as Zelda's behaviour caused was short-lived, but it could well be that in due course its consequences contributed to the note of elegy and loss that would eventually characterize the finished novel. At the end of August, Fitzgerald told Perkins: 'Its been a fair summer. I've been unhappy but my work hasn't suffered from it. I am grown at last' (FP, 76). What is implied is that coping with the Zelda–Jozan affair has been a maturing experience for Fitzgerald the man; but there is a later *Notebooks* entry which at least raises the possibility that for a time the creative intensity of the artist blotted it out:

> I can never remember the times when I wrote anything – *This Side of Paradise* time or *Beautiful and Damned* and *Gatsby* time, for instance. Lived in story.[12]

Despite his determination to get on with his novel, Fitzgerald did not live in complete seclusion in the French Riviera in the summer of 1924. There were trips with Zelda to such fashionable resorts as Cannes, Monte Carlo and Antibes (though at this time in the 1920s the fashionable European still regarded the Riviera as too hot in the summer, preferring the cooler Atlantic resorts such as Dinard and Deauville: it would be largely the Americans of Fitzgerald's generation who would pioneer the idea of the Mediterranean summer vacation).[13] It was probably on such a trip in August that the Fitzgeralds met the couple who would prove their closest friends in France – Gerald and Sara Murphy. The Murphys clearly impressed the Fitzgeralds as Americans of considerable cosmopolitan glamour and style; not rich, they nonetheless lived well, maintaining houses both in Paris and Cap d'Antibes, and both were actively involved in the world of art and culture. Among their many friends were such figures as Pablo Picasso, Fernand Léger, John Dos Passos, Cole Porter, and Archibald MacLeish. Fitzgerald would make use of his relationship with both Murphys in the long-drawn-out writing of *Tender is the Night*.

V

In the middle of June 1924, Fitzgerald was writing to Perkins saying how much he was enjoying *Ariel*, André Maurois's new biography of Shelley, but all his own creative energy was given over to the writing of *Gatsby*. By the end of August he was telling Perkins that 'the novel will be done next week'. But he is not yet prepared to send it off: 'Zelda and I are contemplating a careful revision after a weeks complete rest' (FP, 75). The allusion here to Zelda's involvement is intriguing: the earlier April letter to Perkins, describing Fitzgerald's sense of his deterioration as a writer, had included among the bad habits he had fallen into the need to refer everything to Zelda. This reference makes it clear that Zelda remained involved, and that Fitzgerald continued to attend to her suggestions or criticisms – though it may be the case that the precise stage at which Zelda read what Fitzgerald had written had in fact changed. In any event, the week's rest followed by about two weeks of writing or rewriting allowed Fitzgerald to write to Harold Ober on 20 September telling him that the work was finished: 'I have finished my novel and will send it to you within 10 days or two weeks ...'

And Fitzgerald goes on to express his confidence in the value of what he has written: 'Artisticly it's head + shoulders over everything I've done' (FO, 66). In fact it took a week or two longer – 'the last of the last revision of the novel is being typed' (FO, 67) he told Ober on 19 October – but on 25 October 1924, Fitzgerald was writing to his agent telling him that the completed *Gatsby* was on its way to him, so that a decision could be made about serialization. A couple of days later a letter went off in turn to Maxwell Perkins announcing the despatch of *Gatsby*:

> 'Under separate cover I'm sending you my third novel: *The Great Gatsby* (I think that at last I've done something really my own) but how good "my own" is remains to be seen.' (FP, 80).

(His August letter had told Perkins without equivocation that the new work 'is about the best American novel ever written' (FP, 76).)

Waiting anxiously for responses to his novel from his editor and his agent, Fitzgerald was at this point preoccupied with two issues: the book's title, and its serialization prospects. He was never sure what to call his third novel. Since April at least, Perkins had been pressing him for at least a tentative title so that preparations could go ahead over a cover and dust-jacket. Perkins himself was originally quite keen on the *Gatsby* title: 'I always thought that "The Great Gatsby" was a suggestive and effective title, – with only the vaguest knowledge of the book of course' (FP, 71). *Gatsby* soon became the working title, and it was, as we have seen, *The Great Gatsby* that Fitzgerald announced he was despatching to New York. But the accompanying letter also contained this:

> I have an alternative title:
> *Gold-hatted Gatsby.*
> After you've read the book let me know what you think about the title. (FP, 81)

This was an issue destined to run and run.

The serialization question was essentially one about money. Fitzgerald felt strongly that the serialization of *The Beautiful and Damned* had been a disaster: the changes made by the magazine editors had weakened the novel and thus contributed to its uneven reception both in a critical sense and in terms of sales. *Gatsby* had to be protected from such treatment, whatever the cost. But once again Fitzgerald was now desperately short of money. The cash brought over to France was more or less used up – and during the months of writing *Gatsby* he had been earning nothing. (He felt it was bad luck that none of his recent stories had been picked up by film-makers.) So, as he explained to Ober, he had to return to the short-story treadmill:

> I'm about broke and as soon as the novel gets off I will write a story immediately ... That story will be followed within a month by two more. The first one should reach you by October 20th or a little over two weeks after you receive this letter – and as you have no doubt already guessed I'm going to ask you for an advance on it.

And he goes on to tell Ober that writing these stories he will have movie possibilities in mind: 'I must try some love stories with more action this time. I'm going to try to write three that'll do for Famous-Players as well as for the Post' (FO, 66).

At this time the Fitzgeralds had decided to leave the French Riviera for Italy in the belief that the exchange rate of the dollar against the lira was even more favourable than the dollar–franc exchange. In such a situation, it is not difficult to understand why Fitzgerald should have been anxious to explore serialization possibilities for *Gatsby*. But from the first he recognized that the possibilities were limited. Today's readers no doubt find *The Great Gatsby's* treatment of its characters' sexual behaviour decorous and restrained. In the mid-1920s, however, Fitzgerald knew that his story contained material that put it well outside the moral boundaries of the mass-market magazines such as the *Saturday Evening Post* or any of the magazines aimed at a largely female readership. Thus *Hearst's International*, which had contractual rights to first refusal, was also unlikely to be interested. Fitzgerald's hopes were centred on a magazine called *Liberty*; he told Ober he would accept $15,000 from *Liberty*, as long as the serialization of his short novel was over by the spring of 1925, making book publication by Scribners possible in April. Ray Long, editor of *Hearst's International*, duly turned down *Gatsby*: 'I don't think it quite fits in' (FO, 70), he told the

Reynolds agency. But Jack Wheeler at *Liberty* proved to be equally uninterested: on the very grounds Fitzgerald had known would make his work unacceptable to the mass-market magazines. Wheeler wrote, 'It is too ripe for us. Running only one serial as we do, we could not publish this story with as many mistresses and as much adultery as there is in it' (FO, 70). But this was not the end of the serialization saga. In January 1925, the magazine *College Humor* offered $10,000 for the *Gatsby* serialization rights. Ober was clearly keen for Fitzgerald to accept even though the deal would mean cancelling Scribners' planned April publication of the book. Fitzgerald hesitated, but in the end convinced himself he should turn the offer down. He told Ober his two chief objections were:

(1) That most people who saw it advertised in *College Humor* would be sure that Gatsby was a great halfback and that would kill it in book form.

(2) While $10,000 is no sum to throw away lightly it postpones a turnover from book royalties and probable movie for five months, with the chance of materially decreasing the sale. I dread the gaudy and ill-advised advertising they'd give it. (FO, 74)

Basically Fitzgerald was objecting to the idea of allowing the best book he had written to appear in what he clearly felt was a down-market publication. *College Humor* and *The Great Gatsby* were simply incompatible. For $20,000 he might have swallowed his pride; but in the end he continued to say no. Inevitably he later wondered whether he had done the right thing: 'God! How I hated to turn down that $10,000' (FO, 75) he told Ober in February. Later still, when the financial return from *Gatsby's* success proved so disappointing, he must often have wondered whether he had made the right decision.

VI

When the Fitzgeralds left the French Riviera for Rome in November 1924, they were still awaiting reactions from Perkins and Ober in New York to the manuscript version of *The Great Gatsby*. Just before leaving France, Fitzgerald had written to Perkins telling him he was not satisfied with the existing chapters six and seven, and that he proposed writing in a completely new scene at the proof stage. A previous wire had raised the issue of the title, and the same issue resurfaces in the letter:

> I have now decided to stick to the title I put on the book.
> *Trimalchio in West Egg.*
> The only other titles that seem to fit it are *Trimalchio* and *On the Road to West Egg*. I had two others *Gold-Hatted Gatsby* and *The High-bouncing Lover* but they seemed too light. (FP, 81)

When Maxwell Perkins dashed off his initial response to reading Fitzgerald's manuscript, he took up the question of the title, but he began by saying what Fitzgerald must have hoped and prayed he would: 'Dear Scott. I think the novel is a wonder.' In what follows there is lavish praise for the novel's vitality, its glamour, and underlying thought, 'And as for sheer writing, it's astonishing.' But there is the issue of the title. Various people at Scribners dislike it:

> 'in fact none like it but me. To me, the strange incongruity of the words in it sound the note of the book. But the objectors are more practical men than I. Consider as quickly as you can the question of a change.' (FP, 82)

The so-much-disliked title has to be *Trimalchio in West Egg* – Perkins seems to have forgotten his original preference for *The Great Gatsby*. A week later Perkins wrote Fitzgerald a much longer and more detailed letter full of enormous praise and perceptive criticism of the text. One can only guess at the depth of Fitzgerald's delight and relief: after all his struggles and delays and hackwork he had finally pulled it off. His publisher was telling him he had written a masterly work of fiction. If, as he later told Ober, he owed Scribners its advance on *Gatsby* for almost two years, then the finished work had proved to be more than worth waiting for. Perkins's letter did make some suggestions for possible improvements – he agreed with Fitzgerald that chapters six and seven, including the confrontation scene between Tom and Gatsby in New York's Plaza Hotel, could be improved upon, but he ended with a long list of outstanding elements in the book, telling Fitzgerald prophetically 'these are such things as make a man famous' (FP, 84). Fitzgerald's response from Rome at the beginning of December 1924, is entirely understandable: 'Dear Max: Your wire & your letters made me feel like a million dollars ...' In the long letter that follows Fitzgerald accepts all of Perkins's criticisms and suggestions. He says he will try his best over the title – perhaps by reverting to plain 'Trimalchio' or 'Gatsby'; that he knows how to fix chapters six and seven; that he can also deal with Perkins's concerns over Gatsby's business affairs, and how to get his former history inserted. All these changes Fitzgerald says he will make at the proof stage, and when he has made them the book will 'be perfect' (FP, 86). In the middle of December he is wiring Perkins telling him to make the title 'The Great Gatsby', and Perkins in turn tells him that when Ring Lardner had been told of the 'Trimalchio' title he had instantly balked at it: 'No one could pronounce it', he said (FP, 87). By the end of December Fitzgerald is writing to Perkins once again insisting that he knows exactly what has to be done at the proof stage to make *Gatsby* flawless. He even mentions future plans:

> I've got a new novel to write – title and all, that'll take about a year. Meanwhile, I don't want to start it until this is out & meanwhile I'll do short stories for money (I now get $2,000.00 a story but I hate worse than hell to do them) and there's the never dying lure of another play.

But it is Perkins's unstinting praise of *Gatsby* that is still clearly intoxicating him: 'Anyhow I think (for the first time since The Vegetable failed) that I'm a wonderful writer & its your always wonderful letters that help me to go on believing in myself' (FP, 88, 90). In November Fitzgerald had also told Ober that he was about to start a new novel – 'My loafing days are over,' he wrote, 'I feel now as though I wasted 1922 + 1923' (FO, 69), but, as was normally the case, their letters concerning *Gatsby* remained largely practical and professional. Still Ober did wire his congratulations and sent a letter that Fitzgerald said made him feel 'very good indeed' (FO, 71). He goes on to add a sentence about the improvements that will be made at the proof stage, but then it is back to stories, their placement, and as usual the inevitable problems over money. Fitzgerald's earnings in 1924 amounted to $20,310 – deriving from the sale of eleven stories plus only $1200 in book royalties. Without Ober's constant advances on stories that he was still writing, Fitzgerald knew he could not have survived financially. He was still hoping of course that *Gatsby* would prove a huge success, and thus solve all his problems: he ended his letter of thanks to Ober for his praise of *Gatsby* with 'a prayer that this novel will put me on a financial footing where I won't be such a beggar' (FO, 72). But in the meantime he was keenly aware of just how much he owed to Ober's constant generosity. 'You've been awfully kind about this money,' he wrote in January 1925, 'I don't know what I could have done without it' (FO, 73).

In yet another attempt to economize on living expenses the Fitzgeralds moved to an hotel in Rome around the beginning of December 1924. Back in 1921 they had found little to choose between France and Italy: both countries were unappealing and unrewarding. Now Fitzgerald felt differently: the French Riviera was a great place to be (perhaps because his writing had gone well there) but Italy remained as unattractive as before. In January 1925, he wrote to Ober from Rome telling him: 'I hate Italy and the Italians so violently that I can't bring myself to write about them for the *Post* ...' (FO, 73). This degree of alienation from a country that earlier generations of American artists and writers had found irresistible is difficult to account for. Admittedly the Rome Fitzgerald was living in was the Rome of Mussolini, but there is nothing to suggest that contemporary Italian politics were the source of Fitzgerald's prejudice. Getting himself beaten up by Italian policemen in a drunken escapade presumably did little to make him feel better about Italy and Italians, and soon matters were made worse by both Fitzgeralds falling ill in the wintry cold of Rome. By early February they had decided they should move further south to Capri, in the search for warmer weather. Despite all these problems, work on the revised proofs of *Gatsby* went ahead. The first part of the revision was dispatched from Rome to Perkins on 24 January 1925. Fitzgerald's major concern is that Perkins ensures that the changes are made exactly as Fitzgerald wants them – and that absolutely no other changes be made except in the case of glaring misprints. Around the middle of February, the last part of the revised proof is sent from Capri:

Dear Max:
After six weeks of uninterrupted work the proof is finished and the last of it goes to you this afternoon. On the whole its been very successful labor
(1.)   I've brought Gatsby to life
(2.)   I've accounted for his money
(3.)   I've fixed up the two weak chapters (VI and VII)
(4.)   I've improved his first party
(5.)   I've broken up his long narrative in Chap. VIII (FP, 94)

Fitzgerald's only remaining doubts concerned the old problem of the title. Influenced by Perkins, Zelda, and Ring Lardner he had agreed to settle for 'The Great Gatsby'. But he was still unsure. With the first batch of revised proofs in January he added a postscript saying that his heart told him he should have named the novel *Trimalchio*. But he admits that to reject all the advice he had been given would have been 'stupid and stubborn'. *Trimalchio in West Egg* would have been only a compromise, *Gatsby* alone would have been too much like *Babbitt*, and the postscript ends with the remark – so significant for the novel's future critics and commentators – 'The Great Gatsby is weak because there's no emphasis even ironically on his greatness or lack of it' (FP, 94). This might have seemed like the end of the matter, but as late as March 1925, Fitzgerald was still wiring and writing to Perkins about the title; he thought of going back to *Gold-hatted Gatsby* or *Trimalchio*, and at what was virtually the very last moment, he told Perkins he was crazy about the title *Under the Red, White, and Blue*. Perkins cabled back saying that to change the title now would inevitably delay publication and be psychologically damaging: 'Everyone likes present title' (FP, 272). Fitzgerald reluctantly conceded and *The Great Gatsby* was published in New York on 10 April 1925.

VII

As publication day of *The Great Gatsby* approached Fitzgerald grew increasingly nervous. For months he had been confident that what he had achieved in *Gatsby* was incomparably superior to anything he had done in the past. In October 1924 he told Edmund Wilson 'my book is wonderful' (L, 361); in February 1925, he informed

Ernest Boyd 'It represents about a year's work and I think it's about ten years better than anything I've done. All my harsh smartness has been kept ruthlessly out of it ...' (L, 498). In April, before leaving Italy for Paris, he told John Peale Bishop 'The cheerfulest thing in my life are first Zelda and second the hope that my book has something extraordinary about it. I want to be extravagantly admired again' (L, 377). The previous month he had told Bishop he could now get $2000 per story, but that 'they grow worse and worse', while, buoyed up no doubt by his hopes for the success of *Gatsby*, he aimed to get 'where I need write no more but only novels' (L, 375). Now, however, all these high hopes were to be put to the test. Fitzgerald was understandably jumpy. Writing to Perkins from Capri on the last day of March, he began, 'As the day approaches my nervousness increases' (FP, 98). By publication day he was possessed by doubts and anxieties. On 10 April itself he wrote to Perkins: 'The book comes out today and I am overcome with fears and forebodings.' Still dissatisfied with the Plaza Hotel confrontation scene in chapter VII, and having new doubts about the novel's closing scenes, he is most concerned about the book's possible lack of appeal for women readers, and its focus on the rich:

> Supposing women didn't like the book because it has no impor-
> tant woman in it, and critics didn't like it because it dealt with
> the rich and contained no peasants borrowed out of *Tess* in it
> and set to work in Idaho? (FP, 99)

Fitzgerald can only be half serious here – though for several years he had been complaining that American critics were obsessed with the idea that American fiction should focus on characters close to the soil. As far as women characters are concerned, Daisy, Jordan and Myrtle would surely strike most readers as certainly important. Fitzgerald seems to be searching for alibis just in case the public response to his novel proves disappointing. Earlier in the year, in more confident mood, he had told Perkins he was guessing *Gatsby* would sell 'about 80,000 copies' (FP, 93); and later he would acknowledge that his hope was 'it would do 75,000' (FP, 102). Now, on publication day, he says 'all my confidence is gone' (FP, 99). Perhaps it won't even sell the 20,000 copies necessary to pay Scribners back its advance! Given that *This Side of Paradise* and *The*

Beautiful and Damned, despite reviews that were often lukewarm at best, had both sold close to 50,000 copies, and given too the enthusiastic response of such readers as Perkins, Ober, Ring Lardner, and Roger Burlingame, another of Scribners' editors ('I think that's about the nicest letter I ever received about my work' (L, 498) was Fitzgerald's response to Burlingame), it is quite difficult to understand his change of heart – however prescient in the long run it might prove to be. In a postscript to this letter, Fitzgerald refers to a relative's reaction to a preliminary announcement of the novel – 'It sounded as if it were very much like his others' – and concludes that there are readers 'weary of assertive jazz and society novels' (FP, 100). If so then there is a problem over how to promote *Gatsby*.

The first news reached Fitzgerald, while he was en route from Italy to Paris, in the form of a cable from Perkins on 20 April: 'Sales situation doubtful. Excellent reviews' (FP, 101). To a minor degree, Perkins was being economical with the truth: two unfavourable reviews had already appeared in New York newspapers, one of them headlined 'F. Scott Fitzgerald's Latest a Dud'. But even without knowing of these – untypical – reviews, Fitzgerald was already despondent. 'Your telegram depressed me,' he wrote back to Perkins, and went on to argue that if the book failed commercially it would be for one of two reasons or both:

1st   The title is only fair, rather bad than good.
2nd   *And most important* – the book contains no important woman character and women control the fiction market at present. (FP, 101)

Perkins followed up his telegram with a letter, written on the same day, in which he tried to offer some explanation for the slowness of the novel's sales. He said many in the book-trade had been sceptical, though he was not sure why. One objection had been to the book's length – at 218 pages only, it has apparently struck some distributors as being too short (presumably in terms of value for the reader's money): 'The small number of pages, however, did in the end lead a couple of big distributors to reduce their orders immensely at the very last minute.' (Scribners' initial run for *The Great Gatsby* amounted to 20,870 copies. A second printing of 3000 copies occurred in August 1925, some of which many years later remained unsold.) On the other hand, he says, highly favourable reviews have appeared in such important papers as the *New York Times* and the *Tribune;* other good reviews are anticipated, while the kind of people whose opinion Fitzgerald values are all highly enthusiastic – Gilbert Seldes, Van Wyck Brooks, John P. Marquand, John Peale Bishop. Perkins concludes his letter with yet another unqualified endorsement of *Gatsby's* excellence:

> I know fully how this period must try you: it must be very hard to endure, because it is hard enough for me to endure. I like the book so much myself and see so much in it that its recognition and success mean more to me than anything else in sight at the present time, – I mean in any department of interest, not only that of literature. But it does seem to me from the comments of many who yet feel its enchantment, that it is over the heads of more people than you would probably suppose. (FP, 101)

Whatever the reason, the public reaction to *Gatsby* in the early days after publication was to prove prophetic of the long-term situation: sales remained deeply disappointing, while the responses of critics and friends and fellow-writers were increasingly enthusiastic. The sales of *The Great Gatsby* never even came close to equalling those for *This Side of Paradise* and *The Beautiful and Damned.* Early in May the total sales reached 12,000, 14,000 was attained in early June, 15,000 by the end of the month, 16,000 by early July. By October the figure remained slightly under 20,000; *Gatsby* that is, sold only half as well as Fitzgerald's earlier novels. In the end Fitzgerald's royalties were large enough to pay off his debt to Scribners – but only just. Given that he had once hoped for sales of seventy or eighty thousand, and in consequence a new kind of financial stability that would allow him to go on writing novels, the scale of his disappointment was potentially overwhelming. In fact Fitzgerald coped pretty well. In April to Perkins, and again in June/July to the critic Gilbert Seldes, he did talk about giving up fiction and going to Hollywood to learn the movie business; but this was only if his *next* novel should fail to bring him the economic security to go on being a novelist. 'I can't reduce our scale of living and I can't stand this financial insecurity', he told Perkins. 'Anyway there's no point in trying to be an artist if you can't do your best'

(FP, 102). Fitzgerald's resilience and refusal to despair – it is clear that by the summer of 1925 he is already thinking about a new novel – have to be largely attributed to the deep satisfaction he took from the overwhelmingly positive reaction to *Gatsby* from readers he respected and admired. If *The Great Gatsby* had failed to engage the wider American reading public, it had more than confirmed Fitzgerald's status as a major literary figure among the discriminating and informed. As the ever-supportive Perkins put it to him: 'I think so far as recognition goes, the end will be as it should be, and your position will have greatly advanced, in the eyes of the discriminating public anyway' (FP, 105).

In confirmation of Perkins's view of Fitzgerald's new stature, he had received a range of letters from friends and admirers, all of them congratulating him for what he had achieved in *Gatsby* – and of course many of these letter-writers were also reviewers. Unsurprisingly Edmund Wilson, John Peale Bishop and H. L. Mencken wrote appreciatively and there were letters too from James Branch Cabell, Shane Leslie, Van Wyck Brooks, Gertrude Stein, Edith Wharton and T. S. Eliot. Ernest Hemingway was an enthusiastic reader in Paris. In June, Fitzgerald wrote to Carl Van Vechten thanking him for his positive and perceptive review of *Gatsby*:

> A dozen or more people have been very complimentary about it, largely on account of the writing, but only three or four seemed to have cared to notice what I was driving at and whether or not I approached realizing my intention – but I am consoled by the fact that those three or four have been the people whose appreciation I would rather have than any other Americans (L, 502).

About the same time, Fitzgerald thanked Gilbert Seldes for his review, telling him 'I believe I'd rather your discriminating enthusiasm than anyone's in America ...' (L, 504). Perhaps what was happening was that Fitzgerald had begun to convince himself that the poor sales of *Gatsby* simply reflected his work's artistic subtlety; what he had written was just too fine, too nuanced, for a mass readership to appreciate. And it was certainly the sales issue that lay behind his comment to Marya Mannes in October: 'Thank you for writing me about *Gatsby* – I especially appreciate your letter because women, and even intelligent women, haven't generally cared much for it' (L, 507). Certainly, as has been noted, Fitzgerald had earlier persuaded himself that the novel would not appeal to women readers, but exactly why he thought this is far from clear. Was Zelda perhaps less enthusiastic than he had hoped she would be? Or had he at the back of his mind the common belief that Conrad's work had lesser appeal for women readers? In May 1925 he had told another woman admirer of *Gatsby*, Hazel McCormack, that while the novel was 'far from perfect', it contained all in all 'such prose as has never been written in America before. From that I take heart'. What he now has to do, he goes on, is to combine 'the verve of *Paradise*, the unity of the *Beautiful + Damned* and the lyric quality of *Gatsby*, its aesthetic soundness' into something worthy of the most discriminating admiration (LL, 112). The ideal, at least, was a sound one, and given the new sense of artistic self-confidence produced by the critical enthusiasm for *Gatsby*, one would have thought in no way an unattainable one.

As a final gesture of admiration for what Fitzgerald had achieved in *Gatsby*, Maxwell Perkins arranged for a specially bound copy to be sent to him just before Christmas 1925. On 17 December Perkins wrote:

> I'm sending you for Christmas, or thereabouts, a book I've had especially bound; – for it is among the most original, beautiful, and terrible books of our time, and I want to do it what little honour I can by putting it in that dress into which great books eventually get themselves. – And you ought to have it in that form. (FP, 124)

After the publication of *Gatsby* in April 1925, the Fitzgeralds decided to stay on in Paris. One of the first persons they sought out was Ernest Hemingway, whose early work Fitzgerald knew and admired and whom he had been recommending to Perkins for the previous six months. Fitzgerald was convinced that Hemingway had a brilliant future, and felt that Perkins should make every effort to recruit him as a Scribners author: an outcome finally achieved the following year, largely as a result of Fitzgerald's unstinting effort. Inevitably the two writers, enjoying the good life in Paris, became close friends, and their friendship, despite all its problems and tensions, was destined to endure. At first, as the acclaimed author of *The Great Gatsby*, Fitzgerald was, as it were, the senior partner, but as Hemingway's own career as a writer became increasingly successful, so the nature of the relationship changed. What did not change was the concern they had for each other as professional writers; they did not always agree on aesthetic matters, and could be critical of each other's work, but they were prepared to listen because each knew the other could write.

Fitzgerald's relationship with Hemingway was certainly his closest with another writer, but his record as a promoter of other people's work is a remarkable one – he never seems to have been unwilling to help out those whose writing he liked. Equally, while keeping up with contemporary writing both English and American, he seems always to have kept in mind new authors whom he could recommend to Perkins and Scribners – perhaps a way of saying thank you for all the help and support he had received from his publishers. And perhaps all the more necessary since soon after the appearance of *Gatsby* Fitzgerald innocently gave his editor and publisher cause for alarm. Late in May 1925, Tom Smith, an editor at the publishing firm of Boni & Liveright, who had probably heard of the relatively poor sales of *Gatsby*, wrote to Fitzgerald offering to take on his next novel. Fitzgerald replied at once saying he had absolutely no intention of leaving Scribners – but adding that should anything happen to make his relations with Scribners impossible, then he would come to Boni & Liveright, who were then the publishers of Hemingway and E. E. Cummings. Clearly his intention was that this should be the end of the matter. However, Smith seems to have leaked news of his exchange with Fitzgerald in such a way as to make Maxwell Perkins believe that Fitzgerald was thinking of leaving Scribners. Perkins immediately contacted Fitzgerald, who wired and wrote by return, setting out at length in his letter all the reasons why he had never considered leaving Scribners even for *one single moment*, referring to 'the tremendous squareness, courtesy, generosity and open-mindedness' he had always received from the firm, and mentioning 'the curious advantage to a rather radical writer in being published by what is now an ultra-conservative house' (FP, 108).

Perkins was clearly delighted by Fitzgerald's continuing loyalty, and soon editor and author were getting down to work on their next project. Just as *This Side of Paradise* and *The Beautiful and*

Damned had been followed up by a book of short stories so would be *The Great Gatsby*. By June 1925, Fitzgerald was already deciding which of his recent stories to include. In fact *All the Sad Young Men*, published on 26 February 1926, was a decidedly better collection than his previous two. As early as April Fitzgerald had been telling Perkins that he had 'a book of good stories for the fall' (FP, 102) and, given that the volume included 'Winter Dreams', 'Absolution', 'The Sensible Thing' and the newly-written 'The Rich Boy', he had every reason to say so. The volume sold well for a story collection; in 1926 it had three printings, amounting to 16,170 copies, and Fitzgerald's royalties brought him $3,894. Unlike the previous two collections, however, there was no English edition.

VIII

Ever since completing *Gatsby*, Fitzgerald's need for money had driven him back to the writing of stories for the magazine market. If for any reason he could not go on churning out stories for his agent he was immediately in trouble. Thus when illness prevented him from working for several weeks in Capri in March 1925, he wrote somewhat self-pityingly to Ober; 'I don't know whats the matter with me. I can't seem to keep out of debt. Whenever I get ahead things like this sickness happen. Such is life' (FO, 76). The fatalism of this is probably an accurate reflection of the position Fitzgerald found himself in by the mid-1920s. Despite the frequent resolutions to sort things out, to become more organized and disciplined, he seems to have accepted that there was no way in which his life with Zelda could change fundamentally. Nannies and servants, wining and dining, nights out on the town in bars and night-clubs, were simply necessities – necessities that had to be paid for. His stories were Fitzgerald's meal-ticket – hence the regularity with which his correspondence with Ober was only a variation on the theme of 'Two stories sent will you deposit two hundred' (FO, 82); and 'Thank you a million times for all the kind advances' (FO, 81). Yet from time to time Fitzgerald found himself writing something of more substance. It was also in Capri, for instance, that Fitzgerald began work on what would prove to be one of his finest longer stories – 'The Rich Boy'. But this was not the kind of story that he could throw off in a few days; it proved to be 'a source of much trouble' (FO, 79) and was not finished until August 1925. Based on the life of a friend and Princeton classmate, Ludlow Fowler, Fitzgerald felt that Fowler had to be allowed to see it before publication, but the cuts that Fowler asked for were not in fact made until the story appeared in Fitzgerald's next story collection. 17,000 words long, 'The Rich Boy' might have been expanded – as Matthew J. Bruccoli has suggested – into a short novel of *Gatsby*-like length, thus quickly helping to confirm Fitzgerald's reputation as a serious novelist. But Fitzgerald needed the money, and so 'The Rich Boy' appeared in the *Red Book* early in 1926, the single story earning him $3,500 – more than half the total royalties for *Gatsby*.

In the months after the publication of *Gatsby* Fitzgerald was keen to explore ways of improving his financial position aside from writing more magazine stories. He was insistent, for example, that there should be an English edition of his novel as soon as possible. 'Is Gatsby to be published in England?' he enquired of Perkins, 'I'm awfully anxious to have it published there' (FP, 116). William Collins had been the English publisher of his first two novels and story collections, and thus had first refusal rights to *Gatsby*. After considerable delay, Collins finally decided against publishing an English edition. Perkins quoted to Fitzgerald an extract from his letter of rejection:

> With regard to 'The Great Gatsby', this has perplexed us all here. In a way it is the best book Scott Fitzgerald has done, and yet I think it is the one hardest to sell over here. I do not think the British public would make head or tail of it, and I know it would not sell. It is an awkward length too ... The point is, that the atmosphere of the book is extraordinarily foreign to the English reader, and he simply would not believe in it ... (FP, 121)

From the point of view of potential sales, Collins was almost certainly right. Neither *This Side of Paradise* nor *The Beautiful and Damned* had done particularly well in Britain, and the 'Americanness' of *Gatsby* would have had no special appeal to the average British reader in the mid-1920s. For no doubt identical commercial reasons a second British publisher – Duckworth – also turned *Gatsby* down. Fitzgerald wanted his book to go to Jonathan Cape, but Scribners settled with Chatto & Windus who promised publication in the spring of 1926. When it appeared it received better reviews than any of Fitzgerald's earlier books, but sales were modest.

The other potential source of income from *Gatsby* was of course the film industry. From the beginning Fitzgerald had high hopes of what the movie rights might bring – and a figure as high as $70,000 did at one point seem possible. Fitzgerald's optimistic thinking is suggested by his mentioning to Ober that Erich von Stroheim would be an ideal director for the film, but in the end the rights were sold to Famous Players, who made a silent movie version without Fitzgerald's involvement, for around $50,000; but after the various agents and agencies involved got their share, Fitzgerald's payment was only $13,500.

More surprising, perhaps, was the Broadway success of the stage version of *The Great Gatsby*. Fitzgerald again had no involvement in the dramatization of his novel. The stage adaptation was by a playwright, Owen Davis, and the Broadway producer was William A. Brady. Ober negotiated a satisfactory contract on Fitzgerald's behalf in June 1925; and the play opened at the Ambassador Theatre on Broadway on 2 February 1926. The Fitzgeralds of course remained in France, but both Perkins and Ober saw the stage version and were not unimpressed. Ober's wire to Fitzgerald on 4 February read: 'Audience enthusiastic over Gatsby. Predict real success. Play carried glamor of story. Excellently cast and acted. Reviews all very favorable' (FO, 85). Perkins had seen a pre-Broadway performance in Stamford, Connecticut, and had thought well of it. 'You need not feel ashamed of the play, "The Great Gatsby". Far from it,' he wrote to Fitzgerald. 'Your ideas and the course of the action have been adhered to far more closely than I ever dreamed they would be' (FP, 131). Perkins was unable to attend the play's New York opening, but wrote to Fitzgerald telling him of 'the apparently undoubted success of the first night' (FP, 131). The play was well reviewed and did prove a success. It ran for 112 performances in New York and then went on the road to such cities as Chicago and Detroit. Fitzgerald's share of the box-office receipts amounted to $7630, a sum which helped to keep him more or less solvent during 1926. When the play closed in New York he wrote to Ober:

> Well, its rather melancholy to hear that the run was over. However as it was something of a *succés d'estime* and put in my

pocket seventeen or eighteen thousand without a stroke of work on my part I should be, and am, well content. (FO, 91)

(Fitzgerald is here lumping together his share of the play's box-office and the silent movie rights.)

For 1925, Fitzgerald's total earnings had amounted to $18,333.61. Five short stories earned him $11,025, while book royalties came to just under $5000 including almost $2000 from *Gatsby* after paying off the original advance. In January 1926, the Fitzgeralds left Paris and went to a small spa village in the Pyrenees hoping that a colitis problem Zelda had developed would benefit from the move. From there Fitzgerald wrote to Ober once again thanking him for all his past help and promising that he would do better in 1926:

> I honestly think I cause you more trouble and bring you less business than any of your clients. How you tolerate it I don't know – but thank God you do. And 1926 is going to be a different story. (FO, 85)

A few weeks before, in a mood of even deeper depression, Fitzgerald had written to Perkins telling him that 'work is the only thing that makes me happy – except to be a little tight – and for those two indulgences I pay a big price in mental and physical hang-overs' (FP, 126). At first glance this comment seems strangely paradoxical: how can work and drinking be coupled as 'indulgences'? What Fitzgerald means is in fact quite clear: by 'work' he means his serious work as a novelist (he had been mentioning that he was at work on a new novel), as opposed to his bread-and-butter magazine story writing. Just how huge he felt the gap to be between the two kinds of writing, and the kind of angst he felt over the need to write for a quick financial return, are well brought out by his comments to Ober about 'Your Way and Mine' a story he wrote around the beginning of March 1926: 'This is one of the lousiest stories I've ever written. Just *terrible!*' And he goes on to plead with Ober not to offer it to the *Saturday Evening Post* or the *Red Book* – because these publications would be seen by too many people. '*I feel very strongly about this!*' he wrote (FO, 87). What is truly ironic is that the story was published in the *Woman's Home Companion* the following year, and earned Fitzgerald $1750 – almost as much as his total post-advance royalties for *The Great Gatsby*. Given the Fitzgeralds' apparent total inability to change their hugely expensive life-style, there had to be something self-indulgent about Scott Fitzgerald's attempt to write barely profitable novels rather than vastly profitable magazine stories. Yet not to write his novels would have meant total defeat for Fitzgerald the serious writer. The demands of life would have silenced the voice of art. In any event, by the spring of 1926, Fitzgerald was back in a more cheerful frame of mind. Suddenly, it seemed, things were going rather well: *Gatsby* was doing well on the stage; an English edition was about to appear; a French translation was under way; and *All the Sad Young Men* was doing rather well in New York. In March, Fitzgerald was writing to Perkins in a mood of almost serenity:

> with the play going well & my new novel growing absorbing & with our being back in a nice villa on my beloved Riviera ... I'm happier than I've been for years. Its one of those strange, precious and all too transitory moments when everything in one's life seems to be going well. (FP, 137)

In some ways Fitzgerald had earned the right to this moment. *The Great Gatsby* had been written and published in a relatively short time. And with this novel all of Fitzgerald's early promise had been fulfilled. He had produced a book that would acquire classic status, and had written off those critics who had regarded him as too immature and unintellectual ever to produce major literary work. Of course the failure of *Gatsby* to be a best-seller, and thus solve Fitzgerald's financial problems, was a serious disappointment; but the success of the stage version and the sale of the movie rights were producing enough money to allow him to move on to his next novel without the need to produce a stream of magazine stories. But, as always, Fitzgerald was almost uncannily prescient: this moment in March 1926 would prove all too transitory. And such a moment would never recur in the rest of his literary life.

5
Trailing *Tender is the Night*

In June 1940, a few months before his death, Fitzgerald wrote to his daughter Scottie, a student at Vassar College in New York state, urging her to work hard and not make the kind of mistakes he had done (much of the often moving correspondence between father and daughter repeats this and other self-critical points). He insists that hard work alone has brought him any degree of success:

> What little I've accomplished has been by the most laborious and uphill work, and I wish now I'd *never* relaxed or looked back – but said at the end of *The Great Gatsby*: "I've found my line – from now on this comes first. This is my immediate duty – without this I am nothing." (L, 95)

One might argue that Fitzgerald is underlining his point here by being less than wholly accurate: 'laborious' is about the last word that one would use to describe his writing, and certainly there were times and circumstances in his career when his writing flowed almost effortlessly. But what is chillingly accurate is his recognition that the successful publication of *Gatsby* was the crucial moment in his literary career. By April 1925, he had been a professional writer for just over five years. But apart from the first few months, his professionalism as a writer had existed uneasily alongside his life as a man. He had chosen to marry Zelda because she had become an essential dimension of his dream of success: without her, his triumph was incomplete. But from the very beginning, he sensed that his obligation to their life together might come into conflict with his commitment to writing. As his use of the word here, in the letter to Scottie, makes clear, Fitzgerald experienced a powerful, almost Victorian sense of duty. But after his marriage his problem was in deciding where did his duty lie: to his life with Zelda? or to his art? In the closing years of his life he was quite explicit about the clash between the two. Writing to Scottie in 1938, when he felt she was behaving irresponsibly at school, he described it in some detail:

> When I was your age I lived with a great dream. The dream grew and I learned how to speak of it and make people listen. Then the dream divided one day when I decided to marry your mother after all, even though I knew she was spoiled and meant no good to me. I was sorry immediately I had married her but, being patient in those days, made the best of it and got to love her in another way.... But I was a man divided – she wanted me to work too much for *her* and not enough for my dream. (L, 47)

In the years preceding the publication of *Gatsby* he had found no solution to this problem. What he had done, almost inevitably, was to allow the personal dilemma he had chosen to walk into to become at least a subtext within his novels. *This Side of Paradise, The Beautiful and Damned,* and *The Great Gatsby*, all raise questions about the 'man divided': about the relationship between art and life, about the role of the writer as a figure simultaneously within and without ordinary life and experience, about the need for detachment and the necessity of commitment. But incorporating his problem into his art proved not to be a solution for Fitzgerald's life. Only the critical success of *Gatsby* provided him with a new opportunity. He had proved to himself and to others who mattered that he was much more than a professional writer able to earn big money by writing for the market-place. Writing *Gatsby* he had become a literary artist; he had taken an important place in the literary world; if he had much to do before joining the Henry James's or the Joseph Conrads, at least he was knocking on the door of their house of fiction.

Looking back from the vantage-point of 1940, Fitzgerald recognized the opportunity he had won for himself in 1925. His talent and ability were now beyond dispute; he had a future as a major American novelist. His duty was to seize it: 'from now on this comes first.' All he had to do was to go forward from where *Gatsby* had left him. He had found his 'line'; all that was needed was to pursue it. And within a few months the opportunity, even in financial terms, was there.

As we have already seen, in the months immediately after the publication of *Gatsby* Fitzgerald was back on the treadmill of writing stories for quick money. But early in 1926 the situation changed: the success of the stage version of his novel, added to his share of the movie rights, meant that for a time at least his finances were no longer a daily problem. The consequence of this change is made abundantly clear by Fitzgerald's record of earnings in 1926: his total income was $25,686.05, including book royalties of $2033.20, the play and film return of $19,464.21, and the sale of a mere two stories for $3375. The pressure was clearly off, and a space had been created in which work on a new novel could proceed without interruption.

Fitzgerald's intentions were of the best. At the beginning of 1926 he told Perkins 'this year is going to be different' (FP, 127), and a few weeks later, as noted above, he insisted to Ober that 1926 would be 'a different story' (FO, 85). Within months of the appearance of *Gatsby*, he began planning his next novel. As early as 1 May 1925, when he was still depressed by the poor sales of *Gatsby* and his continuing debt to Scribners, he told Perkins:

> The happiest thought I have is of my new novel – it is something really NEW in form, idea, structure – the model for the age that Joyce and Stein are searching for, that Conrad didn't find. (FP, 104)

In Fitzgerald's Paris, of course, Joyce and Gertrude Stein were established as the presiding figures in the development of a new, modernist prose – for Fitzgerald to cite them as markers, alongside his old master Conrad, is the clearest of indications that he was still buoyed up by the self-belief produced by the critical success of *Gatsby*. In July he tells Perkins that the book 'getting shaped up both in paper and in my head' is called *Our Type* (FP, 116). In August he explains that it is 'about several things, one of which is an intellectual murder on the Leopold-Loeb idea. Incidentally,' he continues, 'it is about Zelda & me & the hysteria of last May & June in Paris' (FP, 120). In October he reports that 'The novel progresses slowly & carefully with much destroying & revision' (FP, 122). In December, feeling depressed, he writes that 'the book is wonderful' and that when it is published he will be 'the best American novelist (which isn't saying a lot) but the end seems far away' (FP, 125–6). Just how far away, not even a depressed Fitzgerald could have guessed. A few days later, in a letter in which he says he is 'very thick' with Hemingway, and also expresses huge admiration for Dos Passos's *Manhattan Transfer*, he repeats – perhaps to keep his spirits up – that his novel 'is wonderful' (FP, 128). In February 1926, reporting to Perkins his receipt of the letter from T. S. Eliot telling him that *Gatsby* represented the first step forward American fiction had taken since Henry James, he adds 'Wait till they see the new novel!' (FP, 134).

Just what the new novel is about is hinted at by a request to Perkins to find out about the legal position of an American who kills another American in France; his plot, he says, is a bit like that of Dreiser's *American Tragedy* (in which a young American plots the death of his girlfriend). And by May 1926, he is telling both Perkins and Ober that his novel will be complete within a matter of months. To Perkins he writes, 'I expect to reach New York about Dec 10th with the ms. under my arm', then turns to the question of serial rights and concludes, 'So book publication would be late Spring 1927 or early fall' (FP, 141). Ober receives the same optimistic account in more detail: 'The novel is about one fourth done and will be delivered for possible serialization about January 1st.' 'It will be about 75,000 words long, divided into 12 chapters', he goes on, 'concerning tho this is absolutely confidential such a case as that girl who shot her mother on the Pacific coast last year' (FO, 89). Then detailed issues are raised about serialization in the *Saturday Evening Post* or *Liberty*, what the serialization fee should be, etc. As late as October 1926, Fitzgerald is still telling Ober that he hopes to hand him the manuscript of the novel in New York, early in January 1927.

What are we to make of Fitzgerald's repeated assertions that he will have completed another novel by early 1927? Obviously making such commitments was a form of attempted self-discipline; the promises provided a target towards which he had to work. After all he had plenty of experience of giving himself deadlines for the delivery of stories for Ober to sell. This worked for his short fiction, so why not for his novel? His obligations to both Perkins and Ober were immense; surely he could not allow himself to let them down by failing to deliver? In this sense the deadlines are aimed more at himself than at anyone else. But his comments also hint at possible problems: the end seems far away, only a fourth is written ... That last comment, made in late April or early May 1926, more or less described the actual state of the manuscript when the Fitzgeralds left France for the United States late in December 1926. The surviving material from this time consists of manuscripts and typescripts of sections of precisely three of the novel's proposed twelve chapters.

There are in fact some links between this material and what would eventually appear as *Tender is the Night*. Not the matricidal plot, which Fitzgerald abandoned, but some of the characters are recognizable as early versions of those appearing in the finished novel: a glamorous American couple (based on the Murphys); an alcoholic composer (based on Ring Lardner); a writer called Albert McKisco (he reappears in *Tender*) who fights a duel with a young Frenchman. But the major question concerns not what Fitzgerald had written, but why he had not written more. Why did he not meet the deadlines he had set himself? He was in the position he had always aimed at – his income from the *Gatsby* versions on stage and screen meant he did not need to drive himself to produce magazine stories. After *Gatsby*, as we have seen, his artistic self-confidence was higher than it ever had been. What was preventing him from building on his success?

The answer has to lie in the life he was living. The months spent on the French Riviera while he was writing *Gatsby*, despite – or could it be because of? – Zelda's involvement with Jozan, was a time of relative tranquillity. But after the Fitzgeralds' return to France from Rome and Capri, life in both Paris and the Riviera seems to have grown increasingly hectic. It was the drinking and partying of Long Island and New York only more so. Both French locations were full of American friends to entertain or be entertained by; as Fitzgerald himself put it wittily to John Peale Bishop in September 1925:

> There was no one at Antibes this summer except me, Zelda, the

Valentinos, the Murphys, Mistinguet, Rex Ingram, Dos Passos, Alice Terry, the MacLeishes, Charlie Brackett, Maude Khan, Esther Murphy, Marguerite Namara, E. Phillips Oppenheim, Mannes the violinist, Floyd Dell, Max and Crystal Eastman, ex-Premier Orlando, Ettienne de Beaumont – just a real place to rough it, an escape from all the world. But we had a great time. (L, 379)

The Hemingways do not appear in this list – but Fitzgerald signs off his letter with the remark that they were coming for dinner. As we have already seen, Fitzgerald and Hemingway had met for the first time only a few months earlier in Paris. But in this period Fitzgerald seems to have spent almost as much time promoting Hemingway's fiction as writing his own. His pre-publication comments and criticisms concerning Hemingway's first novel – *The Sun Also Rises* – were long and detailed, and no opportunity seems to have been lost to further Hemingway's career. On the liner returning to New York at the end of 1926, he wrote to Hemingway telling him that their friendship had been for him the 'brightest thing' that had happened during his stay in Europe (L, 318). (Earlier he had written disparagingly of the Murphys, the MacLeishes, and John Peale Bishop.)

The efforts Fitzgerald made on Hemingway's behalf were at least positive in character. The same cannot be said of most of his activities in this period. As all his biographers make clear, too much of his time was wasted in pointless extravagance and excess, drinking, quarrelling with everyone including his friends, and generally behaving outrageously. Strangely even his sensitivity to others, his ability to understand, to empathize with the emotional condition of those he knew – an ability closely allied to his creativity – seems to have suffered. In the summer of 1925 the relationship between both Fitzgeralds and the Murphys seems to have been of this empathetic kind. Gerald Murphy wrote: 'Currents race between us regardless: Scott will uncover for me values in Sara, just as Sara has known them in Zelda through her affection for Scott' (C, 178). The following summer was different. Employing the Murphys as models for the characters in his novel, Fitzgerald appears to have begun treating them as though they were no more than that – not old friends, but characters he was creating. Sara wrote to him in protest:

'– But you can't expect anyone to like or stand a *Continual* feeling of analysis + sub-analysis, + criticism – on the whole unfriendly – Such as we have felt for quite awhile ...' (C, 196). Given Fitzgerald's drunken throwing of ashtrays, smashing Venetian wine glasses, and punching Gerald, the Murphys might well have felt they were being cast as the villains of his novel.

In the past the bottom line had been that however wild the party, Fitzgerald's creativity had not been seriously impaired. As his principal biographer sums up the situation:

> *Despite the parties* and the drinking and the mental upset Fitzgerald accomplished an impressive amount of work during his first six years as a professional writer – three novels, a play, forty-one stories, and twenty-seven articles or reviews, as well as movie scenarios. This was the most productive period of his life.[1]

As I have tried to suggest, with the critical success of *Gatsby*, Fitzgerald's literary career seemed to have been given a green light; even the financial space he needed seemed to have been provided for a time. But the truth was that when he sailed for New York at the end of 1926, the novel that was supposed to consolidate the success of *Gatsby* was at most one-quarter written. In trying to account for this failure, one struggles to avoid becoming too naively judgemental or censorious of Fitzgerald's disruptive life-style; it is worth remembering that Hemingway too was a heavy drinker while William Faulkner had to dry out in hospital more than once. All three men were professional writers in every sense, but it is Fitzgerald who appears to have found it most difficult to keep his life as a writer in any kind of balance with his life as a man. To write, Fitzgerald needed at least something of the Jamesian or Joycean artistic detachment; he needed to be on his own, focused on his task, relatively undisturbed. But his life with Zelda demanded exactly the opposite: an uninhibited commitment to everything around him, a total engagement with every aspect of an impulsive, improvised life. In the previous six years he had managed to juggle these conflicting needs in such a way as to keep both simultaneously in the air. What 1926 suggests is that the trick was becoming increasingly difficult to pull off. Writing to Scottie of his failings, in that 1940 letter already referred to, Fitzgerald said he wished that after *Gatsby* he'd '*never* relaxed or looked back' (L, 95). Rather than accepting his responsibility to his art, he believed he had relaxed too much and looked back too far. The reasons he did so, I suggest, lie somewhere in his fractured and divided self.

II

The Fitzgeralds arrived in New York from Genoa in December 1926, having spent two and a half years in Europe. There was no manuscript under Fitzgerald's arm for his editor to receive. The family proceeded to Montgomery, Alabama, to spend the Christmas season with Zelda's family. However, in January 1927, a United Artist's producer in Hollywood invited Fitzgerald to come to California to write a comedy screenplay for the actress Constance Talmadge. The financial terms were an advance of $3500 and a further $12,500 on acceptance of the film script. Needing the money, Fitzgerald agreed. In the following two months in Hollywood he wrote the screenplay – a very light-weight affair called 'Lipstick' set in Princeton – and met two people who, for different reasons, impressed him greatly; Lois Moran, a seventeen-year-old actress, and Irving Thalberg, the powerful young studio head of MGM. Fitzgerald paid flattering attention to the attractive Lois, saying that he admired her disciplined dedication to her acting career – she would become the major source for Rosemary Hoyt in *Tender is The Night*. Thalberg, much later, would be the inspiration for the protagonist of *The Last Tycoon*. But if Fitzgerald's art in the end gained some creative sustenance from this first visit to Los Angeles, which, perhaps ominously, he described to his cousin Ceci (Mrs Richard Taylor) as 'a tragic city of beautiful girls' (L, 435), his life gained nothing. He and Zelda quarrelled bitterly over Lois Moran (was Fitzgerald getting his own back over Edouard Jozan?) and the studio rejected the script of 'Lipstick'. The $12,500 was thus not forthcoming. The $3500 advance having been overspent on Hollywood high living, Fitzgerald returned east worse off than when he left.

The problem of where to live in America was solved by the decision to rent Ellerslie – a large, many-roomed, nineteenth-century mansion near Wilmington, Delaware. Zelda suggested that 'The squareness of the rooms and the sweep of the columns were to bring us a judicious tranquility.'[2] In fact 'tranquillity' was never to be the dominant note of the Fitzgeralds' time at Ellerslie. In the early days there Fitzgerald may well have attempted to get on with his novel: he certainly knew that Maxwell Perkins was waiting anxiously to hear that progress was being made. In January 1927, Perkins had been saying that a decision about a title was required because the novel 'will before so very long begin to appear in Liberty' (i.e. in serial form), and in April he is worrying about getting ahead with a suitable book-jacket (FP, 146–7). Harold Ober, too, had every reason to believe that the novel was nearing completion. On 2 January, Fitzgerald had wired from Montgomery (perhaps he was making a New Year resolution): 'I can finish novel by May first but would like until June first if possible' (FO, 93). From Hollywood, he had even written: 'Expect to finish novel before April 1st' (FO, 94). Even Hemingway was given unrealistic target dates for the novel's completion: 1 July in an April letter, 1 December in a November one. As time passed, and his novel remained no nearer completion, Fitzgerald learned the wisdom of ceasing to name precise dates: an August 1929 letter to Hemingway simply refers to the ever-present, ever-unfinished novel as 'old faithful' (L, 324). Back at the beginning of 1928, however, Fitzgerald was writing to Perkins apologizing for all the delays and trying to explain them. Perkins's growing anxiety is clear in his letter of reply. 'We can surely count on your novel for the fall can't we? It must be very nearly finished now' (FP, 150). That was January, and in July Fitzgerald – by then briefly in Paris – was still trying to be reassuring: 'The novel goes fine. I think its quite wonderful ... will be done *sure* in September' (FP, 152). Finally, in November 1928, Fitzgerald dispatched the first two chapters of his novel from Ellerslie to Perkins in New York. The Scribners editor must have experienced more than a little relief at actually having at least part of a manuscript in his hands – with the promise that two more chapters would follow shortly. Perkins unsurprisingly responded with enthusiasm to the material he had been sent, which was probably a version of the 1926 material concerning the American protagonist travelling in Europe with his mother, and told Fitzgerald the book should appear in the spring of 1929. However, when the Fitzgeralds left Ellerslie for good and sailed for Europe once again in March 1929, no further chapters had been sent to Perkins.

Some at least of the reasons for Fitzgerald's failure to make much progress with his novel at Ellerslie in the 1927–29 period are easy enough to identify. Life at Ellerslie was far from tranquil. The usual round of parties and entertainment was soon in full swing; early guests included Lois Moran and her mother. There were also regular trips up to New York, often to the Plaza Hotel. As Zelda put it: 'We come up for a weekend, then wake up and it's Thursday.'[3] Perkins worried that Fitzgerald was heading for some kind of nervous breakdown. Then of course there was the perennial problem over money. The income from the *Gatsby* productions having gone, and the trip to Hollywood proving a financial disaster, Fitzgerald had no alternative but to return to the commercial short-story market. For what it was worth, that market would at least prove even more remunerative than in the past. In the course of 1927 Fitzgerald received another advance from Scribners – against his new novel – of just under $6000, but his main source of income took the form of advances from Ober and the Reynolds Agency. These sometimes ran at a rate of one per week. Thus for example he received $500 on 1 September 1927, $500 on 8 September, $500 on 15 September, $300 on 22 September. In October 1927, he borrowed $1450; in November, $2200; and in December $2650. These sums seem worryingly large but of course were being offset against the remarkably generous returns from the stories he was writing. His first story of 1927 was 'Jacob's Ladder', written in June. In July Paul Reynolds was writing to say the *Saturday Evening Post* had taken it with enthusiasm (Ober had been away ill):

We have sold your story entitled 'Jacob's Ladder' to the Post for Three Thousand Dollars ($3,000.00). They say they like the story tremendously, and are going to be very much disappointed if you don't do a lot more for them just as good. (FO, 98)

Clearly based on Fitzgerald's encounter with the young Lois Moran, 'Jacob's Ladder' concerns a man in his thirties helping to make a sixteen-year-old girl a film star, but finding himself dropped from her life when she becomes a success. Fitzgerald responded to the *Post*'s enthusiastic demand for more such stories with a further four before the end of 1927. One result was a rise in his price to $3500 which the *Post*'s editors were clearly more than willing to pay. Having accepted a story called 'Magnetism', one wrote:

It is a splendidly handled story. We like it so much in fact that we hope Mr Fitzgerald will decide to do at least one more short story before settling down to the final grind on the serial.

This *Post* editor at least clearly felt that Fitzgerald was wasting his time writing serious fiction. Another of these stories – 'The Bowl' – concerned American football, and Fitzgerald visited Princeton to watch the football team at practice. Earlier in June, he had written 'Princeton', a rather nostalgic article for *College Humor*. With this burst of creativity Fitzgerald's earnings for 1927 reached a new high of $29,757.87. The five *Post* stories brought in $15,300, while his total book royalties were a mere $153.23. The rest of his book earnings of $5911.64 were accounted for by Scribners' generous advance on his novel. His *Ledger* summary for the year was: 'Total loss at beginning. A lot of fun. Work begins again.'

The work that Fitzgerald had in mind must have been the *Post* stories he was writing in the second half of the year. And it is noticeable that in this period there are fewer complaints in his correspondence about the burden of writing magazine stories. One suspects that in a situation where progress on the novel was more or less at a standstill, where Fitzgerald might even have been feeling that his creativity was blocked in relation to his serious fiction, his ability to produce *Post* stories – and their enthusiastic reception – must have been at least professionally reassuring. Certainly in the following year, 1928, Fitzgerald's major writing achievement had nothing to do with the novel that would be *Tender is the Night* – rather it was a short story series which, in the eyes of some of his admirers at least, rather blurred the distinction between his purely commercial writing and his 'serious ' fiction.

Zelda Fitzgerald had begun ballet lessons in Philadelphia while at Ellerslie, perhaps in reaction to her husband's implication that, as compared to the hard-working, disciplined Lois Moran, she had never bothered to make serious use of any of her undoubted abilities. Partly to pursue Zelda's ballet training under the noted teacher Lubov Egorova, the Fitzgeralds left Ellerslie in April 1928, to spend the summer in Paris. This visit was made financially viable by the new series of stories that Fitzgerald had begun to write in January of that year.

The series in question was the group of Basil Lee stories whose strongly autobiographical nature has been referred to in the opening chapter. The first of these stories, 'The Scandal Detectives', was written in January 1928, and in the following twelve months or so another eight were produced. The third story (in terms of the series' chronology) – 'The Freshest Boy' – was written before the Fitzgeralds left for Paris, and the second – 'A Night at the Fair' – in France in April. (Fitzgerald wired Ober successfully to get the *Post* to delay publication so that the series' linear chronology could be maintained.) What is striking is the ease with which Fitzgerald produced all these stories; while his novel made little if any progress, by returning to his own early memories, he seemed to release a spring of creativity. Of course while Fitzgerald knew that these were 'light', commercial magazine stories – earning in the end no less than $31,500 – they were also sufficiently vivid, evocative and entertaining to appeal to a wide range of readers. Among the most enthusiastic were Maxwell Perkins and Harold Ober.

At the end of June 1928, Perkins wrote to Fitzgerald in Paris: 'I got from Ober your three boys' stories, and read them with great interest.' Unsurprisingly, given the non-appearance of the promised novel, he goes on: 'Won't you have a book of them sometime?' And he proceeds to praise in particular the evocative power of certain passages:

> That magical quality of summer dusk for young boys I have never before seen evoked. I hope you will be doing some more of these stories. (FP, 151)

On this last point Ober was in complete agreement. The *Post* had taken the first three stories and the editor was asking for more. In August 1928, Ober acknowledges receipt of the fourth story, 'He Thinks He's Wonderful', describes it as 'a very attractive story' which he is confident the *Post* will want, and goes on:

> I think you will have to write two or three more of these stories for I shall never be satisfied until I hear more about Basil, and I think everyone who reads the stories feels the same way.

Significantly he concludes, 'They will make an exceedingly interesting book, I think' (FO, 116).

Like Perkins, Ober had received regular reassurances from Fitzgerald about progress on his next novel: a Paris wire of 3 June 1928, for example, read, 'Two more chapters finished all completed August' (FO, 113). But, once again like Perkins, Ober was clearly beginning to have less and less faith in these authorial deadlines. For both men, then, the idea of a different Fitzgerald book had obvious attractions. The Basil Lee stories were giving Fitzgerald no problems of any kind; they were appearing regularly and were being well received. Why not maintain Fitzgerald's momentum as a productive author by having a new book by him out in 1929? Fitzgerald did not respond to Ober's book suggestion, but a letter to Perkins in July does indicate that he too saw the possibility of an eventual Basil Lee book: 'I plan to publish a book of those *Basil Lee* Stories after the novel' (FP, 152). But for Fitzgerald it is that final phrase that is crucial. He was not prepared to entertain the possibility of publishing such a book *before* his novel had appeared. His reasoning is apparent in the same letter: the publication of a major novel would make it possible for him to follow it soon after with a 'lighter' work without in any way damaging his reputation as a serious writer. As he explained to Perkins: the Basil Lee stories, perhaps with one or two more serious ones, would make 'a nice *light* novel, almost, to follow my novel in the season *immediately* after, so as not to seem in the direct line of my so-called "work"' (FP, 152). No more was said about a Basil Lee collection in 1928, but the idea was not one that Perkins and Ober were prepared to abandon, and in due course it would resurface.

While Zelda was pursuing her ballet training in Paris throughout the summer of 1928, Fitzgerald's creative energies were absorbed by his work on the Lee stories. He did at this time meet Sylvia Beach and James Joyce as well as Thornton Wilder and the young French writer André Chamson whose work he persuaded Scribners to publish; he also renewed contact with his old friend John Peale Bishop and saw something of Gerald and Sara Murphy. But the essentially disorganized, serendipitous pattern of his life remained exactly as before; he drank excessively and twice ended up in a Paris jail. By September 1928, the Fitzgeralds were back at Ellerslie in Maryland, bringing with them a Paris taxi-driver theoretically employed as a kind of chauffeur-butler but soon acting mainly as Fitzgerald's drinking partner. Nevertheless, that autumn, as well as continuing the Basil Lee series, Fitzgerald wrote 'The Last of the Belles', a story in which for the last time he drew heavily upon his memories and experience of the American South for theme and setting. Fitzgerald's earnings for 1928 amounted to $25,732.96: seven stories were sold to the *Saturday Evening Post* for $22,050. His book income was $2272.96, but almost all of this was in fact yet another Scribners advance against his next novel.

Fitzgerald's constant willingness to help other writers, promoting their work, and trying to arrange publication, has already been noted. Thus the correspondence with Maxwell Perkins from Paris is full of proposals and suggestions about books and authors Scribners might consider taking on. Acting as a kind of voluntary European agent for Scribners presumably helped Fitzgerald cope with his growing sense of guilt over the lack of progress on his novel. (At one point Perkins wrote to thank him for his help over new books and authors adding wryly: 'But the book we really want to publish is your book' (FP, 156).)

In early 1929, however, Fitzgerald's impulse to be of use to other writers found an outlet much closer to home. In addition to her commitment to ballet-dancing, Zelda had begun to demonstrate further her determination to be a serious person by becoming a writer in her own right. In earlier years she had written some articles as well as most of a story published as her husband's; now in February 1929, Fitzgerald helped devise a plan for Zelda to write six story sketches about different types of girls for *College Humor*. Zelda would write them but Fitzgerald would help to 'fix them up'. The pieces appeared in the magazine under the names of both Fitzgeralds. This was not male chauvinism on Fitzgerald's part. It was simply business – Fitzgerald's name had to be there for the sale to be made. When another story by Zelda (revised by Scott) – 'The Millionaire's Girl' – appeared a year later in the *Saturday Evening Post* solely under Fitzgerald's name, he asked Ober for an explanation. Ober, who may well have genuinely thought that Fitzgerald was the author of this story, replied he had dropped Zelda's name because he feared that jointly authored, *College Humor* might have made contractual trouble over their ongoing 'girl' series. More ominous was Fitzgerald's comment to Ober in October 1929, that in writing the *College Humor* series, Zelda was drawing upon their 'common store of material', and that the originals of the types of girls she had described, 'I had in my note-book to use'. (FO, 146).

III

The Fitzgeralds' lease on Ellerslie ran out in the spring of 1929 and they decided to return to Europe. This would prove to be their fourth and final visit. One motive was Zelda's desire to resume her ballet lessons under Egorova; another perhaps Fitzgerald's hope that his blocked work on the novel would benefit from a return to its geographical location. Perkins was still of course waiting to see the promised third and fourth chapters of the novel; when about to leave Fitzgerald wrote to say he would work on them aboard ship and send them to New York when they docked at Genoa (the journey to Paris was being made via the Mediterranean). In the event nothing was sent. Fitzgerald's comments to Ober were vaguer and more wishful: on the point of departure, saying 'goodbye for several months,' he wrote, 'I hope to God I'll have the novel soon' (FO, 130). On arrival in France, insisting that he was 'happy to be back', he said, 'I hope to God the novel will be done this summer' (FO, 132).

The Fitzgeralds would remain in Europe for the next two and a half years, but in all that time Fitzgerald's progress on his novel would remain painfully slow. Neither in Paris, nor on his favourite Riviera, did he find the new source of creative inspiration that was now so obviously necessary to get the novel moving towards completion. One has to suspect that the problem was at least in part the failure of the central matricide plot to engage with any kind of personal emotional reality. That personal immediacy had made the Basil Lee stories easy to write; its absence was perhaps making the novel impossible to write. The result is that the narrative of Fitzgerald's literary life during his final European years is one of growing unhappiness over his inability to write his serious work, balanced by a steady output of short fiction which was if anything increasingly successful in commercial terms.

Fitzgerald's loss of the kind of aesthetic self-confidence that the critical success of *Gatsby* had earlier inspired, and his more general sense of despondency is well indicated by an exchange of letters with Hemingway in September 1929. Having arrived in Paris in

April, Fitzgerald assumed that his old intimacy of 1925–26 with Hemingway would be resumed. In fact the situation was changed. Hemingway was no longer the young writer trying to make his way, inevitably impressed by the successful author of *The Great Gatsby*. Himself increasingly successful, he was less inclined to condone Fitzgerald's form of disruptive alcoholism. Nonetheless he did agree to act as he had over *The Sun Also Rises* and show Fitzgerald a typescript of his new novel, *A Farewell to Arms*. Characteristically, Fitzgerald had no trouble in finding enough time to read it carefully and write a detailed, nine-page commentary. Full of praise, the report also contained sharp criticisms. Hemingway rejected some of Fitzgerald's suggestions, but acted on others. Despite further complications in their friendship caused by Fitzgerald's failure to pay proper attention while acting as timekeeper for a notorious boxing bout between Hemingway and the Canadian novelist Morley Callaghan, Hemingway in 1929 did his best to reassure Fitzgerald that he was a fine writer, telling him that the parts of the new novel he had seen were as good as all but the very best bits of *Gatsby*. But Fitzgerald was not in a frame of mind to be receptive. On 9 September, from Cannes, where the Fitzgeralds spent much of the summer, he wrote a letter to Hemingway full of self-pity and blaming himself for what he calls the 'dissipation' that was preventing his getting 'serious work done'. In two and a half months in Cannes he had written one short story and 20,000 words on the novel – 'which is superb for me of late years –' and his one consolation was that 'the *Post* now pays the old whore $4000 a screw'. More interestingly, he advanced a version of a theory of human experience which would soon begin to appear in his writing in a variety of forms: broadly the notion that individuals had only so much personal and emotional energy, which could therefore be used up too early. As a writer, he tells Hemingway, perhaps he has nothing left to say:

> it is possible that the 5 years between my leaving the army and finishing *Gatsby* (1919–1924) which included 3 novels, about 50 popular stories and a play and numerous articles and movies may have taken all I had to say too early, adding that all the time we were living at top speed in the gayest worlds we could find. (L, 326)

In his reply Hemingway refused to be drawn into discussing such theoretical issues. His advice is simply to forget about the stories – 'which arent whoring. They're just bad judgement' – and just get on with the novel until it is finished:

> Oh Hell. You have more stuff than anyone and you care more about it and for Christ sake just keep on and go through with it now and dont please write anything else until it's finished. It will be damned good –[4]

In this exchange Fitzgerald is, as always, totally dismissive of his work as a short-story writer. In fact his output in the form in 1929 was not without merit. He wrote in all seven stories for the *Post* and Ober thought extremely highly of several of them. Of 'The Swimmers' – one of several stories based around marital problems, a subject which was emerging as a major fictional preoccupation – he wrote, 'I think it is the ablest and most thoughtful story you have ever done' (FO, 142). Only a month or two earlier he had called 'At Your Age' 'the finest story you have ever written' (FO, 137) – a judgement he had acted upon by persuading the *Saturday Evening Post* to raise Fitzgerald's short-story price to its massive $4000 peak. (An index of just how vast a sum this was is given by the statistic that the average annual income of an American college teacher in 1929 was $3056.) In 1930 'At Your Age' would appear in the Modern Library's volume of *Great Modern Short Stories* – though Fitzgerald wanted to be represented by 'The Rich Boy', and was annoyed, for once, by Scribners' refusal to grant permission. However, from Fitzgerald's point of view, the only rationale for the *Post* stories was as before the creation of sufficient financial space to allow him to give uninterrupted attention to his novel.

Boosted by his soaring *Post* price, Fitzgerald's earnings for 1929 amounted to $32,448.18 – eight Post stories brought in $27,000 and Zelda's story sketches added $2430. Such figures were enough to create the desired space, and indeed there is some evidence that as the year went on Fitzgerald was renewing his efforts to make progress with the novel. His reports to Perkins and Ober are constantly upbeat. In June he told Perkins: 'I am working night & day on novel from new angle that I think will solve previous difficulties' (FP, 156). The new angle involved the abandonment of the matricide plot and a new focus on a Hollywood film director and his wife a trip to Europe who meet a Lois Moran/Rosemary Hoyt-type character travelling with her mother. (Two chapters of this new version of the novel survive in typescript.) Ober – who had just left the Reynolds Agency and set up on his own – is told in October: 'I've sworn not to come back without the novel which is really drawing to a close' (FO, 153), while in November Fitzgerald reported to Perkins: 'For the first time since August I see my way clear to a long stretch on the novel' (FP, 158). In December Fitzgerald insists once again to Ober that he is 'Working like hell on novel' (FO, 163). But Ober's repeated requests that he be sent a portion of the manuscript so that he can begin seriously to negotiate serial rights produce no result.

The pattern of Fitzgerald's literary career in the following year, also spent in France, would prove to be little different from that of 1929. Short stories and articles would continue to be written, but the novel would remain stymied. A letter to Perkins in January 1930, suggests something of Fitzgerald's own weariness with the project:

> because I don't mention my novel it isn't because it isn't finishing up or that I'm neglecting it – but only that I'm weary of setting dates for it till the moment when it is in the Post Office Box. (FP, 161)

Ober on the other hand was notified in March that part of the book would soon be dispatched to him, and he was quick to pass on such good news to Perkins. Perkins in turn wrote instantly to Fitzgerald in terms clearly designed to encourage him to be as good as his word:

> Harold Ober yesterday gave me reason to hope that a large part of your novel would be here before long. I'll tell you when we get that into our hands, and a publication date set, we'll let loose everything we have got in the way of salesmanship and advertising. Everyone here is impatient to get that book and what is more, there is no author who commands a more complete loyalty than you do. (FP, 165–6)

No doubt it was the failure of the promised portion of the novel to arrive that now persuaded Fitzgerald's editor and his agent it was time to pursue a different way forward. Their idea was to revive the idea of a book based on the Basil Lee stories. In April, Ober wrote to say he had been talking to Perkins about the necessity for Fitzgerald to have a book out that autumn: 'Unless you are almost positive that the novel is going to be ready, don't you think it might be well to let them do the Basil Lee stories?' (FO, 166–7). He goes on to say that of course it would be better 'to get the novel out this autumn, if it can be done ...' but the hint of scepticism here clearly explains why both men had decided that any book would be better than none.

Ober's other suggestion had been that the magazine serialization of the novel should be allowed to begin before the text was complete. Fitzgerald was outraged by both these suggestions. With some justice he felt that the proposals implied that his mentors were giving up on him. He replied to Ober:

> I know you're losing faith in me + Max too but God knows one has to rely in the end on one's own judgement. I could have published four lousy, half baked books in the last five years + people would have thought I was at least a worthy young man not drinking myself to pieces in the south seas ...

But such work would have represented 'the hurried and the second rate'. Concerning the stories, his argument is that these are *Post* stories and nothing more – his novel is something else entirely:

> These *Post* stories *in* the *Post* are at least not any spot on me – they're honest and if their *form* is stereotyped people know what to expect when they pick up the *Post*. The novel is another thing – if, after four years I published the Basil Lee stories as a book I might as well get tickets for Hollywood immediately. (FO, 168)

Fitzgerald's message to Perkins was identical: a Basil Lee book would ruin his reputation as a serious novelist. On 1 May he told his editor:

> Harold Ober wrote me that if it [the novel] couldn't be published this fall I should publish the Basil Lee stories, but I know too well

by whom reputations are made & broken to ruin myself completely by such a move ...

He alludes to the idea, spelled out to Hemingway the year before, that he had written too much too early: 'I wrote young & I wrote a lot & the pot takes longer to fill up now but the novel, my novel, is a different matter than if I'd hurriedly finished it up a year and a half ago.' Other novelists, such as Dreiser and Thornton Wilder, had let years pass between novels, and he concludes: *'I know what I'm doing* – honestly, Max' (FP, 166). Having received Fitzgerald's letters, both Perkins and Ober dropped the idea of any book appearing before the novel. Ober even got the editor of *Liberty* to agree to everything that Fitzgerald wanted: more time to complete the novel to his satisfaction; no requirement to send over any part of the manuscript; no serial to begin until the text is complete; no cuts. 'You are entirely right about the novel,' wrote Ober, 'and I think you are right not to bring out the Basil Lee stories until after the novel is published.' 'I have lots of confidence in you,' he goes on, 'and I am sure that the novel when it appears is going to be as good a piece of work as you or anyone else has done' (FO, 170).

Just before this exchange took place, Fitzgerald had had to deal with a new situation that would have a major impact on the writing of the novel that would be published as *Tender is the Night*. In February 1930, the Fitzgeralds had left Paris for a brief vacation in Algiers. Zelda's account of the reasons for the trip was: 'It was a trying winter and to forget bad times we went to Algiers.'[5] Little seems to have been forgotten, however, and Zelda was soon worrying over having abandoned her ballet lessons even for a short time. Back in Paris, her nervousness increased, and in April she experienced her first psychological collapse. She entered the Malmaison clinic outside Paris on 23 April, and discharged herself on 11 May. However her condition worsened, and on 22 May she entered another non-specialist clinic in Switzerland. After consultations there on her mental state she was diagnosed as schizophrenic and moved to the Prangins clinic on Lake Geneva in early June. Fitzgerald settled in Lausanne to be near her, but made regular visits to Paris to see Scottie. In November, after a lengthy silence, he wrote to Ober explaining all the difficulties that had overtaken his life: problems over his own health (an old lung weakness had resurfaced), Scottie's appendicitis, and of course Zelda's breakdown. At the end of the letter he added: 'Havn't touched novel for four months, save for one week' (FO, 172).

Despite all his personal and familial problems, and despite the draining concern over his inability to get ahead with his serious writing, 1930 was not an unproductive year for Fitzgerald. For the *Post* he wrote seven stories, five of which tapped effectively into the same area of early personal emotional memory as had served him well with the Basil Lee stories. The series of five Josephine Perry stories emerged out of his remembered relationship with Ginevra King, his girlfriend in the early Princeton years. Josephine is a Chicago debutante, from a wealthy family; she engages in a series of romantic relationships that lack emotional honesty or integrity. The fifth story, entitled 'Emotional Bankruptcy', allows Fitzgerald to expand on his growing interest in the notion of the individual who has used up her emotional resources to the degree that a real relationship is unsustainable. However, successful as they are, the Josephine stories do not match the controlled power of 'Babylon Revisited', universally seen as one of Fitzgerald's finest stories, written in December 1930. Reflecting in some way Fitzgerald's redefined link with his daughter, given her mother's illness, the story is a moving account of a failed father–daughter relationship. What this story makes clear is that Fitzgerald, under whatever personal pressures, was still capable of producing fiction of the highest order. Also written around this time was 'One Trip Abroad', a story concerning a young American couple who go to pieces during a visit to Europe meant to be culturally enriching, and who end up in a Swiss clinic. The story, which Fitzgerald did not reprint, seems clearly to anticipate the final shape of *Tender is the Night*. If these stories were impressive so too were Fitzgerald's earnings in 1930: his total income was $33,090.10 – the seven *Post* stories brought him $25,300, while his book income of $3789.94 was once again almost wholly made up of yet another advance on the novel from Scribners.

Zelda Fitzgerald's illness had inevitably piled further pressure on Fitzgerald's always shaky finances; the costs of her treatment in the Swiss clinic, where she remained from the summer of 1930 until September 1931, were extremely high. Fitzgerald could pay only with what his pen produced and there is something heroic about the way in which he accepted the task. No less than 17 stories were sold in the 1930–31 period. Inevitably no doubt, their quality was uneven. As we have seen, some of the 1930 fiction was up to his highest standard, but May 1931 finds Ober writing to say that the *Post* editors are increasingly uneasy over his recent work: the last three stories have not been 'up to the best you can do' (FO, 176). They suggest that stories with an American setting might be more appealing to their readership. Ober himself was almost certainly experiencing growing uneasiness over what was happening to Fitzgerald's career as a writer. There is the ongoing problem over the novel, clearly now no closer to completion. 'I think you ought without fail to have a novel out in 1932', he writes, and goes on with a hint of asperity: 'now is the time for you to get down to hard work and finish the novel' (FO, 177). More positively, in the absence of the novel, Ober appears to have been looking for new ways forward for Fitzgerald. In November 1931, he wrote to say that the editors of *Cosmopolitan* were extremely interested in getting a twenty or thirty thousand word novelette from Fitzgerald; and in January 1932, he reports that the magazine would offer $5000 per story for six chosen out of eight or four out of six, as well as at least $10,000 for the novelette.

Fitzgerald's father had died in Washington in January 1931. Fitzgerald made a quick trip across the Atlantic to be present at the funeral. Dick Diver makes this trip in *Tender is the Night*, but 'On Your Own', the story that Fitzgerald wrote drawing on this experience at the time, was rejected by a range of magazines. The reason for this uniformly negative reaction to a highly competent story is not now self-evident; but it may lie in the female protagonist's sense that her European experience has brought her a sophistication of manners lacking in America. An essay entitled 'The Death of My Father' also remained unfinished. With another article, Fitzgerald had more success. In a letter to Perkins in May 1931, referring to a history of the United States from 1900 to 1925 that Scribners were then publishing, he said that the credit for naming the twenties decade the Jazz Age belonged to him. Perkins wrote back that he was right, and added that the editor of *Scribner's Magazine* was about to invite him to contribute an article on the subject. Fitzgerald's autobiographical piece 'Echoes of the Jazz Age' appeared in the magazine's November 1931 issue.

Fitzgerald's unstinting efforts to meet his new financial obligations succeeded to the degree that 1931 was the earnings high-point in his literary career. His total income was $37,599. Nine stories – eight published by the *Post* – brought him $31,500. Book royalties amounted to a mere one hundred dollars. Towards the end of 1930 Zelda's condition improved and she began again to write stories – one of these, 'Miss Ella', was accepted by *Scribner's Magazine* and published in December 1931. The improvement continued during Fitzgerald's absence at his father's funeral, and in the spring and summer of 1931 all the bitterness, antagonism, mutual recriminations and accusations which had overflowed during or after discussions with Zelda's doctors, seemed to disappear entirely. The family were allowed to enjoy days out together, and even longer expeditions, and Zelda's letters to Fitzgerald in this period are full of love and tenderness. The improvement continuing, Zelda was judged well enough to leave the Prangins clinic in September 1931, and the Fitzgeralds sailed for America. Fitzgerald's *Ledger* summary for this, his thirty-fourth year, was: '*A Year in Lausanne. Waiting. From Darkness to Hope.*'

IV

Back in America the Fitzgeralds rented a house in Montgomery, Alabama, and thought of settling there. One reason for returning to her home town was Zelda's desire to be near her parents, particularly as Judge Sayre was unwell, but Fitzgerald probably also wanted to conciliate the Sayre family, some of whom at least were inclined to blame him for Zelda's breakdown. That autumn in Montgomery Fitzgerald wrote two more *Post* stories, and on the proceeds determined to settle down to yet another attempt at completing his novel. In November, however, his plans were upset by an offer from Hollywood. Irving Thalberg at MGM was keen to recruit Fitzgerald to write a screenplay from a novel called *Red-Headed Woman* as a vehicle for their current star Jean Harlow. Fitzgerald was reluctant to leave Montgomery at this point and turned down MGM's initial offer of $750 per week; $1000 a week was still not enough to tempt him, but when the figure reached $1200 per week for six weeks (plus return railway fare) he felt he had to accept. The outcome, however, of this, his second trip to Hollywood, was little more successful than his first in 1927. He fell out with his collaborator, and although he completed his screenplay within five weeks the studio chose not to use it. (The film was eventually made with a screenplay by Anita Loos.) Nonetheless he returned to Montgomery with almost $6000 and as he explained to Ober: 'I'm not sorry I went because I've got a fine story about Hollywood which will be along in several days' (FO, 181). The story was 'Crazy Sunday' concerning which Fitzgerald wrote to *Cosmopolitan* – the magazine which had expressed such interest in his work – saying they could have it once the *Post* turned it down, but adding that he could not write a novelette for them at the present time. The *Post* duly declined 'Crazy Sunday' as involving a morally unconventional ending unacceptable to its readership, but Fitzgerald's somewhat satirical account of Hollywood and some of its leading figures also proved too much for *Cosmopolitan* to take on. 'Mr Hearst's policy man' as the magazine's editor described him to Ober felt that Fitzgerald's story might offend the influential Hollywood people with whom Hearst – the powerful Californian publisher – was affiliated. 'Crazy Sunday' was eventually published by H. L. Mencken in the November 1932 *American Mercury*. (It also appeared in *The Best Short Stories of 1933* volume.)

In January 1932, after his return from Hollywood, Fitzgerald wrote to Perkins explaining that he was finally in a position to get on and finish his novel:

> At last for the first time in two years & 1/2 I am going to spend five consecutive months on my novel. I am actually six thousand dollars ahead. Am replanning it to include what's good in what I have, adding 41,000 new words & publishing. (FP, 173)

How he had arrived at such a precise word count is difficult to say, but in any event his plans were about to be disrupted once again. While Fitzgerald was in Hollywood working on 'Red-Headed Woman', Zelda had begun writing a novel while also sending her husband almost daily letters full of loving warmth and tenderness. However, she suffered from asthma in Montgomery and in December visited Florida hoping that warmer weather would do her good. For the same reason she returned to Florida with Fitzgerald in January 1932. During the return trip, however, she experienced a second serious mental collapse and decided she needed to be back in hospital. As a result, on 12 February 1932 she entered the Phipps Psychiatric Clinic which was part of the Johns Hopkins University Hospital in Baltimore. With Zelda hospitalized in Maryland, Fitzgerald could not remain indefinitely in Alabama. Hence in May 1932, he rented La Paix a large, 15-room Victorian frame house outside Baltimore. Once again he was back in a situation of the severest financial pressure – which he could only begin to meet by writing for his established commercial market. In the April-May period of 1932 he wrote three stories for the *Post* including 'What a Handsome Pair!', a story about competitive and non-competitive married couples, which clearly originates in Fitzgerald's sense of his own marital situation; two other *Post* stories followed later in the year, both based on Fitzgerald's experience of·hospital life. (He was treated for typhoid fever in Johns Hopkins Hospital in August; in the next five years he would be treated there for alcoholism and his chronic inactive tuberculosis on another eight occasions.) However, like other magazines, the *Saturday Evening Post* was not immune to the major downturn in America's economic life which, after the boom times of the 1920s, was producing the great depression of the 1930s. Authors' receipts were falling and Fitzgerald's proved to be no exception: in 1932 his story price fell first to $3000 then to $2500. As a result his total earnings for 1932 reached only $15,826 – the lowest figure since 1919. Six short stories earned him $14,805, while he received $480 as yet another advance on *Tender is the Night*.

1932 also saw the emergence into Fitzgerald's literary life of another Zelda-linked unsettling factor. The new disturbance concerned not Zelda's health but her ambition as a writer. From his earliest reactions to her stories and sketches there had been hints that Fitzgerald was concerned about the similarity between his material and Zelda's, and perhaps even about likenesses between her writing style and his. (Fitzgerald was not wholly wrong about this. After his death, when Edmund Wilson collected the non-fictional material by Fitzgerald that was published in 1945 as *The Crack-Up*, even the critically acute Wilson included two articles, 'Auction – Model 1934' and "Show Mr. and Mrs. F. to Number –"', which were in fact exclusively Zelda's work.) That concern now flared up into an angry dispute.

The novel that Zelda had begun writing in Montgomery while Fitzgerald was in Hollywood was completed with surprising speed while she was in the Phipps clinic in Baltimore. Her next step was to send the manuscript direct to Maxwell Perkins at Scribners without showing it to Fitzgerald. When he learned what had happened he was furious, and wired Perkins to do nothing until he received a revised version of the text. Different factors contributed to Fitzgerald's outrage which was undeniably excessive even if not totally incomprehensible. Here he was struggling year after year to complete his novel while his wife dashed one off in a matter of weeks. Much more seriously, Zelda's novel – which would be published as *Save Me The Waltz* – proved to be deeply autobiographical and thus touched on material and situations that Fitzgerald planned to use in *Tender is the Night*. He was clearly terrified that readers would in some way see *Save Me The Waltz* as having pre-empted his own so long-delayed novel. The situation was further complicated by the involvement of Zelda's doctors, and questions about what was desirable in terms of her mental health. The Baltimore doctors were inclined to agree with the argument that Zelda's experiences shared with her husband were 'common property' when it came to writing about them. But Fitzgerald refused to concede this point and insisted that there be significant changes to Zelda's text before it could be considered for publication by Scribners. The name of the novel's male protagonist, for example, was changed from Amory Blaine (the hero of *This Side of Paradise*) to David Knight, but the evidence does not survive to let us see just how extensive the revisions to Zelda's original version in fact were. Once the changes he had insisted on were made, Fitzgerald was ready to do his best to promote Zelda's novel. She had apologized for going straight to Perkins with the text saying that she knew that Fitzgerald was so busy with his own novel that he would not want to be disturbed. He did not really believe this, but having got his own way over the text, he told Perkins that the necessary revisions were only minor and that 'it is a fine novel' (C, 290). Zelda more or less reserved her position saying that she had agreed to the changes only because they represented aesthetic improvements. The novel's 'real story', she said, 'was the old prodigal son' – presumably she means the narrative of Alabama Knight's marriage, experiences in Europe, and final return to her home in

Montgomery – but that *'the other material ... is nevertheless legitimate stuff which has cost me a pretty emotional penny* to amass' (C, 290–1). In other words she was not prepared to agree that her psychological breakdown was owned in terms of fiction by her writer husband. *Save Me The Waltz* was published by Scribners in October 1932. Selling only some 1400 copies it was a commercial failure; and the reviews it received were largely unfavourable. But the implications and consequences of this entire episode, and of Fitzgerald's attitude and behaviour in particular, in relation to his literary life, were, as we shall see, in no sense over.

In the summer of 1932 at La Paix, despite Zelda's health problems and all the furore over *Save Me The Waltz*, Fitzgerald did get down to serious work on his novel. Indeed it is not impossible that Zelda's productiveness gave still greater urgency to his need to get his own book completed. A *Ledger* entry for August 1932 reads: 'The novel now plotted + planned, never more to be permanently interrupted', while the plan itself extends over 16 detailed pages. Much of it is entirely new. The old matricide idea has been abandoned, and likewise the newer opening concerning the American film producer and his wife en route to Europe. The new plot focuses on a psychiatrist who marries his patient. The planned movement of the novel reveals the psychiatrist going 'more and more to pieces'; he is a secret drinker, and although he is 'a communist-liberal-idealist' he is corrupted by the bourgeoisie and becomes a man 'divided in himself'. When he is 'socially the most charming and inwardly corrupt' he has an affair with a young actress he meets on the Riviera but does not really love. In the end his wife is cured of her illness and, despite being guilty of a murder, is brought together with another 'strong + magnetic man' by her failing husband. Despite its title, 'The Drunkard's Holiday', the heroine being guilty of murder, and a few other details such as the idealist doctor sending his son to be educated in the Soviet Union, this description is instantly recognizable as strongly akin to the published version of *Tender is the Night*. Fitzgerald was also very clear about the precise structure of the novel: it 'will be a little over a hundred thousand words long, composed of fourteen chapters, each 7,500 words long, five chapters each in the first and second part, four in the third – one chapter or its equivalent to be composed of retrospect.'[6]

In the novel that Fitzgerald now went on to write he did of course incorporate material, usually revised and rewritten, from the various earlier drafts. But to a very large extent what he was writing was a new work. As we have seen, the apparently interminable delay in his writing another novel to follow up the success of *The Great Gatsby* was the result of a series of factors in his day-to-day life: his constant need for large sums of money, his increasingly out-of-control drinking, his deteriorating relationship with Zelda, then Zelda's illness itself. But all along there had been another problem: Fitzgerald never appears to have been entirely happy with what the new novel was about – the plots and characters he variously had in mind seem never to have possessed him imaginatively. One suspects that the fundamental problem was that his own experience was insufficiently involved. In that situation, even if the personal circumstances of his life had been altogether more favourable, then he would still have had major difficulties in getting ahead. What is different about this final version of his novel is that it draws heavily on Fitzgerald's awareness of his own recent life with Zelda; the emotional problems confronting Dick and Nicole Diver have their origins in Fitzgerald's increasingly anguished relationship with Zelda. In the earlier versions of the text, the glamorous American couple living on the Riviera had been based on Gerald and Sara Murphy. In the published version – dedicated to the Murphys – this is only partly true: like most of the characters in the novel, the Divers are now composite figures, their Murphy origins subsumed within the Fitzgeralds. After *Tender is the Night* was published John O'Hara was right to insist to the less than happy Murphys that the Divers were not them:

> Sooner or later his characters always come back to being Fitzgerald characters in a Fitzgerald world. . . . And of course as he moved along, he got farther away from any resemblance to the real Murphys. Dick Diver ended up as a tall Fitzgerald.[7]

The main point remains that it was by refocusing the plot and central characters of his novel into areas of his own experience that Fitzgerald was finally able to rediscover the creative and imaginative energy to go ahead and complete his book.

With Zelda initially dividing her time between the Phipps Clinic and La Paix, Fitzgerald worked steadily at his novel through the second half of 1932. Even when Zelda was discharged from the clinic at the end of June – though remaining under medical supervision – nothing changed, because the Fitzgeralds' lives remained largely separate. There were occasional visitors, but no more parties, and they rarely went out together. Fitzgerald was concerned that Zelda seemed to be withdrawing from any kind of family life, but at least he was able to get on with his writing. An indication of his renewed sense of professional discipline is given perhaps by his decision in this period to rearrange all the material in his *Notebooks* into 23 sections in alphabetical order. Each section has a heading – Anecdotes, Bright clippings, Conversations and things overheard, Descriptions of things and atmospheres, and so on through the alphabet. Edmund Wilson's published version of the rearranged *Notebooks* in his 'Crack-Up' volume covers almost 150 pages – which indicates that Fitzgerald's own undertaking had been a substantial one. As 1932 passed into 1933, he continued to work on his novel, but inevitably he was still confronting financial problems to the degree that at one point he was forced to borrow from his mother. In the course of 1933 he did sell three stories to the *Post*, which earned him $7650, but the commercial market for short stories was changing just at the time when Fitzgerald was becoming less able and less happy to write for it. Ober wrote to him in August 1933, saying that 'all the magazines have been harder to please this year than ever before'. And he goes on to argue that part of the problem is Fitzgerald's own previous success; he is always in competition with himself: 'An editor expects every story to compare favorably with some story of yours which he has considered your finest story.' But he also suggests that they have made a mistake in not maintaining the impression that the *Post* is lucky to get a Scott Fitzgerald story: 'I think we have let the *Post* feel that you were rushing out stories in order to get some money' (FO, 198–9). Ironically, 'One Hundred False Starts', with its suggestion that there are limits to any author's creativity – 'mostly, we authors must repeat ourselves – that's the truth'[8] – also appeared originally in the *Saturday Evening Post*, but whatever the reason, Fitzgerald was finding it increasingly difficult to go on churning out saleable commercial stories. As a result the writing of the final stages of *Tender is the Night* was largely financed by advances from Perkins and Ober. An advance of $4200 came from Scribners in 1933 – making a grand total since 1927 of something around $16,000 – and Ober made available $4000 which was to be repaid out of the novel's serial rights. These rights had in fact been given over to the magazine *Liberty* back in 1926, but in the intervening years the ownership of that magazine, as well as its editorial team, had changed, and Ober was confident that in a strict legal sense *Liberty* no longer had a right to Fitzgerald's text. However, he agreed with Fitzgerald that there was a kind of moral obligation which they should meet; in the event *Liberty* agreed to cancel the old contract.

Late in 1933, Fitzgerald made steady progress with the novel. On 25 September he wrote to Maxwell Perkins from La Paix saying that he was ahead of schedule:

> The novel has gone ahead faster than I thought. There was a little set back when I went to the hospital for four days but since then things have gone ahead of my schedule, which you will remember, promised you the whole manuscript for reading November 1, with the first one-fourth ready to shoot into the magazine (in case you can use it) and the other three-fourths to undergo further revision. I now figure that this can be achieved by about the 25th of October. I will appear in person carrying the manuscript and wearing a spiked helmet. (FP, 181)

As this passage indicates, Fitzgerald had made a tentative agreement with Perkins to have *Tender is the Night* serialized in *Scribner's Magazine* in four sections. The terms eventually agreed were $10,000, six thousand of which were to go towards meeting Scribners' advances, while the remaining four thousand would be paid to Ober who would use the money to fund Fitzgerald's needs as required. Before these arrangements were confirmed, however, the situation appeared to change when Ober reported that the editor of *Cosmopolitan* was extremely interested in serializing Fitzgerald's novel and would pay between $30,000 and $40,000 for the rights. Perkins responded to this development with characteristic generosity. He agreed that as Fitzgerald had not had a novel out for so long, and as his stories had been appearing only in popular magazines, it would be good for his reputation to have the serial appear in a high-class magazine (meaning *Scribner's*); but he did not believe that appearing in *Cosmopolitan* would damage the novel's prospects – certainly not to a degree that would outweigh the financial advantages. Fitzgerald should not undertake to do anything that was to his own disadvantage out of a sense of loyalty to Scribners. Fitzgerald had mentioned in his letter that he wanted above all to avoid finding himself in a situation where, having completed *Tender is the Night*, he had to return immediately to grinding out stories for the *Saturday Evening Post*. Perkins agreed wholeheartedly: 'Escape from that is the main thing' (FP, 185). The details of Ober's negotiations with *Cosmopolitan* do not survive, but the deal did not materialize. A letter from Fitzgerald to Perkins a week or two later thanks him for the gesture 'of coming up two thousand' (presumably to the $10,000 finally agreed with *Scribner's Magazine*), and reports that 'negotiations with *Cosmopolitan* were of course stopped . . .' (FP, 186).

Just as he had promised, Fitzgerald delivered the text of his new novel to Perkins in New York in October 1933. Fixing on an appropriate title proved once again to be a problem. 'The Drunkard's Holiday' had (fortunately) been abandoned; other possibilities were 'Doctor Diver's Holiday: A Romance' or plain 'Richard Diver'. In November, however, Perkins received a telegram from Fitzgerald announcing he had 'definitely decided on title'. On the telegram itself Perkins wrote: 'Tender is the Night, A Romance' (LL, 242). With his fourth novel at long last complete, Fitzgerald was inevitably concerned about how best to maximize his financial return. Serialization was in place, but Fitzgerald talked to Perkins about the possibilities of his book becoming a Book Club choice. He also wrote to Chatto & Windus in London urging simultaneous American and English publication, and mentioning that T. S. Eliot of Faber & Faber was interested in the book. (Eliot had in fact written to him saying that Chatto was a good publisher but adding that if he were free to do so he might send his manuscript elsewhere.) He had high hopes too concerning stage and film rights, particularly as Clark Gable had recently expressed interest in a talkie version of *The Great Gatsby*. Another plan was to have *Gatsby* itself reissued in Bennett Cerf's Modern Library series; Fitzgerald clearly felt that the two novels would usefully support each other. As he had done with *Gatsby*, he also took a strong interest in how Scribners were proposing to advertise his new work; he wanted the publicity to stress that the author 'is anything but through as a serious novelist' (FP, 187). However, he could not bring himself to approach Eliot – whom he had met at a dinner-party earlier in 1933 when the poet had been lecturing at Johns Hopkins University – to ask for an endorsement of the author of *The Great Gatsby*'s new work. What Fitzgerald did do was write to Victor Llona, who had translated *Gatsby* into French, suggesting the possibility of a French translation of *Tender is the Night*. In the end *The Great Gatsby* did appear as a Modern Library book in 1934 – with an introduction by the author that Fitzgerald subsequently wished to change – but none of his other hopes or expectations were realized. Film and theatre versions of *Tender is the Night* were produced but at the time they were unable to attract any commercial backing and so never materialized on stage or screen. A French translation of the book did not appear until 1951; and Chatto's English edition, when it appeared in September 1934, attracted little attention. (D. W. Harding did review it in an oddly self-contradictory manner in the critically rigorous journal *Scrutiny*.) Hence the serialization fee plus his royalties on the book's sales remained Fitzgerald's only sources of income from *Tender is the Night*.

The novel was serialized in *Scribner's Magazine* in four instalments, beginning in January 1934. Inevitably there were differences between the serial and book versions. Fitzgerald made revisions in the proofs for the serial, and subsequently revised the serial for the book. The serial text has twelve chapters; only the book has the division into Books I, II, and III. Six short scenes in the serial are dropped from the book. Occasionally the language of the book is slightly more explicit about sexual matters. Fitzgerald naturally believed that the book text was superior to that of the serial – and he worried that reviewers might well have read only the serial version. In a letter to Edmund Wilson in March 1934 – before the book was published – he made his point about the superiority of the later version: '... yet I could wish that you, and others, had read the book version rather than the magazine version which in spots was hastily put together', and he goes on to mention several of the scenes that will be omitted as irrelevant, as well as 'innumerable minor details'. 'I have driven the Scribner proofreaders half nuts but I think I've made it incomparably smoother,' he concludes (L, 366). Another problem with the serial version had been the length of the four sections. In January and February 1934, Perkins suggested the omission or shortening of specific scenes – the Paris railway station shooting scene, or the arrest scene in Cannes – but Fitzgerald argued effectively against these proposals, even insisting instead on a slight expansion of the arrest scene. In March he wrote requiring that there be no interference with his use of italics: 'I know exactly what I am doing,' he told Perkins, 'and I want to use italics for *emphasis* ...' (FP, 193). Working on the proofs of the serial and on the book text simultaneously, Fitzgerald knew he was making things difficult for the printers: 'This is an awful mess,' he told Perkins, 'all the result of haste and nobody's fault except mine' (C, 326–7), but in all these exchanges Fitzgerald comes over very much as the professional writer, wholly confident of the rightness of his aesthetic judgements.

On the crucial question of how successful *Tender is the Night* would be with the reading public Fitzgerald was rather less confident. In January 1934, he articulated his doubts to Maxwell Perkins:

> The novel will certainly have *success d'estime* but it may be slow in coming – alas, I may again have written a novel for novelists with little chance of its lining anybody's pockets with gold. The thing is perhaps too crowded for story reachers to search it through for the story but it can't be helped, there are times when you have to get every edge of your finger-nails on paper.... it is a book that only gives its full effect on its second reading. Almost every part of it now has been revised and thought out from three to six times. (FP, 189)

On 4 March, however, perhaps buoyed by some of the favourable reactions to the early instalments of the serial – he had told Chatto & Windus the book was 'getting an extraordinary response here' (C, 324) – he sounds rather more optimistic:

> I don't think there is a comparison between this book and The Great Gatsby as a seller. The Great Gatsby had against it its length and its purely masculine interest. This book, on the contrary, is a woman's book. (FP, 194)

Making that last point – that *Tender is the Night* was a woman's book – Fitzgerald may have been influenced by early responses to the first instalments of the serial version which had praised in particular the treatment of Nicole Diver. Replying to an enthusiastic letter from Cameron Rogers, a biographer, Fitzgerald said he had been surprised by readers' responses to Nicole – he had assumed that Dick Diver would be very much the centre of attention (C, 322). Illustrations for the serial version had been provided by Edward Shenton – Fitzgerald admired them so much that some were incorporated into the book form – who wrote to Fitzgerald full of praise for what he had achieved: 'It's the best thing that's been written since "The Great Gatsby",' he said (C, 319). Soon too Fitzgerald was able to enjoy overwhelmingly positive responses from other admiring friends and fellow writers. Having read only the first instalment, John Peale Bishop wrote:

> ... your gifts as a novelist surpass those of any of us. It is so skilful, so subtle, so right that I have only praise for it. You get the whole romance of that period, which is now like history. (C, 321)

About the same time, Archibald MacLeish wrote even more enthusiastically: 'Great God Scott you can write. You can write better than ever. Believe it. Believe It – not me' (C, 323). Having read the second instalment the novelist Louis Bromfield wired his congratulations. In a letter of thanks Fitzgerald wrote: '... maybe I am going to have some sort of *succès d'estime* out of it. A writer's praise is worth that of a hundred critics, don't you think?' (C, 325–6) After the appearance of the first two instalments Fitzgerald received a different kind of letter from a reader – Pauline Reinsch, – in Madison, Wisconsin – one listing a series of errors in the French and German usage in the text. Characteristically Fitzgerald urged Scribners to send proofs of instalments three and four to Ms Reinsch so that she could correct them.

Tender is the Night was published by Scribners on 12 April 1934, exactly nine years and two days after Fitzgerald's previous novel, *The Great Gatsby*. Its sales were respectable but far short of the figures Fitzgerald had achieved in the early 1920s with *This Side of Paradise* and *The Beautiful and Damned*. The first printing of 7600 copies sold out quickly, and was followed by two more printings of 5075 and 2520 copies. In April and May *Tender is the Night* occupied tenth place in the *Publishers Weekly* best-sellers lists. The book was widely and on the whole well reviewed. Bruccoli tells us there were twice as many favourable as unfavourable reviews. But *Tender is the Night* could not be described as an unquestioned critical success. Favourable reviewers often expressed reservations; even perceptive critics such as Edith Wharton, Clifton Fadiman, William Troy, Henry Seidel Canby and J. Donald Adams worried over the presentation of the principal character Dick Diver. The book had been so long in coming that perhaps it was inevitable there should be something anti-climactic about its actual appearance. Few reviewers were as unequivocally positive as Gilbert Seldes:

> [Fitzgerald] has gone behind generations, old or new, and created his own image of human beings. And in doing so has stepped again to his natural place at the head of the American writers of our time.[9]

Inevitably disappointed by the general public reception of his novel, Fitzgerald must have taken some comfort from the richly appreciative letters he received from such friends and fellow authors as James Branch Cabell, Carl Van Vechten, John O'Hara, Robert Benchley, John Dos Passos, Thomas Wolfe, G. B. Stern, Mabel Dodge Luhan, Bennett Cerf and Christian Gauss.

However, even among Fitzgerald's friends, there were those who questioned the degree of success his novel had achieved. Hemingway clearly simultaneously admired and disapproved of the book. But his disapproval almost certainly had its origins in the closeness of his relationship at this time with the Murphys – and with Sara Murphy in particular. His argument with Fitzgerald was over the presentation of the Divers; his assumption was that the Divers were a portrait of the Murphys and what he objected to was Fitzgerald's readiness to depart, as he saw it, from the truth about the Murphys. Fitzgerald's response was to advance his theory of the 'composite' nature of characters in fiction: the novelist had to be free to adapt the characteristics of different real people in creating fictional characters – and this presumably is what he believed he had done. In this particular exchange, Fitzgerald's position appears to be the more persuasive one, and with the passage of time Hemingway came to think increasingly highly of *Tender is the Night*.

In 1935 in a letter to Maxwell Perkins he asked how Fitzgerald was, and went on: 'A strange thing is that in retrospect his Tender is the Night gets better and better.'[10] Later still he wrote again to Perkins praising the novel: 'It's amazing how <u>excellent</u> much of it is ... much of it is better than anything else he ever wrote ... reading that novel much of it was so good it was frightening.'[11] When *Tender is the Night* appeared, Sara and Gerald Murphy reacted very much as Hemingway did. Fitzgerald had dedicated the novel to them, but they remained unhappy about the way he had made use of them in portraying Dick and Nicole Diver. Yet with the passage of time their hostility too seems to have faded, and Gerald in particular came to admire what Fitzgerald had written.[12]

As had been the case with *Gatsby*, Fitzgerald felt that even those who had admired *Tender is the Night* had not really understood what he had been attempting to achieve. In letters to friends such as Mencken, Bishop and Hemingway, he did attempt to explain aspects of the form and structure of his novel. To Bishop he explained that whereas *Gatsby* was a 'dramatic' novel, *Tender is the Night* is a 'philosophical, now called psychological' one: to compare the two would be like 'comparing a sonnet sequence with an epic'. If *Gatsby* was in the vein of *Henry Esmond* then *Tender is the Night* was more like *Vanity Fair* (L, 383). To Mencken he wrote insisting that apart perhaps from the opening Rosemary section, everything in the novel is the result of 'a *definite intention*' (L, 529). And to all three correspondents he goes into considerable detail in defending the final pages of the novel describing Dick Diver's disappearance into anonymity in upper New York state. The 'dying fall' atmosphere is what he is aiming to create, and its source, he tells Hemingway, is Conrad's idea in the Preface to *The Nigger of the Narcissus*:

> that the purpose of a work of fiction is to appeal to the lingering after-effects in the reader's mind as differing from, say, the purpose of oratory or philosophy which respectively leave people in a fighting or thoughtful mood. (L, 329)

Despite his willingness to justify and defend what he had done in *Tender is the Night*, Fitzgerald was nonetheless deeply disappointed by its only modest success. His royalties earned him just over $5000

– well short of what he needed to pay off his debts – and, as has already been noted, his hoped-for interest from Broadway or Hollywood had failed to materialize. It was his feeling that his book was somehow not winning the reception it deserved that encouraged him to look for explanations for what had gone wrong. In May 1934, he received a letter from the critic Malcolm Cowley who was 'deeply impressed' by the book and had reviewed it favourably. But in the course of his letter Cowley suggested that readers with whom he had talked had been confused by the reverse chronology of the book – the beginning with Rosemary and the subsequent going back in time to the earlier history of Dick Diver. A simple linear chronology would have been better (C, 366). Fitzgerald did not respond to Cowley's suggestion at the time, but he eventually came to agree that this proposed reordering of the sections of *Tender is the Night* did represent an improvement. Hence he suggested to Bennett Cerf, editor of the Modern Library series, in 1936, and to Maxwell Perkins two years later, that his novel should be reissued with this revision of its structure. However neither Cerf nor Perkins found the notion viable, and it was not until 1951 that Malcolm Cowley arranged the publication of *Tender is the Night* in its restructured form, arguing with some justice that his edition represented the author's final version.

Writing to Perkins almost a year after the original publication date Fitzgerald had admitted that *Tender is the Night* might have been an even better book had he not been so alcohol-dependent when he was working on it:

> A short story can be written on a bottle, but for a novel you need the mental speed that enables you to keep the whole pattern in your head and ruthlessly sacrifice the sideshows as Ernest did in "A Farewell to Arms." If a mind is slowed up ever so little it lives in the individual part of a book rather than in a book as a whole; memory is dulled. I would give anything if I hadn't had to write Part III of "Tender is the Night" entirely on stimulant. If I had one more crack at it cold sober I believe it might have made a great difference. (FP, 218–9)

But despite this admission, Fitzgerald continued to think that the novel was better than its reception in 1934 had indicated. In 1938 he wrote to Perkins suggesting it would benefit his reputation if some of his work were back in print. *Tender is the Night* was particularly in his mind:

> – that book is not dead. The *depth* of its appeal exists – I meet people constantly who have the same exclusive attachment to it as others had to *Gatsby* and *Paradise*, people who identified themselves with Dick Diver. Its great fault is that the *true* beginning – the young psychiatrist in Switzerland – is tucked away in the middle of the book. If pages 151–212 were taken from their present place and put at the start the improvement in appeal would be enormous. In fact the mistake was noted and suggested by a dozen reviewers. (FP, 250–1)

Whatever view one takes on the preferred structure and chronology of *Tender is the Night*, Fitzgerald's sense of the enduring worth of his book has been proved right. *Tender is the Night* does not possess the brilliant poetic economy of *The Great Gatsby*, but through its greater scope it illuminates the conflicting values and changing mores of post-World War I America in an unparalleled manner. As a less dramatic but more psychological novel it also provides, through its account of the decline and fall of its doctor/scientist protagonist, a penetrating exploration of the lineaments of its author's literary life. Dick Diver's role as doctor/scientist is analogous to Fitzgerald's role as artist. The doctor who marries his patient, Dick Diver is destroyed by the resulting confusion of roles: the objectivity and detachment of the medical scientist are incompatible with the involvement and commitment of the husband and lover. On this point the text is finally quite explicit: 'the dualism in his views of her – that of the husband, that of the psychiatrist – was increasingly paralyzing his faculties.'[13] And in this context *Tender is the Night* is an exploration of a problem that Fitzgerald increasingly felt was centrally and dangerously present in his own experience. This too is the reason the novel itself provides the best explanation of why it took so long to write.

6
Experiencing *The Crack-Up*

With the writing of *Tender is the Night* at last completed, Fitzgerald left La Paix and moved to a rented house in Baltimore in December 1933. In the previous month Zelda and he vacationed in Bermuda, but the hoped-for rest and recuperation after the final effort involved in finishing the novel were spoiled by a recurrence of his lung infection. This disappointment was an ominous herald of Fitzgerald's increasingly troubled situation in the next stage of his literary life. In fact the years between the publication of *Tender is the Night* and the decision to move to Hollywood in 1937 would prove the most difficult and demoralizing of Fitzgerald's life. His problems seemed to multiply relentlessly. It was increasingly clear that Zelda's mental health would never be fully restored; Fitzgerald's own health, undermined by his continuing drinking problem, was uncertain; Scottie was growing up and the costs of her education had to be met, on top of Zelda's hospital bills. More worrying still, he was having to face the fact that the old trick of sitting down and churning out a money-winning *Saturday Evening Post* story was becoming increasingly difficult to perform. Creative vitality was giving way to creative exhaustion, and Fitzgerald felt more and more that with the passing of his youth his life was running down – 'getting ready for the end' as he once put it to a friend.[1]

In December 1934, Harold Ober found it necessary to write to his client urging him to get back on track by giving up the damaging habits he had fallen into. 'I hope you won't mind,' writes Ober, 'if I read you a little lecture.' He contrasts the present situation with the old days:

> Up to a couple of years ago if you had sent me word that a story
> would arrive on a certain date, I would have been as certain that
> the story would arrive as that the sun would rise the next day.
> Lately when you have wired me that a story would be sent on a
> certain date I have no faith at all that it will come.

Worse still, Fitzgerald has begun to contact editors directly, making
promises, and then not keeping them. Ober tells him to stop all
writing or telephoning to editors – or movie executives: 'Sometimes
I think it would be better if you would take the telephone out of
your house entirely.' Fitzgerald apparently often telephones when
he has been drinking and this simply adds to the legend always
ready to crop up: 'that you are never sober' (FO, 206–7).

Fitzgerald's initial reaction to this indictment from his literary
agent was an act of contrition: he wrote to Ober accepting all his
criticisms and agreeing to follow his advice. Next day, however, he
had second thoughts and entered a self-defence protesting that all
his troubles were not related to his drinking. In this 'compact
"apologia pro sua vita"' he referred to the bad times of the winter of
1930–31: Zelda's collapse, her family's attacks on him, and her
recurring illness. Then he felt that his literary reputation 'was at its
very lowest ebb'; he was 'completely forgotten' and that fact was
'rubbed in by Zelda's inadvertently written book'. From this point
on his one aim had been at whatever cost to get his novel finished.
With financial help from Ober, Perkins, and his mother, he had
achieved this, 'but at the end it left me in the black hole of Calcutta,
mentally exhausted, physically exhausted, emotionally exhausted,
and perhaps, morally exhausted.' Nonetheless, his personal circumstances were so demanding that he could not allow himself a
moment's respite:

> No sooner did I finish the last galley on the last version of the
> last proof of the book proof of 'Tender is the Night' than it was
> necessary to sit down and write a *Post* story. (FO, 209)

In this situation there is clearly much that is honest and fair
comment both in Ober's criticism and Fitzgerald's defence. But even
if one accepts Fitzgerald's explanation of the sources of his difficulties as a man, there is no denying their increasingly damaging effect

on his work as a writer. After *Tender is the Night* was finally completed, he seems to have been uncertain about how his writing career should go forward. Various projects are considered but most are either never taken up or soon abandoned. Ring Lardner had died from tuberculosis and alcoholism in September 1933 at the age of forty-eight; Fitzgerald wrote a moving tribute to him which appeared in the *New Republic*, attracting appreciative letters from Dorothy Parker, John O'Hara, and other friends. Fitzgerald's piece is far from a conventional encomium; he insists that Lardner's achievement, fine as it was, was less than it might have been; the narrowness of the world of baseball, about which he originally wrote, always constrained him, making it difficult for him to communicate all that he had learned about human experience. No doubt, in thinking about their friendship in the Great Neck days, Fitzgerald was alert to the troubling parallel between their respective careers in subsequent years. Scribners decided it would be an appropriate time to bring out a selection of Lardner's work and Maxwell Perkins invited Fitzgerald to help choose the material and write an introduction; however the need to press ahead with *Tender is the Night* forced Fitzgerald to decline. A week or two earlier, in September 1933, he had written to Perkins mentioning plans for his 'next book' (i.e. after the publication of *Tender*). It might be either 'an omnibus collection of short stories' or the long-contemplated volume of Basil and Josephine stories (FP, 182). Neither of these projects materialized. A more bizarre idea emerged in the middle of the following year. Gilbert Seldes had edited the Ring Lardner selection for Scribners and when it appeared Fitzgerald wrote to him proposing that they consider a stage production of some of Lardner's one-act plays alongside a couple of macabre Grand Guignol plays. Needless to say, nothing came of this suggestion. Much more interesting – but little more likely to have been put into effect – was Fitzgerald's suggestion to Christian Gauss that he be invited to Princeton to give a series of lectures 'on the actual business of creating fiction' (L, 406). In the unlikely event of its being willing to take a chance, the Princeton English Department could have been offering a course in creative writing almost a generation before such courses became commonplace in America's academia. Other 1934 ventures included an attempt to persuade Clark Gable, whom Fitzgerald had met in Baltimore, to make a new sound movie version of *The Great Gatsby*, and the writing of a film scenario (never used) for George Burns and Gracie Allen who were also on tour in Baltimore. Invited at this time by Malcolm Cowley to contribute to a *New Republic* feature called 'Good Books That Almost Nobody Has Read' (April 1934), Fitzgerald did respond: his choices included Nathanael West's *Miss Lonelyhearts*, as well as two books by friends – Edmund Wilson's *I Thought of Daisy* and Thomas Boyd's World War I novel, *Through the Wheat*.

A major focus of Fitzgerald's own writing in the period immediately after the appearance of *Tender is the Night* proved to be even more ill-judged than those projects that failed to materialize. In the middle of 1934, prompted perhaps by memories of his childhood enjoyment of *Ivanhoe* alongside his continuing enthusiasm for history itself, he came up with the idea of a story series set in ninth-century France; even more bizarrely the stories' hero would be based on Hemingway. Ober had great difficulty selling this idea to magazine editors: most turned it down, he reported to Fitzgerald, because they were sure that their readers' expectations of a Fitzgerald story were that it would be about modern society. Nonetheless, as always, he encouraged Fitzgerald to continue, telling him he had 'an exceedingly good book in this material' (FO, 206). Unfortunately Ober was quite wrong – undertaking to write these stories, which he hoped would eventually come together to make a historical novel, is one of the rare occasions when Fitzgerald's literary judgement failed him completely. The stories read at best like contributions to a magazine for boys' adventure stories; the characters are mere outlines and the historical context lacks substance. Ober eventually succeeded in selling the idea of the series to the *Red Book*, and three stories appeared between October 1934 and August 1935; but Fitzgerald struggled to produce them on time. The editor of the *Red Book* was unhappy about the delay between receiving the first and second stories and even when he had the third, Ober told Fitzgerald, 'he hasn't any real faith when he will get the following stories. I don't think you can blame him for feeling this way' (FO, 206).

Fitzgerald did in the end write one more story in the series but the *Red Book* chose not to publish it. Despite this failure, the idea of turning the series into a historical novel remained very much in Fitzgerald's mind. As late as October 1935, he was still trying to interest Perkins in a plan to make the series into a Scribners book – or even two books. Perkins expressed polite interest but nothing came of the idea. Fitzgerald's increasing worry that he had used up all his material, that there was nothing left in his life to write about, best explains why he thought medieval history could provide him with fresh subject-matter. But perhaps the failure on this occasion of the critical sense that normally operated so sharply in relation to his commercial market writing can only be fully understood in the context of the more general forms of uncertainty and self-doubt he was experiencing in this period.

Earlier in the summer of 1934, Fitzgerald had managed to produce three more stories for the *Saturday Evening Post*. Each was bought for $3000, but the *Post* was not satisfied that they were up to the expected Fitzgerald standard. With his reputation at the *Post* becoming increasingly less secure, Fitzgerald was pleased to find a market in the new magazine *Esquire*, edited by Arnold Gingrich. Gingrich was a huge admirer of Fitzgerald's prose and thus was ready to take whatever Fitzgerald sent him. The problem, however, was money: Gingrich's maximum payment was no more than $250. *Esquire's* first Fitzgerald publications were two personal articles written by Zelda, polished by Fitzgerald, and credited to both. Two stories by Fitzgerald followed, as well as 'Sleeping and Waking', an autobiographical piece that heralded the much more controversial 'Crack-Up' articles that would appear in *Esquire* in 1936. Despite his growing problems, Fitzgerald's earnings in 1934 amounted to $20,032.33; eight stories were sold for $12,475; income from book royalties was negligible, but he received another advance of about $6500 from Scribners.

II

Scribners had followed up the publication of Fitzgerald's first three novels with a volume of his short stories. Perkins was anxious to maintain this pattern after the appearance of *Tender is the Night*, urging Fitzgerald to put together a volume of some kind as quickly as possible. Fitzgerald had earlier talked of the possibility of either an 'omnibus' collection of his stories, or a 'Basil and Josephine' book. In May 1934, discussing the make-up of a book to appear in the autumn, these reappeared as his first two suggestions; the others were for a collection of new (i.e. uncollected) short stories, or a collection of more autobiographical pieces including 'Echoes of the Jazz Age' and the still unpublished 'My Lost City'. Unsurprisingly, Perkins's preference was for a book composed of the Basil Lee and Josephine stories – as long as Fitzgerald could get the material together quickly. Such a book, he wrote, 'would be very much liked and admired' (FP, 199). His second choice would be Fitzgerald's third suggestion – the collection of new stories.

Within a few days of hearing from Perkins, however, Fitzgerald was having second thoughts about a Basil and Josephine volume; the doubts that had deterred him in the past resurfaced. The stories, he told Perkins, 'are not as good as I thought'; 'they would require a tremendous amount of work and a good deal of new invention to make them presentable.' Then there was the danger that critics and readers might take the book to be a kind of inferior novel and so damage further his critical reputation. Finally many of the stories' best ideas and phrases had already been transferred to *Tender is the Night*. Fitzgerald's decision was to go for the new collection of his stories while agreeing to include within it some of the Basil and Josephine material; Perkins was invited to help with the selection (FP, 199). Fitzgerald worked at the volume over the summer and autumn of 1934, but progress was slow. Perkins was anxious that the book should appear as quickly as possible so as to benefit from the renewed interest in Fitzgerald's writing produced by the publication of *Tender is the Night*; he even argued that the story collection would make reviewers think again about *Tender*. He suggested that Fitzgerald was worrying too much about the odd phrase that might appear both in *Tender is the Night* and an earlier short story – Hemingway did not seem to mind about such a thing happening in his work. What was making Fitzgerald's progress with the story collection so slow was not really the laborious business of checking repetitions of phrases between the stories and the text of *Tender is the Night*. Rather it was a whole series of problems – his own and Zelda's health, his constant financial worries and the oppressive weight of the debts he was incurring, his sense of emotional and creative exhaustion, his alcohol dependence and the recent, guilt-inducing tensions in his relationship with Zelda, which were bearing down upon him in this period of his life. But he took advantage of Perkins's reference to Hemingway to assume the aesthetic high ground: if he was being slow it was because he had to get everything right. He had 'a great sense of exactitude' about his work – and the fact that 'Ernest has let himself repeat here and there a phrase would be no possible justification for my doing the same.' Hemingway might be able 'to afford a lapse in that line', but he couldn't, and anyway he had to be 'the final judge of what is appropriate in these cases' (FP, 207). Fitzgerald eventually told Perkins he had made a big mistake in imagining he could have his story collection ready for publication in the autumn of 1934; a more realistic date would be the early spring of 1935. Perkins had no option but to agree, and after slow progress through the winter of 1934–35, with much chopping and changing about which stories to include, the volume called *Taps At Reveille* (Fitzgerald had his usual problem over deciding on a suitable title) finally appeared in March 1935. The print run was just over five thousand copies and Fitzgerald dedicated the volume to his agent, Harold Ober. Reviews were mainly favourable, but the sales were not such as to require a second printing.

In June 1934, Fitzgerald had had to make a desperate appeal to Max Perkins for an immediate loan of a thousand dollars. And of course he had never lost sight of the different kind of debt he owed Perkins for his unswerving support and loyalty throughout his entire writing career. These were the considerations that made it essential that he try to explain to Perkins how he had had to disappoint him over the timing of the publication of *Taps at Reveille*. This he attempted to do in a long letter of November 1934:

I know you have the sense that I have loafed lately but that is absolutely not so. I have drunk too much and that is certainly slowing me up. On the other hand, without drink I do not know whether I could have survived this time. In actual work since I finished the last proof of the novel in the middle of March, eight months ago, I have written and sold three stories for the *Post*, written another which was refused, written two and a half stories for the *Redbook*, rewritten three articles of Zelda's for *Esquire* and one original for them to get emergency money, collaborated on a 10,000 word treatment of "Tender is the Night," which was no go, written an 8,000 word story for Gracie Allen, which was also no go, and made about five false starts on stories which went from 1,000 to 5,000 words, and a preface to the Modern Library edition of "The Great Gatsby", which equalizes very well what I have done in other years. (FP, 210)

If one also includes the work he was doing on the stories for the *Taps* collection, then on the face of it Fitzgerald's case is a strong one. Nonetheless the truth of the matter remains that in 1934 Fitzgerald's literary career was moving into crisis. Even the best of the work he produced that year was of no more than journeyman level; there were too many false starts, too many projects that went nowhere; and the idea that he could turn to the writing of fiction about medieval France was proving fundamentally misconceived. The appearance of *Gatsby* in the Modern Library series was a plus, but Fitzgerald himself was dissatisfied with the preface he wrote for it – and while Bennett Cerf would have accepted a revised version the occasion did not arise, because sales did not justify a second printing. In his self-justificatory letter to Perkins, Fitzgerald makes much of his own poor health as a major factor affecting his literary work: the kind of energy he had ten, or even five, years ago is just no longer there. But even that physical exhaustion, exacerbated of course by his drinking habit, almost certainly had its origins in a deeper emotional and psychological level of potential breakdown. Fitzgerald's difficulty in seeing the way forward for his literary career after *Tender is the Night*, the various failed or failing projects he undertook, the difficulties he experienced over shaping the material to make up *Taps at Reveille* – alongside his worsening alcohol problem and declining physical condition – are all symptomatic of the ever more anguished personal position he was beginning to recognize he had reached. For years he had juggled more or less successfully the two roles he consciously wished to play: his role as a man – lover and husband, father and friend – and his role as professional artist-writer. Since his decision to win back and marry Zelda, the task had never been an easy one, but he had contrived, as it were, to keep the different plates spinning on their sticks. But the events of 1930–31, and the immediately following years, made the balancing act more and more difficult to sustain. Zelda's breakdown in particular seemed increasingly to pit the two roles dramatically against each other; sustaining the loving, supporting role of the man was now only possible at the expense –

in terms of money, time, energy, emotional resources – of the needs of the serious artist-writer. Inevitably, at different moments and in different moods, Fitzgerald reacted in different ways: loving, concerned, responsible, the ideal husband and father at times, his sense of exasperated frustration could, at others, explode in anger and cruel vindictiveness.

In the early years of Zelda's illness, the overwhelmingly dominant reality of Fitzgerald's literary life was the absolute necessity to finish writing his long-awaited fourth novel. Unless he could do that, he knew his career as a serious writer was over. André le Vot, Fitzgerald's French biographer, has an interesting passage in which he tries to sum up the nature of the position Fitzgerald worked himself into when he was finally finding it possible to complete *Tender is the Night* towards the end of 1933:

> The man receded before the storm of responsibilities he faced, toward Zelda, Scottie, the *Post*, his creditors; five years, he complained, had estranged him from himself to the point that he no longer knew exactly who he was or even if he was still anyone at all.[2]

In other words, in order to finish his novel, Fitzgerald had had to give up one of his roles – his role as a man; to complete his novel he had become, in the phrase he himself would use a year or two later, 'a writer only'. In 1933 and 1934 this was the threatening dilemma that was haunting and undermining Fitzgerald's literary life: the circumstances of his life as a man were increasingly challenging his continued existence as a writer. No wonder he found himself beginning to struggle to survive.

III

But exactly such a struggle characterizes Fitzgerald's literary life between 1934 and 1937. Early in 1935, he left Baltimore for North Carolina. Zelda was then in the Sheppard Pratt hospital just outside Baltimore, but this time it was Fitzgerald's own health that necessitated the move. His lung problem had resurfaced and he was told he might benefit from a period in the mountain air of North Carolina. For two weeks he stayed at the Oak Hall Hotel in Tryon, but the tests he underwent on his return to Baltimore showed a continuing deterioration in the condition of his lungs; he decided to return to North Carolina for the summer. This time he chose the rather grand Grove Park Inn near Asheville. Now more than ever money was Fitzgerald's overwhelming concern. Just before leaving Baltimore he wrote to Ober on the subject of the possible dramatization of *Tender is the Night* adding:

> I am half crazy with illness and worry, and in a state where each aggravation only adds to the accumulation of anxiety, strain, self pity, or what have you. (FO, 218)

This was exactly the state of mind that was going to prevail for the next two years. Nonetheless, Fitzgerald had no option but to try to survive financially by continuing to write. Independently of both Perkins and Ober, he tried at this time to interest Chatto & Windus in London in a book of his stories. His suggestion was not an English edition of *Taps at Reveille*, but rather a volume of 21 stories selected from his three earlier collections as well as the new one. Such a volume, he thought, might appeal to 'the library patron' in England, and help to build up his English public since he believed there was 'nothing in my work which is necessarily unintelligible or antipathetic to the British mind' (C, 401–2). Chatto, however, chose not to pursue the idea.

With no real hope of any further return from his published work, Fitzgerald needed desperately to produce and publish new material. But this was proving increasingly difficult to do. The concentrated bursts of creativity which had allowed him to produce short stories perfectly geared to the requirements of the mass magazine market had at last become impossible to attain. In September 1936, he would tell Perkins, 'I have to admit to myself that I haven't the vitality that I had five years ago' (FP, 231). Discussing his writing plans with Ober in the summer of 1935, he argued that even in his best years there was a limit to what he could achieve: 'Even in years like '24, '28, '29, '30 all devoted to short stories I could not turn out more than 8–9 top price stories a year.' 'All my stories,' he goes on,

> are conceived like novels, require a special emotion, a special experience – so that my readers, if such there be, know that each

time it'll be something new, not in form but in substance, it'd be far better for me if I could do pattern stories but the pencil just goes dead on me.... (FO, 221)

Fitzgerald was no doubt right in asserting that he had never written 'pattern' stories, but unfortunately a 'special emotion' or a 'special experience' was just what much of his recent work – the French history stories, for example – precisely lacked. In fact in this period Fitzgerald came increasingly to feel that he had no special new emotions or experiences about which to write; those from the past, on the other hand, had already been fully exploited. (In the auto-biographical 'Afternoon of an Author' he would refer to 'the increasing necessity of picking over an already well-picked past'.)[3] Hence to keep up the production of saleable new short stories was now virtually impossible. In May 1936, he noted in a letter to Ober that he was constantly having to rewrite such material as he was producing: 'Every single story since *Phillipe I* [the first of the medieval tales] in the Spring of 1934 two years ago I've had to write over.' What that meant was a doubling of his work, and no oppor-tunity for a break; debts press, so while revising one story he had to start another. 'This business of debt is awful,' he continues,

> it has made me lose confidence to an appalling extent. I used to write for myself – now I write for editors because I never have time to really think what I <u>do</u> like or find anything to like. (LL, 299)

In fact, even if Fitzgerald felt he was now writing only for editors, he was experiencing less and less success in satisfying them; in 1935 and 1936 his work was rejected far more frequently than in the past. One answer, he believed, was to come up with a subject idea that could be used in a story series – like the successful Basil and Josephine group. Such linked stories could be written more quickly and sold more profitably. But the ideas he came up with, such as a single father bringing up his daughter, and the experiences of a hospital nurse, proved to have at best only limited appeal. In the summer of 1936, Fitzgerald, wisely or not, admitted to a fiction editor at the *Saturday Evening Post* that he seemed to have lost his old ability to write short fiction:

Somewhere about the middle of "Tender is the Night" I seemed to have lost my touch on the short story – by touch I mean the exact balance, how much plot, how much character, how much background you can crowd into a limited number of words ... In the last two years I've only too often realized that many of my stories were built rather than written. (LL, 301)

Even more telling than this admission, perhaps, is the role that Ober now came to play in 'editing' some of Fitzgerald's stories. In a manner unthinkable in the past, Ober sends his author lists of proposed textual amendments or improvements – which Fitzgerald often appears to accept. Ober felt, for example, that a story called 'The Pearl and the Fur' contained 'a great many improbabilities'; understanding that Fitzgerald didn't feel able to do any more work on the story, he and his assistant had 'tried to fix up the most glaring inconsistencies' (FO, 264). A long list of suggested improvements follows. In a follow-up letter Ober half-apologizes for his intervention, but insists on the need for further changes:

I hope you know that no one reads your stories with more pleasure and with more partiality than I do and that I wouldn't suggest your making changes in a story unless it seemed to me important that you should do so.

However it is his final comment that in most significant: 'I am sure you want me to use my best judgment and so far I think we have agreed very well on the changes that are advisable to make in your stories' (FO, 267). That Ober should have come to play such an interventionist role in relation to Fitzgerald's short fiction is a perfect illustration of the loss of confidence and general sense of creative decline that had overtaken his once prize client.

After making the decision to return to Hollywood in mid-1937, Fitzgerald was more than ready to acknowledge just how disastrous the previous two or three years had been. In October 1936, he admitted to Perkins he had been hoping all along that Hollywood would come to his financial rescue by buying the movie rights to *Tender is the Night*; or alternatively that the novel would be as successfully dramatized as *Gatsby* had been. Denied such sources of income he had no option but to return to 'this endless *Post* writing'

– or go to Hollywood (FP, 233). A little later he described 1936 to Perkins as 'my least productive & lowest general year since 1926'. He had sold only four stories, and written eight *Esquire* pieces. 'Stories', he admits, 'are somehow mostly out of me unless some new source of material springs up.' 1937 has begun equally badly – the 'same damn lack of interest, staleness . . .' (FP, 235). In letters to some of his oldest friends the same points recur: he has decided to go back to Hollywood because the experiences of recent years have drained him of life and energy of all kinds – physical, emotional, and creative. On his way west in July 1937, he tells his cousin Ceci that 'for the present and for over 3 years the creative side of me has been dead as hell' (L, 438). And a month earlier, to his old St Paul friend Oscar Kalman – who had helped him out financially some months before – he provided a full account of the 'two years' mess' that reached its lowest point in the fall of 1936':

> A prejudiced enemy might well say it was all drink, a fond mama might say it was a run of ill-luck, a banker might say it was not providing for the future in better days, a psychiatrist might say it was a nervous collapse . . .

but its effect 'was to fantastically prevent me from doing any work at the very age when presumably one is at the height of one's power' (L, 569). Committed to Hollywood in mid-1937, Fitzgerald knew very well that since the publication of *Tender is the Night* in 1934, his literary career had fallen into an apparently irreversible decline.

Fitzgerald was right to look back on the years between 1934 and mid-1937 as the low-point in his literary career. But as in the past, despite all his problems of failing health, alcoholism, extreme financial pressures – alongside his commitment to maintaining Zelda in private care and Scottie in private education – and declining creativity, he continued through these years to struggle to write. In 1935, while living either in Baltimore or North Carolina, Fitzgerald produced seven stories: two were published in the *Saturday Evening Post*, two in *McCall's*, the others in the *American Magazine*, *Liberty*, and *Esquire*. But Ober had to work hard to place these stories. The *Post* two were part of the proposed 'Gwen' series about a father–daughter single parent situation which Ober reported the *Post* was definitely interested in. Two more Gwen stories were written, but the *Post* lost interest and only one of them was published in Fitzgerald's lifetime. His proposal of a radio series based on the same father–daughter theme was considered by CBS – he had earned $700 for a short anti-war radio script called 'Let's Go Out and Play' – but in the end not pursued. No more successful were the continuing attempts to produce a commercially viable dramatization of *Tender is the Night*, to interest Hollywood in a movie version of the novel, or to persuade Maxwell Perkins that the French medieval stories could become one or even two books. Just how precarious Fitzgerald's position was at the end of 1935 he indicates in a wry commentary written from a Hendersonville hotel to Ober:

> I am getting accustomed to poverty and bankruptcy (In fact for myself I rather enjoy washing my own clothes + eating 20 cents meals twice a day, after so many years in the flesh pots ...)
>
> I arrived here weak as hell, got the grippe + spat blood again (1st time in 9 months) + took to bed for six days. I didn't dare see the Ashville doctor till I got this story off + wrote a $200 article for Gingrich on which I've been living. (FO, 233)

(The Gingrich article was in fact the first of the three 'Crack-Up' autobiographical essays which *Esquire* published in 1936.) Ultimately Fitzgerald's earnings for 1935 amounted to $16,845.16. The seven stories earned $14,725, the remainder coming from Scribners and the material published in *Esquire*. In November 1935, Ober had visited Hollywood, and in December he was writing to Fitzgerald suggesting that he might consider working there. Ober's concern for Fitzgerald was both genuine and personal – he was already beginning to act as a kind of foster-father to Scottie – but there must have also been a growing worry over the money Fitzgerald owed him. Hollywood, he suggests, would allow Fitzgerald to get out of the hole he is currently in, and in due course would provide him with the financial freedom to write a novel when he is ready to do so. Replying on 31 December 1935, Fitzgerald equivocates: he is not inclined to go to Hollywood now, but he might 'if there was no choice'. He feels that working on other people's stories doesn't suit 'what qualities I have', and he insists that 'no single man with a serious literary reputation has made good there'. He would need a good technical man to work with, and to find such a person would require a lucky break, but 'unless some such break occurs I'd be no good in the industry'. And he ends by talking darkly of either being able to pull out of his present situation in the next few months or of going under – 'in which case I might start again in some entirely new way of my own' (FO, 241). Ober did not respond, and for the moment the notion of solving Fitzgerald's financial problems by moving west to Hollywood was dropped.

IV

The publication of the three 'Crack-Up' essays in *Esquire* in 1936 at least gained for Fitzgerald a flurry of renewed public interest. These straightforwardly autobiographical pieces, begun in Hendersonville, North Carolina, as we have seen, to obtain what Fitzgerald calls 'emergency money' from Arnold Gingrich, attempt to explain in depth what has gone wrong in their author's life and literary career. They end with Fitzgerald declaring that from now on he will give up all attempts to be a man and instead become 'a writer only'. Clearly there were many readers who were struck by the starkly dramatic contrast between their memories of the Fitzgerald they had read in the 1920s and the account he was giving of himself now. While the pieces were appearing, Fitzgerald told Gingrich, he had received commendatory letters from Alec Woollcott, Julian Street, G. B. Stern, Nancy Hoyt, James Boyd, and others – as well as letters from 'old friends'. What he did not say was that at least some of the letters from old friends were decidedly hostile. John Dos Passos, for example, wrote:

> I've been wanting to see you, naturally, to argue about your Esquire articles – Christ, man, how do you find time in the middle of the general conflagration to worry about all that stuff? ... We're living in one of the damndest tragic moments in history – if you want to go to pieces I think it's absolutely o.k. but I think you ought to write a first rate novel about it ...[4]

In late March 1936, Fitzgerald wrote to Sara Murphy about the 'Crack-Up' essays:

If you read the little trilogy I wrote for *Esquire* you know I went through a sort of 'dark night of the soul' last autumn, and again and again my thoughts reverted to you and Gerald, and I reminded myself that nothing had happened to me with the awful *suddenness* of your tragedy of a year ago, nothing so utterly conclusive and irreparable. (L, 445)

The reference here is to the death from meningitis of Baoth, the Murphys' fifteen-year-old elder son exactly a year previously (their second son Patrick would die from tuberculosis in January 1937 – Fitzgerald wrote: 'Fate can't have any more arrows in its quiver for you that will wound like these ... The golden bowl is broken indeed but it *was* golden; nothing can ever take those boys away from you now' (L, 446–7)). But Fitzgerald could not deflect Sara's inevitable criticism of *The Crack-Up*. In April she wrote to say he should have known all along that 'life' at some point would betray him:

Do you *really* mean to say you honestly thought [quoting from the first 'Crack-Up' article] "life was something you dominated if you were any good?" Even if you meant your *own* life it is arrogant enough, – but life! ... rebelling, dragging one's feet & fighting every inch of the way, one must admit one can't *control* it – one has to *take* it, – + as well as possible – That is all I know. (C, 429–30)

Close friend of the Murphys as Fitzgerald was, Hemingway at this time was perhaps an even closer one; and certainly the view of life expressed here by Sara Murphy is one that Hemingway would have endorsed. Unsurprisingly, then, Hemingway shared Sara's disapproval of the 'Crack-Up' articles which he regarded as a form of whining in public. Subsequently he even went so far as to incorporate his contempt into his own fiction. In the posthumously published *True at First Light*, the protagonist lies awake at night and remembers 'how Scott Fitzgerald had written that in the something something of the soul something something it is always three o'clock in the morning'. He remembers that the Fitzgerald quotation 'had occurred in a series of articles in which he had abandoned this world and his former extremely shoddy ideals and had first referred to himself as a cracked plate'. Having successfully recalled the quotation, he discusses it in the morning with another character who asks why Fitzgerald had picked especially on three in the morning: 'I think it is just fear and worry and remorse ... I think what he meant was his conscience and despair.'[5] As will be noted below, this was in fact the second time that Hemingway had used and abused Fitzgerald in his own fiction, but apart from the general unpleasantness, what is intriguing here is Hemingway's suggestion that *The Crack-Up* reflects Fitzgerald's remorse, conscience, and despair. As will emerge, my own view is rather similar.

Whatever the views of Fitzgerald's friends (and both Maxwell Perkins and Harold Ober have to be included among those made uneasy by their publication), the 'Crack-Up' essays in *Esquire* had certainly made an impact. Clearly there were still readers interested in Fitzgerald and his life. In March 1936, he received a letter from Simon & Schuster enquiring about the possibility of his writing a book based on the autobiographical articles then appearing. Fitzgerald immediately contacted Scribners. He reminded Perkins that he had thought about a book based on his autobiographical sketches of the 'How to Live on $36,000 a Year' type several years before; now 'the interest in this *Esquire* series has been so big' perhaps Scribners would be interested in reconsidering the idea? If not, should he pursue the Simon & Schuster possibility? (FP, 227) Perkins replied suggesting that Fitzgerald write a book of reminiscences along the lines of 'Echoes of the Jazz Age' (which he called 'a beautiful article') rather than a purely autobiographical one. On the other hand he wouldn't be against an autobiographical book which could include the material in the *Esquire* pieces:

> Couldn't you make a really well integrated book? You write non-fiction wonderfully well, your observations are brilliant and acute ... Whatever you decide, we want to do, but it would be so much better to make a book out of the materials than merely to take the articles and trim them, and join them up, etc. (FP, 228)

For the rest of 1936, the idea of a book of reminiscences or of a more purely autobiographical kind (and eventually the distinction between the two would become blurred) would keep resurfacing. Fitzgerald's immediate reaction to Perkins's suggestions was a negative one: a new book of the reminiscence kind would be a much bigger undertaking than what he had in mind. He does not have the time to write such a book. Meantime he already has 60,000 words of a personal kind that he could collect and revise to make a book. Perkins, in his turn, remained unconvinced: the book of reminiscences was the better plan. A few weeks later Fitzgerald wrote 'Afternoon of an Author' for *Esquire* – another purely autobiographical piece. Arnold Gingrich responded with such enthusiasm to this article that Fitzgerald was encouraged to think again about publishing a book-length collection of such pieces. He asked Perkins in June to 'reconsider the matter' (FP, 230). His editor replied as before – while making it clear that Scribners would indeed be prepared to publish such an autobiographical collection if Fitzgerald went ahead with it.

Earlier in 1936 Fitzgerald had considered another project that he felt might be financially rewarding. In 1930 he had met the manager of a leading Russian ballerina; the manager was now in the US trying to get the ballet star a film contract. Fitzgerald conceived the idea of writing a screenplay for her. Ober was reasonably encouraging but warned Fitzgerald against spending time on the project before an actual contract was in place: he would be better advised to continue work on the Gwen story series. In the end the ballet film idea was not pursued. As always Fitzgerald returned to short-story writing as the only possible way of maintaining any degree of financial viability. But, as has been noted, even this kind of writing was proving ever more difficult to sustain. *Esquire* published several stories – most of poor quality – but the mass-circulation magazines were proving less and less interested in his work. 'Trouble' – from the aborted series about a nurse and not published until March 1937 – would prove to be his last *Saturday Evening Post* story. 'Thumbs Up', a Civil War story involving torture and the assassination of Lincoln, was turned down by 13 magazines before being accepted by *Colliers* – on condition that Fitzgerald revise it. (It was finally published in June 1940 as 'The End of Hate'.)

Fitzgerald also experienced trouble in other forms in 1936. In July his physical condition suffered another blow when he broke a shoulder attempting a dive in his hotel swimming-pool; the shoulder was put in plaster, but Fitzgerald made the situation worse by falling over in his bathroom while still wearing the cast. In August he had to face a blow which, while not physical, was probably even more damaging to his personal well-being. The August edition of *Esquire* which contained his 'Afternoon of an Author' piece, also contained a new short story by Hemingway called 'The Snows of Kilimanjaro'. About a dying writer, the story near its beginning makes a cruelly dismissive reference to 'poor Scott Fitzgerald' and his romantic awe of the rich. Wholly understandably, Fitzgerald was hurt and dismayed by this needless attack on him. Hemingway may possibly have felt that the frankness of the 'Crack-Up' articles had somehow opened the door to such a use of his old friend's name, but he can hardly have been surprised to receive Fitzgerald's measured letter of protest. In the event, when 'The Snows of Kilimanjaro' appeared in Hemingway's next collection of stories, it was Maxwell Perkins who insisted that he drop Fitzgerald's name. A few weeks later, in September, Fitzgerald had to face yet another humiliating crisis of a personal kind. A reporter from a popular New York newspaper persuaded him on his fortieth birthday to let himself be interviewed in his room in the Grove Park Inn in North Carolina when he had been ill and drinking. The resulting story was inevitably lurid and sensational: Fitzgerald was portrayed as a despairing drunk. When he read the story in the newspaper Fitzgerald was so devastated that he swallowed enough morphine to kill himself – only to vomit it up before it could affect him. He admitted what had happened to Ober and, as always, his agent did his best to reassure him: the *New York Evening Post* was 'a very cheap paper and very few people read it'; and he was certain that Fitzgerald was 'going to write other fine novels and many fine stories – better ones than you have ever done before' (FO, 281).

In mid-September 1936, Fitzgerald, after a lengthy silence, wrote to Maxwell Perkins recounting all his problems of the summer – omitting the newspaper interview fiasco, but including the death of his mother which had occurred in August. In terms of work the 'total accomplished for one summer has been one story – not very good, two *Esquire* articles, neither of them very good' (FP, 231). As a result of his mother's death, Fitzgerald stood to inherit just under $23,000, and it is this apparent change in his circumstances that Perkins focuses on in his reply. The money represents Fitzgerald's 'big chance' – 'you have never been free from financial anxiety'. Now he should plan to live economically for eighteen months or two years and write 'a major book' (FP, 232). The following month

Perkins wrote again urging Fitzgerald to plan a book now that would get him out of all his difficulties, even suggesting that the book of reminiscences he had previously recommended might be the best way forward. In fact Perkins was underestimating the depth of Fitzgerald's financial problems. Almost all of his mother's inheritance would go on simply paying off existing debts – there was no financial cushion upon which he could relax and write. Writing back to Perkins he rejected the idea of a biographical or autobiographical book saying he had a novel planned, or at least conceived, which would take two years of free time to write. No such time is available. He needs to earn at least $18,000 a year to cover Zelda's hospital bills and meet the rest of his expenses; he sees no way of achieving this other than either 'this endless Post writing' or Hollywood. He feels he has got himself 'completely on the spot', and what the next step is, he writes, 'I don't know' (FP, 233–4). This is the mood which appears to have dominated Fitzgerald for the rest of 1936 and into the opening months of 1937. Perkins, like Ober, tries his best to reassure and support him throughout this period. Indeed in March 1937, Perkins wrote to say that he had only pushed the idea of a book of reminiscences as a way of getting Fitzgerald to deal finally with the past and thus be in a position to move on to something entirely fresh. Fitzgerald's earnings for 1936 amounted to $10,180. Four stories earned $7650; nine *Esquire* pieces brought in $2250, and royalties amounted to $81.18.

Fitzgerald's income continued to decline in the early months of 1937. His requests for small advances from Ober, who was growing increasingly uneasy about his role as banker, become more and more anguished as he struggles to come up with cash for daily living expenses. He tells Ober that every day brings demands and bills and threats of legal suits 'from all over hell'. 'Some matters as buying razor blades + even cigarettes have grown serious' (FO, 309). He did write one excellent article – 'Early Success' which appeared in *American Cavalcade* – but *Esquire* had become effectively the only market for his stories. Most of these were of indifferent quality but 'Financing Finnegan' – a barely fictionalized account of Fitzgerald's own financial dependence on Perkins and Ober – is distinguished by its nicely judged note of self-deprecation. Nonetheless Fitzgerald's income in the first half of 1937 fell to less than $3500. His position was now an impossible one. He could no longer pretend that his writing could earn him enough even to pay his daily bills. He had cut his personal expenses to the lowest level possible, but as he explained to Perkins, ideas suggested by close friends such as 'sending my daughter to a public school, putting my wife in a public insane asylum' would shatter the last vestiges of self-respect (FP, 234).

By June 1937, Fitzgerald's debt to Ober was well over $12,000. Fortunately, whether out of concern for his own or his client's financial interest, Ober had kept alive the possibility of a Hollywood job for Fitzgerald. Back in August 1936, he had had a meeting in New York with Edwin Knopf of MGM assuring him that Fitzgerald was willing and able to do a good job in Hollywood. Knopf knew of Fitzgerald's less-than-successful previous visits to Hollywood, and was worried both by reports of his drinking and by what the writer himself had said in the 'Crack-Up' articles. Reporting this meeting to Fitzgerald, Ober could not resist repeating his disapproval of the autobiographical essays: 'I think those confounded Esquire articles have done you a great deal of harm and I hope you won't do any more' (FO, 279–80). In any event in June 1937, Ober arranged for Fitzgerald to come up to New York from North Carolina to meet Knopf to discuss the Hollywood possibility. The meeting went well, and the outcome was that Fitzgerald was offered a screenwriting job by MGM at a salary of $1000 a week for six months, with an option for renewal at a figure of $1250 per week. In his current situation Fitzgerald could not do other than accept.

Despite the fact that over the preceding months Fitzgerald had been at best hesitant and wary over the prospect of Hollywood, he did not approach his new job in a defeatist or cynical mood. Having made his decision, he seems to have decided to act in a thoroughly professional manner. Writing to Scottie on board the westbound train, he reviewed his previous Hollywood failures, acknowledged his mistakes, and expressed his determination to profit from them on this occasion. He was sure that as a writer he could succeed in Hollywood: 'Given a break I can make them double this contract in less than two years' (L, 31). A letter to Anne Ober, written a few days later, has something of the same commitment and confidence. Having listed all the stars he has met or seen, he goes on: 'And this is to say I'm through. From now on I go nowhere and see no one because the work is hard as hell, at least for me, and I've lost ten pounds'. (L, 572).

Is this the voice of the new, slimmed-down 'writer only' Fitzgerald whose existence is announced at the end of the 'Crack-Up' series? A qualified 'yes' is perhaps the best answer.

As we have seen, some of Fitzgerald's oldest friends and most loyal supporters had been upset and dismayed by the publication of the three 'Crack-Up' essays. But the very strength of that reaction is an index of the pieces' value: what was upsetting and dismaying was the harsh authenticity of Fitzgerald's self-examination, the facing of truths however unpalatable. The original occasion of the essays obviously was Fitzgerald's identified need for what he called 'emergency money', but that in no way detracts from their honesty: 'The Crack-Up', 'Handle With Care' and 'Pasting It Together', provide an unparalleled insight into their author's own sense of his literary life and its problems. At the end of the third essay Fitzgerald's conclusion is that he has to change: the balancing-act is no longer possible, the plates have fallen off their sticks, the conjurer has missed the trick. Surrounded as it is with cynicism and self-deprecating irony, Fitzgerald's final statement nonetheless is that he has stopped trying to be both man and writer; instead he has become a writer only. Of course it is tempting to dismiss the distinction itself as too obvious and simplistic to be of value, and the conclusion to be only a momentary outburst occasioned by disillusionment and depression. In my view, however, what Fitzgerald is saying here merits much closer attention. The tension between the two roles of man and writer that he now makes explicit had been present throughout his entire career; more significantly the decision to become a writer only is relevant not only to the present and future, but, to a degree which most commentators have failed to recognize, to the past as well. However much he disapproved of them, Hemingway had sensed conscience, guilt and remorse in the 'Crack-Up' essays. *He was right to do so.*

V

Fitzgerald prefigured what was to come in the 'Crack-Up' essays in 'Sleeping and Waking' published in *Esquire* at the end of 1934. 'Sleeping and Waking' is a straightforwardly autobiographical piece the initial tone of which is relatively light and entertaining. Towards its conclusion, however, where Fitzgerald begins to drama- tize the impact of the insomnia he is experiencing, there is a sudden switch to an altogether more disturbing and ominous note. Just as he will write 'there was not an "I" any more' in the second 'Crack- Up' essay, so now his sense of identity is lost:

> The character who bears my name has become blurred. In the dead of the night I am only one of the dark millions riding forward in black buses toward the unknown.

His past life has become nothing but a landscape of horror and waste:

> – Waste and horror – what I might have been and done that is lost, spent, gone, dissipated, unrecapturable. I could have acted thus, refrained from this, been bold where I was timid, cautious where I was rash.
>
> I need not have hurt her like that.
>
> Nor said this to him.
>
> Nor broken myself trying to break what was unbreakable.[6]

Relief finally comes in the form of sleep, dawn, and the promise of a new day, but in the darker and deeper self-examination of 'Sleeping and Waking' Fitzgerald had in a sense found a new line, a new source of creative material, that he would carry forward into the 'Crack-Up' essays.

What has to be remembered, however, is that the new line has its own history. It is not quite as new as it seems. The 'Crack-Up' essays are certainly new in the sense that they represent a direct and public analysis of Fitzgerald's flawed life and career. But they are in no way his first attempt to analyse and understand the pattern of his life. A major effect of Zelda's breakdown, from the earliest days in France and afterwards, was to compel Fitzgerald to look hard at their life together in order to try to understand what had gone so badly wrong. Inevitably such attempts at objective self-analysis often become merely exercises in self-justification, attributing blame, denying liability, or rebutting charges. In Fitzgerald's many exchanges with Zelda herself and her different psychiatrists and doctors in France and America, this is the pattern of uncomfortable self-analysis that emerges. Obviously none of this material was meant for publication (though from the beginning the professional writer aspect of Fitzgerald made him perfectly aware of its potential fictional use). The various letters, statements and exchanges were intended for Zelda and her doctors alone; but the nature of the insights and self-understanding this material contains is often highly relevant to the issues that the 'Crack-Up' pieces publicly confront.

In the document headed 'Written with Zelda gone to the Clinique', which may or may not have been sent to Zelda when she was in the Prangins clinic in 1930, Fitzgerald provides an early account of what he believes had gone wrong in their relationship. He goes back to the period of the writing of *Gatsby* in 1924, 'with no one believing in me' and 'before the end, your heart betraying me' (a reference to Zelda's relationship with the French aviator), a period of intense unhappiness transformed by the critical success of the novel: 'I was a success – the biggest man in my profession everybody admired me.' Then buoyed by the money that the stage and movie versions of *Gatsby* brought in, he let things slide: 'I thought then that things came easily – I forgot how I'd dragged the great Gatsby out of the pit of my stomach in a time of misery.'

He drank too much in face of Zelda's being 'endlessly sick'. From then on in Paris, at Ellerslie in America, and back in Paris and the Riviera, their lives were increasingly at odds: 'You were going crazy and calling it genius – I was going to ruin and calling it anything that came to hand,' while those on the outside 'guessed at your almost meglomaniacal selfishness and my insane indulgence in drink'. And Fitzgerald ends by referring back, somewhat obscurely, to *The Beautiful and Damned*, apparently crediting himself with having guessed right about their own futures when describing the decline and fall of the lives of Gloria and Anthony Patch in the novel: 'I wish the Beautiful and Damned had been a maturely written book because it was all true. We ruined ourselves – I have never honestly thought that we ruined each other.'

Zelda was not so sure. Her extended account of their life together, produced in the same period, is a quite extraordinary and moving document; written with a kind of hard lucidity, it is full of vividly evoked detail and suffused emotion, and much of it compares favourably with most of Zelda's formal creative writing. What the account brings out is the constant confusion and disarray in the Fitzgeralds' life together, brought on in the main by Scott's compulsive drinking. At Juan-les-Pins in the summer of 1926 'there were too many people and too many things to do: every-day there was something and our house was always full.' There is a disturbing reference to some unspecified but frightful incident in Genoa. Fitzgerald disliked her ballet training because 'you saw it made me happy'. And his drinking was responsible for his failure to get on with his work: '... you know the real reason you couldn't work was because you were always out half the night and you were sick and you drank constantly' (C, 245–50). Towards its close, Zelda's narrative does become less controlled and coherent, but it remains both vivid and disturbing.

In these descriptions of the Fitzgeralds' marriage, occasioned by the doubts and fears and guilts brought on by Zelda's first breakdown, there is no direct statement that it was specifically Fitzgerald's career as a writer that was under threat as a result of their life together. Zelda understandably insists that it was Fitzgerald's drinking that was destroying his literary career, but Fitzgerald himself does not concede this. Yet when he insists that 'we ruined ourselves' rather than each other, what he appears to have in mind in his own case at least, is the collapse of his career as 'the biggest man' in his profession. In the still more bitter exchanges, and the letters of explanation and justification to the different doctors involved in treating Zelda, which were to follow in 1932 and 1933, it was the threat he believed Zelda had come to be to his continued survival as a serious writer that most infuriated Fitzgerald. As a husband and lover (or as a man) he would do everything in his power to help Zelda recover, but as a writer he would guard and defend his own position at whatever cost to hers. This is why Fitzgerald reacted with such violence and bitterness to Zelda's attempt, after she had been compelled to abandon her ballet training, to make a career for herself as a novelist. He had already insisted that their life together had drained him of confidence and self-esteem; his sense of his inferiority, he believed, had made him socially dysfunctional; now even his identity or existence as a writer was under threat.

In March 1932, just after Zelda had completed *Save Me The Waltz*, and despatched it direct to Maxwell Perkins, Fitzgerald wrote several letters to Dr Mildred Squires at the Henry Phipps clinic indicating just how angry, frustrated, and threatened he felt by what Zelda had written. Early in the first letter (14 March 1932) he mentions the novel he himself has been working on for the last four years, except that 'Since the spring of 1930 I have been unable to proceed *because* of the necessity of keeping Zelda in sanitariums.' Zelda had heard the 50,000 words he has managed to write and has used some of this material in her own book: 'one whole section of her novel is an imitation of it.' Worse, the way in which she has written of their life together, and particularly of him as 'a somewhat anemic portrait painter' puts him in an absurd position and her in a ridiculous one: 'this mixture of fact and fiction is simply calculated to ruin us both, or what is left of us, and I can't let it stand.' (At this point the protagonist of Zelda's novel is still called Amory Blaine.) His books had made Zelda a legend, but her 'somewhat thin portrait' of him has the single intention of making him 'a non-entity'. He is not sure how to proceed, but 'this is pretty near the end'. Zelda's mother blames him for her incarceration but he is the one forcing himself to write 'to pay for such luxuries as insanity', while the current 'atmosphere of suspicion' makes it increasingly difficult for him to write the kind of *Saturday Evening Post* stories needed to go on earning the necessary money (LL, 209–10). Throughout this tirade one is struck by the degree to which Fitzgerald's concern appears to be for the potential damage Zelda's novel will do to his professional status as a writer. This is why he 'can't let it stand'.

A week or two later, Fitzgerald wrote again to Dr Squires raising the possibility of a separation from Zelda – this being the condition of his own survival. On the subject of her continued writing he says he is unable to depart from his 'professional attitude'. And the letter quickly returns to the central theme that her writing is being achieved at his expense:

> I have reached the point of submersion if I must continue to rationalize the irrational, stand always between Zelda and the world and see her build this dubitable career of hers with morsels of living matter chipped out of my mind, my belly, my nervous system and my loins. (LL, 210–11)

A third letter to Dr Squires, written after Zelda had agreed to make the changes in *Save Me The Waltz* that Fitzgerald had demanded, reiterates Fitzgerald's complaints about her writing. She has achieved 'something fairly good, at everybodys cost all around, including especially mine', but writing the novel has been bad for her because it has meant the recapitulation of all the experiences that led up to her illness. (Clearly thinking along similar lines, Fitzgerald would later urge Zelda not to read *Tender is the Night*.) As a result of 'her desire for self-expression' (made possible by her 'very expensive' stay in the clinic) they are farther apart than they have ever been since she became sick – but this time Fitzgerald has no sense of guilt whatsoever. His request is that Zelda be not allowed to write any more '*personal stuff* while she is under treatment'. *Save Me The Waltz* can be regarded as safely over and done with; the necessity is that Zelda '*mustn't* start another personal piece of work – she spoke today of a novel "on our personal quarrel & her insanity"'. If she does go ahead he would stop supporting her:

> Should she begin such a work at present I would withdraw my backing from her immediately because the sands are running out again on my powers of endurance – I can't pay for the smithy where she forges a weapon to bring down on mine and Scotty's &, eventually, her own head, for all the pleasant exercise it may give her mental muscles. (LL, 212–14)

The undeniable bitterness and intensity of feeling underlying all these letters are best understood, I believe, in relation to Fitzgerald's feeling that Zelda's desire for 'self-expression' was above all a threat to his own standing as a serious writer. After more years than he liked to remember he had still to finish *Tender is the Night*. He could not allow Zelda to do the job for him.

In fact over the summer of 1932 Fitzgerald became increasingly convinced that he was engaged in an artistic struggle for survival with Zelda. His letters to Dr Adolf Meyer, director of the Phipps clinic, and Dr Thomas Rennie, a psychiatrist involved in Zelda's treatment, make the point quite explicitly. In a long letter to Dr Rennie in October, Fitzgerald argued that Zelda had come to regard herself as the superior artist: 'she has come to regard me as the work horse and herself as the artist – the producer of the finer things such as painting, uncommercial literature, ballet etc ...'. Thus she subconsciously does not want him to complete *Tender is the Night* successfully; rather she wants to be allowed to begin another novel of her own, which will use the material from their personal lives that *Tender is the Night* is bound to include. She has agreed to wait for *Tender is the Night* to be completed before beginning her next novel, but she is in fact afraid that the successful completion of his novel will mean she cannot write hers. Astonishingly, then, Fitzgerald concludes that Zelda feels his writing is menacing hers: '"I'm as good or better than he is"' (LL, 219–21). One can hardly imagine a situation in which writing and creativity could be interpreted more unequivocally as the root cause of tension and psychological breakdown in a relationship. At this point at least Fitzgerald has effectively persuaded himself that the whole problem over Zelda is about nothing other than his status as a writer. Writing in April 1933, to Dr Meyer, whom he suspected of sharing the view that his drinking was at least partially responsible for Zelda's breakdown, Fitzgerald still insists that Zelda's writing, unless strictly limited and controlled, is harmful to both herself and him:

> the question of her work I must perforce regard from a wider attitude. I make these efforts possible and do my own work besides. Possibly she would have been a genius if we had never met. In actuality she is now hurting me and through me hurting all of us.

Zelda, he continues:

> is working under a greenhouse which is my money and my name and my love.... So she is mixed up – she is willing to use the greenhouse to protect her in every way, to nourish every sprout of talent and to exhibit it – and at the same time she feels no responsibility about the greenhouse and feels that she can reach up and knock a piece of glass out of the roof at any moment ... (C, 306–9)

What these letters to Zelda's doctors make clear is that Fitzgerald was coming increasingly to feel that his wife's needs as an ill person – sometimes agreed to by her doctors – were in direct conflict with what he regarded as his legitimate needs as a professional writer. At stake apparently was her survival as a mentally active person or his survival as a successful writer. Only a collision of interests as sharp as this can explain the intensity of the antagonisms between the two that emerge in this period. In the months after the publication of *Save Me The Waltz*, with Zelda's health apparently improving, their relationship seems to become still more distrustful and hostile. In the draft of an unsent letter (perhaps to Dr Rennie) headed 'Sequence of Events', Fitzgerald sketches out his relationship with Zelda in late 1932 and early 1933. He mentions the problems over *Save Me The Waltz*, the professional harm it caused, his own poor health, Zelda's lack of sympathy, her ability to play 'the innocent and injured' with a doctor who doesn't know the situation, and goes on:

> As I got feeling worse Zelda got mentally better, but it seemed to me that as she did she was coming to the conclusion she had it on me, if I broke down it justified her whole life – not a very healthy thought to live with about your own wife.

Working furiously on his novel during the day, he says he has been unable to sleep and needs alcohol to keep going. The result has been a particularly violent confrontation:

> Finally four days ago told her frankly & furiously that had got & was getting a rotten deal trading my health for her sanity and from now on I was going to look out for myself and Scotty exclusively and let her go to Bedlam for all I cared.

'Next day', writes Fitzgerald, 'I phoned you and made an appointment' – and most readers will agree that he is indeed the one who now seems to need medical advice.[7] But how is the depth of such animosity to be explained? My view once again is that what Fitzgerald was finding almost impossible to cope with was the threat that he believed Zelda represented to his own continued existence as a major writer. He was still struggling to finish *Tender is the Night*. With his help *Save Me The Waltz* had been published. But now he was sure Zelda was planning another novel that would again involve the kind of *personal* material – insanity, and

psychiatry – that he was using in *Tender*. It is his fury at this possibility more than anything else that fuels the bitterness and
hostility running through the extraordinary 114-page document in
which a stenographer recorded a confrontation between Fitzgerald
and Zelda, in the presence of Dr Rennie, at La Paix a few months
later, in May 1933.

Dr Rennie must have hoped that a 'frank exchange of views'
between Fitzgerald and Zelda over the causes of the tension in their
relationship would lead to better understanding and eventually to
some degree of resolution. If so, he must have been disappointed.
The points at issue between the two emerge more than sufficiently
clearly, but clarification brings only increased hostility. At the end
of this emotional marathon nothing has been resolved. What does
emerge is that the question of Zelda's writing is far and away the
most contentious and divisive issue. Right at the start Fitzgerald
insists on his status as a professional writer and the struggle
involved in his achieving and maintaining that position:

> The whole equipment of my life is to be a novelist. And that is
> attained with tremendous struggle; that is attained with tremen-
> dous nervous struggle, that is attained with a tremendous
> sacrifice which you make to lead in any profession.

Zelda by contrast is merely an amateur: 'She has certain experiences
to report but she has nothing essentially to say.' Whereas she is 'a
third-rate writer and a third-rate ballet dancer' he is 'a professional
writer with a huge following'. Indeed he is 'the highest paid short
story writer in the world'. Zelda at this point interjects not unrea-
sonably that he seems to be 'making a rather violent attack on a
third-rate talent, then ...' Fitzgerald does allude to the writing of
Save Me The Waltz:

> one of the agreements that we had was about a certain affair,
> which was writing novels, in which I said that you had written a
> novel that I considered plagiaristic to me, unwise in every way,
> and that it should not have been written, because I have a certain
> public weight ...

But the focus of his anger is clearly not that past affair, but rather the new novel he is sure Zelda is writing now. This work will damage him still further because he is certain it involves material about insanity and psychiatry and therefore will be seen, should it appear before or at the same time as his new novel, as being in direct competition with his. It is this scenario – imaginary as it is – that seems to impel Fitzgerald's most extreme demands. He believes that Zelda has already written thirty or forty thousand words of her new work: he gives Dr Rennie a package of material which he says he has not read. It is a story about the mad Nijinski, based on a clipping he says he gave to Zelda. Zelda agrees that her novel does involve psychiatry. 'It is a story of Nijinski going crazy on a cattle boat,' interjects Fitzgerald. 'Dr Rennie,' replies Zelda, 'it is what I want to write. It is a very emotional novel, and that is the whole purpose of the thing, and the reason for it.' Fitzgerald insists that in writing this novel Zelda is breaking the agreement she had made with him and her doctors not to write on anything to do with insanity. They have apparently agreed that this is a bad idea on strictly medical grounds. But quite clearly the real issue for Fitzgerald is Zelda's use of material which he regards as exclusively his. At an earlier stage Zelda's doctors had been inclined to accept her view that she had as much right to write about shared experiences as Fitzgerald had. Fitzgerald himself had never acceded to this, and now states his position in uncompromising terms:

> Everything that we have done is mine – if we make a trip – if I make a trip to Panama and you and I go around – I am the professional novelist and I am supporting you. That is all of my material. None of it is your material.

Dr Rennie now seems to go along with this. He intervenes to say that for Zelda to write about psychiatric topics in a personal way is not a good idea; and he reminds her that she had agreed not to do so for five years at least.

After a series of unpleasant exchanges between the Fitzgeralds about their marriage, Fitzgerald's drinking – Zelda insists that when he is drunk Fitzgerald is constantly arguing that she is ruining his life – trips to New York, and their sex-life, Fitzgerald returns obsessively to the topic of Zelda's writing. Having just conceded that he 'may be hypersensitive to what I consider logical, from the traditions of my profession', he nonetheless demands that Zelda stop writing:

> I want you to stop writing fiction.... Whether you write or not does not seem to be of any great importance.
> Zelda: I know. Nothing I do seems to be of any great importance.
> Fitzgerald: Why don't you drop it then?
> Zelda: Because I don't want to live with you, because I want to live someplace that I can be my own self.

Zelda has already said that she would rather live in an insane asylum than 'submit to Scott's neurasthenic condition and be subjected to these tortures all the time'. So inevitably the question of divorce comes up and Zelda is inclined to say yes to the idea 'because there is nothing except ill will on your part and suspicion'. Equally Fitzgerald has already admitted to his drinking, neurasthenia, and bullying, but for him none of this is the real issue. He refuses to give up drinking, for example, because to do so would be taken to mean that he was conceding that his drinking has been the cause of Zelda's problems. When Zelda presses him to go on talking about *his* weaknesses, he immediately returns to the old charge: 'To express yourself you assume the right to ruin me, is that right?'

It is at this point that Zelda makes perhaps her shrewdest contribution to the whole encounter:

> What is the matter with Scott is that he has not written that book and if he will ever get it written, why, he won't feel so miserable and suspicious and mean towards everybody else.

Later Zelda explains that her desire to write is all about self-respect and self-esteem: 'I want to write and I am going to write.' But she does not want to write 'at Scott's expense'. So for the moment she will agree

> not to do anything that he does not want, a complete negation of self until that book is out of the way, because the thing is driving me crazy the way it is, and I cannot do that.

But after that she must be allowed to do what she wants to do. Only by writing can she place herself 'on a more equal footing than we are now'; she 'simply cannot live in a world that is completely dependent on Scott when he does not care anything about me and reproaches me all the time ...' But to hear Zelda talk about independence and equality seems only to infuriate Fitzgerald still further; he insists that such ideas are proof of 'the wholly Amazonian and the Lesbian personality'. He remains adamant that her writing has to stop. She may say she is willing to put off writing another book but he does not believe her – because she has said that before without meaning it. What she is saying now means only that he 'will have to write this whole book in the next three months with the sense that you wait hating me, waiting for me to get away'. 'I want my own way,' insists Fitzgerald. 'And I want the right of my own way,' retorts Zelda. But that is exactly what Fitzgerald cannot allow:

> And you cannot have it without breaking me so you have to give it up. It all comes to the same thing: I have to sacrifice myself for you, and you have got to sacrifice yourself for me, and no more writing of fiction.

Even if instead of a novel, Zelda chooses to write a play, it cannot be about psychiatry, it cannot be set in Switzerland, nor on the Riviera, and whatever the idea is it will have to be submitted to Fitzgerald for his approval. The interview ends with Zelda saying that when Fitzgerald finishes his book, they had better divorce because she 'cannot live on those terms' and 'cannot accept them'.

Scott Fitzgerald's writing of whatever kind is always a pleasure to read. The same cannot be said of this disturbingly unpleasant document. There is a rawness of emotion and a level of antagonism present here that seem to drive Fitzgerald in particular to more and more extreme positions. But if humanly damaging, this confrontation illuminates to an unparalleled degree the precise nature of the dilemma Fitzgerald was facing at this critical point in his literary career. It is Dr Rennie, no doubt unwittingly, who is responsible for pinpointing the central issue. Late in the interview, he asks Zelda the following question: 'Mrs Fitzgerald, what is the paramount thing in your life, to create, or married life? I really think you will have to decide this.'

The next entry appears as a parenthesis: '(A lapse of about a minute when no one spoke.)' No wonder. Dr Rennie is asking Zelda to choose between her putative life as a writer and her life as a married woman. Fitzgerald could not have been so obtuse as not to see how the same question might be asked of him. When he breaks the silence it is to say 'That is the question'. Then he goes on, somewhat obscurely, 'You see, there is an awful lot of water that has run under the bridge on your side and my side.' Does he mean that this essential choice between art and life has long been an underlying issue between them? Zelda responds by insisting on her personal need to write, but Rennie returns to the idea that for her there is a choice to be made between her life as a writer and her life as a married woman:

> Would life for you as a creative artist compensate you for your life without Mr Fitzgerald, if you were given the opportunity to really go on for the next twenty years and be an outstanding woman writer of this country, doing it alone? Would that mean enough when you were sixty?

Again there is a lapse of about a minute when no one speaks. Finally Zelda replies: 'Well, Dr Rennie, I think perhaps that is a sort of a silly question.' What is silly is Rennie's patriarchal assumption that it is only a woman writer who could be asked to confront such a choice between art and life – with the expectation that she will inevitably choose to repudiate art. Fitzgerald knew a great deal better. Ever since his marriage to Zelda he had struggled to find a satisfactory way of combining his life as a writer with his life as Zelda's husband. His long-drawn-out failure to complete *Tender is the Night* had been teaching him just how difficult that task was. He was even confronting the possibility that it was an impossible one. Now here was his wife threatening his very existence as a serious writer. She was planning another novel – which would carry the Fitzgerald name – on the same psychiatric theme as his own unfinished novel, and she was writing it using *his* material. It could only be a disaster if such a novel appeared around the same time as his. In these terms one can at least begin to understand why Fitzgerald felt such outrage and anger. Had Dr Rennie had the awareness to put his original question to Fitzgerald he might well have replied that yes, life without Mrs Fitzgerald would indeed be compensated for by confirmation of his position as an outstanding writer of his country. His actual response to Zelda's comment on the silliness of the Rennie question was: 'Suppose I said, "I am going to sacrifice you, that is what I am going to do at any cost, I have got to develop my personality?"' (Like 'self-expression', 'develop my personality' is code for pursuing one's art.) Zelda's response is, 'That is what you have said all along, and that is what you have done.'[8] But here at least she is being less than fair. Fitzgerald has not in fact sacrificed her, and even now he is only supposing he might. He has accepted his responsibilities – particularly since Zelda has been ill – and has struggled to sustain them. He is furious now because Zelda in his view is both ignoring what he has done, and undermining his status as a professional writer. In April 1936, in the final 'Crack-Up' essay, he will announce to the world his intention to transform himself into a different kind of person:

> So, since I could no longer fulfill the obligations that life had set for me or that I had set for myself, why not slay the empty shell who had been posturing at it for four years? I must continue to be a writer because that was my only way of life, but I would cease any attempts to be a person – to be kind, just or generous.

And his conclusion is that the transformation has been effected:

> I have now at last become a writer only. The man I had persistently tried to be became such a burden that I have "cut him loose" with as little compunction as a Negro lady cuts loose a rival on Saturday night.[9]

In fact it was in the past, not in the future, that Fitzgerald came closest to becoming the 'writer only' figure he adumbrates here. It is difficult to read the record of the confrontation between him and Zelda on that day in May 1933 without concluding that he had indeed ceased to be kind, just or generous. But just as it is difficult to see that Fitzgerald actually became a wholly different kind of man or a wholly new kind of writer after April 1936, so it is impossible to regard his treatment of Zelda in May 1933 as permanently changing his concern for her well-being.

That in fact the opinions and attitudes articulated by Fitzgerald in May 1933, in the confrontation with Zelda, were extreme and exaggerated is confirmed by subsequent events. The anger and violence in his voice, his determination to make Zelda submit to his will ('It has got to be an unconditional surrender on her part') reflect above all the threat he thought he perceived in her writing to his own still incomplete *Tender is the Night*. Zelda's perception that it was the unfinished state of his own novel that was responsible for much of Fitzgerald's anger proved in fact to be quite accurate. Once *Tender is the Night* was completed and published Fitzgerald's attitude towards her writing changed completely; he was soon back at Maxwell Perkins trying to persuade him to publish more of her stories. Indeed as early as March 1934, Fitzgerald had decided there was no longer a problem over Zelda's writing. At this time Zelda had moved from Baltimore to a new clinic – Craig House in Beacon, New York state – and Fitzgerald wrote a series of letters to Dr Jonathan Slocum, her physician, attempting to describe her condition. In a letter dated 22 March 1934, he takes up the topic of her writing:

> As to her writing: there is no longer any competitive element involved. [Dr Slocum had asked for and received a copy of the transcript of the confrontation of May 1933. He may well be the person who wrote on the cover sheet of the Princeton library's copy of the report: 'This is the most outrageous thing I have ever *read*. Dr Rennie is worse than Mr Fitzgerald!'] There was a time when she was romping in on what I considered "my" material, disguising her characters under such subtle names as F. Scott Fitzpatrick, when I thought she was tearing at the very roots of my profession, in other words, of our existence. She finally got the idea and desisted, but rather bitterly. At any rate all that element of competition in material which I had to turn into money, or if possible, into art, and which she was competent to turn only into essentially inefficient effort, we can now assume to be in the past.[10]

The episode itself, as Fitzgerald is arguing here, may well have been relatively shortlived, but its significance is enduring. Seen in relation to all the other factors contributing to the crisis in his career occurring in the 1934–37 period, the issue of Zelda's writing is a major factor driving Fitzgerald towards understanding that all the burdens of his life as a man – economic, marital, familial, emotional – were making it increasingly difficult for him to survive as a writer. He had managed to finish *Tender is the Night* – but only just – and the struggle to continue as a writer was an increasingly exhausting one. The truth was he had arrived at the position – latent in his literary career ever since his marriage to Zelda – when the conflict between the two roles he had always tried to play was finally paralysing and destroying his creativity itself. In such circumstances, it is easy to understand why his attitude towards the position of the artist should move towards the ideas of objectivity, detachment and non-involvement in life, which are finally articulated in the 'Crack-Up' articles. If only he could attain something of the impersonal, onlooker status of such masters as James and Joyce, then his problem would be solved. If his commitment to all the multifarious demands of life could be replaced by a single-minded devotion to art, then the draining away of his remaining creative resources could be staunched.

In a spring 1933, note to Mrs Margaret Turnbull, his neighbour at La Paix, clarifying his views on the greatness of writers which they had discussed the previous evening, Fitzgerald includes a sentence which hints at the harsh professionalism he was coming to see the artist as requiring: 'To me the conditions of an artistically creative life are so arduous that I can only compare to them the duties of a soldier in war-time' (L, 455). Even more revealing is a letter to the same recipient Fitzgerald wrote only a few months before beginning the 'Crack-Up' essays. Mrs Turnbull had written to him of 'life being made up of hope, and a little fulfillment'. Fitzgerald responds in violent disagreement:

> The hell it is – too much fulfillment from a man's point of view, if he has been one of those who wanted to identify himself with it utterly. It's so fast, so sweeping along, that he walks stumbling and crying out, wondering sometimes where he is, or where the others are, or if they existed, or whether he's hurt anybody, but not much time to wonder, only sweeping along again ... (L, 459)

This is a wonderful and frightening picture of Fitzgerald himself in the darkest period of his literary life. He is the man who has experienced too much fulfilment, who has identified himself utterly with life, and found himself irresistibly swept along by it. Alone in expensive or shabby hotels in North Carolina, no wonder he questions his own and others' existence, his capacity for harming others – Zelda, Scottie, Beatrice Dance (with whom he had been having an affair) – in the few moments he has when not wrestling over yet another recalcitrant story or article. It is his life that has made the palace of art so difficult to reach. In the spring of 1936, after the 'Crack-Up' pieces had been written, Fitzgerald wrote again to Mrs Turnbull clarifying a previous conversation. The theme this time is the difference between those who are 'tender-minded' and those who are 'tough-minded'. The terms have a particular relevance to artists:

> I think perhaps the creative worker has the privilege of jumping from one attitude to the other, or of balancing on the line. I am continually surprised both by my softness and by my hardiness.
> (L, 461)

The argument of *The Crack-Up* was that Fitzgerald had been insufficiently 'tough-minded', but that henceforward he would change. And in some respects perhaps he did.

I have already argued that in the final version of *Tender is the Night* Fitzgerald had already addressed the artist-man dilemma in the character of Dick Diver. Certainly there is good reason to see Diver as a portrait of the scientist-doctor who is destroyed by becoming a husband-lover. And the tragedy is that what is morally admirable is professionally suspect. This is the sense in which, unrecognized by John Dos Passos, Fitzgerald had indeed written a novel about 'going to pieces'. But after *The Crack-Up* Fitzgerald is more specific about the kind of tough-mindedness that is demanded of the professional writer – and the moral issues that might be involved. In the introduction to Andrew Turnbull's 1965 edition of Fitzgerald's letters to his daughter, Scottie herself tried to account for her father's often difficult behaviour by seeing it as a necessary consequence of being a writer. 'Why are writers insufferable people?' she asks, and the first and most important answer she offers is that writers are inclined to treat real people with the same kind of freedom as the characters they invent:

The rest of us accept our fellow beings at face value, and swallow what we can't accept. Writers can't: they have to prod, poke, question, test, doubt, and challenge, which requires a constant flow of fresh victims and fresh experience.[11]

For writers, that is, all of life and experience is no more than fresh material for them to use – or perhaps abuse. In 'Author's House' (1936), another *Esquire* piece involving a form of personal allegory, Fitzgerald appears to concede the point. The author in the piece has perpetrated a somewhat unpleasant joke at the expense of a very naive reader of one of his stories, which he now regrets:

> But it's too late ... You can pay a little money but what can you do for meddling with a human heart? A writer's temperament is continually making him do things he can never repair.[12]

In August 1935, writing to James Boyd about his recent love affair with Beatrice Dance, Fitzgerald makes what is in essence the same point in his own voice:

> Still it's done now and tied up in cellophane and – and maybe someday I'll get a chapter out of it. God, what a hell of a profession to be a writer. One is one simply because one can't help it. (L, 548)

Of course there had been occasions in the past when Fitzgerald's friends and acquaintances had been less than happy about his readiness to make use of them in his fiction. One recalls again, for example, Sara Murphy's complaint in 1926 that Fitzgerald's constant scrutiny of Gerald and her in relation to the novel he was writing was destroying their friendship: '– But you can't expect anyone to like or stand a *Continual* feeling of analysis + sub-analysis, + criticism – on the whole unfriendly – Such as we have felt for quite awhile ...' (C, 196). And even in the darkest and tensest days of 1933, when his marriage to Zelda seemed to be on the point of disintegration over the issue of her continued writing, Fitzgerald seems in the case-history headed 'Self-Expression' (his code again for Zelda's writing) to have been sketching out a fictional work based on the situation.[13] What the 'Crack-Up' period represents, then, is no more than an explicit recognition of facts that Fitzgerald had always understood: being 'kind, just and generous' had never been a necessary part of being a writer. But, as the tone of the ending of the final 'Crack-Up' essay makes abundantly clear, he remained uneasy over the moral posture of the disengaged, wholly professional, objective writer. But if there was a moral problem here for Fitzgerald the man, there was also an aesthetic one for Fitzgerald the writer.

What that problem was, Fitzgerald had allegorized several years before in a story called 'Outside the Cabinet-Maker's' written and published in 1928. The story is about a man and his six-year-old daughter (Fitzgerald and Scottie) sitting in a car outside a cabinet-maker's shop in which the man's wife is ordering a doll's house for their daughter. While they wait, the man creates a fairy story, based around the cabinet-maker's shop, complete with a King, Queen, Prince, Princess, Witch and Ogre. The little girl is enchanted by the story – but the man is aware that he can no longer share that enchantment:

> The man was old enough to know that he would look back to that time – the tranquil street and the pleasant weather and the mystery playing before the child's eyes, mystery which he had created, but whose luster and texture he could never see or touch any more himself.... For a moment he closed his eyes and tried to see with her but he couldn't see – those ragged blinds were drawn against him forever.[14]

The artist-writer, that is, is outside the experience, the observer only. In the 'Crack-Up' articles, Fitzgerald writes bitterly of his own over-involvement with life and experience, of his inability to distance himself from the objects of his horror or compassion. Hence his decision to make a clean break, to cease to be the man he had tried to be, and become instead a 'writer only'. But the kind of writer Fitzgerald had always been was one who took his creative start from being inside, not outside, the cabinet-maker's. As he had put it in the passage from 'One Hundred False Starts' (1933), quoted much earlier, 'Whether it's something that happened twenty years ago or only yesterday, I must start out with an emotion – one that's close to me and that I can understand.'[15] Fitzgerald's art, that is, crucially arose out of involvement with life, not detachment from it. In the same article, Fitzgerald insisted on his professionalism:

> I am thirty-six years old. For eighteen years, save for a short space during the war, writing has been my chief interest in life, and I am in every sense a professional.[16]

In *The Crack-Up* Fitzgerald is finally reasserting and redefining his professionalism. Writing remains his chief interest, but the new 'writer only' professionalism requires an abandonment of that involvement with life which apparently had come close to destroying him. What *The Crack-Up* does not indicate is the source of the new kind of art that the new professionalism clearly demands. Fitzgerald's dark night of the soul – the years in his literary life between 1934 and early 1937 – while hardly providing their solution, at least had the benefit of clarifying the problems he was facing as both man and writer.

7
Leaving *The Last Tycoon*

Fitzgerald approached his third and final period as a Hollywood screenwriter in a thoroughly professional manner. He believed he could make a success of the job and was determined to do so. Older and wiser than in the past, he was ready and willing to commit himself unequivocally to whatever the work involved. There would be no question of his posing as the superior artist victimized by the crass commercialism of the Hollywood movie machine. In mid-1939, replying to a query from a young would-be writer about possible Hollywood opportunities, he made the point more or less directly:

> there was a period when the eastern writer was suspect – he was 'high hat,' he did not know the medium, and wouldn't take the trouble to learn it – ... but I believe that time is gone. (L, 606)

That time had certainly gone for Fitzgerald himself; he had arrived in Hollywood fully prepared to take whatever trouble was required to work successfully in the new medium.

Despite this professional commitment, however, in the three and a half years between his arrival in California in July 1937, and his death in Los Angeles in December 1940, Fitzgerald's opinions on Hollywood would remain decidedly ambivalent. As a writer he found it difficult to adjust to a situation where a team of writers was expected to collaborate on the same script; and he found it equally difficult to accept that a producer-director could arbitrarily intervene at any time and rewrite dialogue or scenes. More generally he recognized that what made for success in Hollywood had more to do with good luck, personality, and friends and contacts than with anything concerning aesthetic values or purely artistic achievement. He knew too that success in the movie industry could slip away almost as quickly as it might arrive. But despite all this, there can be no doubt that at least from mid-1937 to the end of 1938, Fitzgerald tried his hardest to become the kind of screenwriter the film industry would admire and reward.

The contract that Fitzgerald signed with MGM in 1937 made specific provision for him to work on his own writing in between assignments from the studio. In July, Fitzgerald wrote to Edwin Knopf, the producer who had hired him, setting out in detail the work he was currently engaged on, pointing to six stories and two articles ('Early Success' and 'My Lost City') sold but still unpublished, as well as a nearly finished play ('Institutional Humanitarianism', never published nor produced). His idea may well have been to impress on Knopf that despite his recent difficulties he was in no sense finished as a writer. As it turned out, while 1937 did see the publication of six stories, two articles and a poem, his work for the studio was so intense that throughout the second half of 1937 and in 1938 he had no free time to continue with new work of his own. As a result, 'Financing Finnegan' in *Esquire* was the only story to appear in 1938. The publishing record, that is, confirms the fact that in the first year and a half of his final visit to Hollywood, all of Fitzgerald's creative energies were devoted to his attempt to establish himself as a reliable and successful screenwriter.

For a variety of reasons, however, including bad luck, occasional drinking binges, and difficulty in adjusting to the kind of collaborative writing that was often required, Fitzgerald in the end, despite his best efforts, failed to break through as a big-time Hollywood film writer. Initially all went pretty well. He worked on *Three Comrades*, a Joseph Mankiewicz film, based on a novel by Erich Maria Remarque. Fitzgerald's script seemed to gain the director's approval but nonetheless another writer was brought in – inevitably Fitzgerald fell out with him – and at a late stage Mankiewicz himself made many changes in Fitzgerald's script. Deeply disappointed, he predicted that the film, in its altered state, would be a flop. In fact *Three Comrades* proved to be both a commercial and a critical success, gaining for Fitzgerald the only screen credit – the absolute prerequisite for success in Hollywood – of his film-writing career. As a consequence of the success of *Three Comrades*, MGM raised Fitzgerald's salary to $1250 per week for the year 1938. In the end MGM would pay Fitzgerald no less than $85,000, and it has to be said that rather than exploiting or damaging Fitzgerald's creativity, Hollywood was his saviour at least in economic terms. He had arrived in Los Angeles with debts well in excess of $20,000 – to Ober, Perkins, Scribners, hospitals, doctors, etc. – and it is impossible to believe that with his continuing obligations to Zelda and Scottie he could ever in such circumstances have returned to the writing of what he regarded as serious literature. The Hollywood money, on the other hand, meticulously divided between his various creditors, in the end made that return possible – even if, as we shall see, in a somewhat paradoxical manner.

After *Three Comrades* Fitzgerald worked hard over a four-month period on the script of 'Infidelity', a vehicle for the star Joan Crawford. The film, however, eventually ran into what proved to be insurmountable censorship problems and was never made. After a brief spell on an unfinished 'Marie Antoinette' project, he was assigned to a film called *The Women*, based on a successful play by Claire Booth Luce; Fitzgerald was eventually teamed with his old friend Donald Ogden Stewart but in the end both men were replaced by Anita Loos and Jane Murfin. Fitzgerald's final significant assignment from MGM was to write a screenplay for *Madame Curie*, in which Greta Garbo was expected to star. He worked on the script from November 1938 to January 1939, at which point plans to produce the film were shelved. In the final three weeks of his MGM contract in that January, Fitzgerald's task was to revise and polish some scenes in *Gone With The Wind*.

By the end of January 1939, when MGM decided not to renew his contract, Fitzgerald recognized that his dream of becoming a big man in Hollywood was over. Working like a true professional, he had spared no effort, but success had again eluded him. In the winter of 1939 he wrote to Scottie in semi-jocular tones admitting that this was so:

I'm convinced that maybe they're not going to make me Czar of the Industry right away, as I thought 10 months ago. It's all right, baby – life has humbled me – Czar or not, we'll survive. I am even willing to compromise for Assistant Czar! (L, 63)

His admission of defeat to Gerald Murphy was more direct: 'My great dreams about this place are shattered' (L, 448), he wrote in the spring of 1940. For the remaining two years of his life Fitzgerald worked as a freelance Hollywood writer, picking up whatever employment he could get at whatever salary he could command. Early in 1939 he did not help his position by throwing away an excellent script opportunity in the most egregious of manners. With the young writer Budd Schulberg he was hired by the director Walter Wanger to produce a screenplay for *Winter Carnival*, a film based on the annual student celebration at Dartmouth College in New Hampshire. On the flight east, Fitzgerald embarked on a drinking binge which lasted for almost two weeks and got him fired from the project. Despite the notoriety of this episode (Schulberg eventually wrote about it in his 1950 novel *The Disenchanted*) Fitzgerald remained sober for most of the final Hollywood years; Sheilah Graham, who became his lover in this period, insists that he was drinking only in nine months out of the three and a half years during which they were together. (Less forgivably, his drinking bouts more than once coincided with trips east to see Zelda and take her away on brief holidays: on such occasions it was Zelda who ended up having to protect and look after Fitzgerald.)

On a freelance basis Fitzgerald worked for brief periods on films such as 'Air Raid' (never made) and Samuel Goldwyn's *Raffles*. And in 1940 he was hired by Twentieth Century Fox to prepare a screenplay from Emlyn Williams's play *The Light of Heart*. From time to time he came up with proposals for films, sometimes based on existing stories of his own – but none of these were picked up by producers. In the summer of 1940, however, he was commissioned by an independent producer, at $500 a week, to write a film script based on his own 1931 story 'Babylon Revisited'. Once again the film was not made – though a new version, not using Fitzgerald's script, was finally produced in 1954.

In summary, Fitzgerald's third and final Hollywood visit was a mixture of success and failure. He had returned there in 1937 for one reason only – to make enough money to ensure his economic survival. In this at least he more or less succeeded. But his goal of establishing himself as a successful studio screenplay writer was not achieved. He made every effort to adjust to the circumstances of Hollywood writing, but in the end probably remained too much the individual artist to fit in. Frances Kroll's memoir has provided us with an unforgettable image of Fitzgerald's failure to belong in the world of Hollywood. She describes walking along Sunset Boulevard side by side with Fitzgerald in late 1940:

> He was wearing a dark topcoat and a grey homburg hat. As we kept pace, I looked over at him and was chilled by his image, like a shadowy figure in an old photograph. His outfit and pallor were alien to the style and warmth of Southern California – as if he were not at home here, had just stopped off and was dressed to leave on the next train.[1]

II

MGM's decision not to renew Fitzgerald's contract for a second year, at the beginning of 1939, gave him the time and opportunity to return to his literary career. Not of course that his work on films had ever completely blanked out his existence as a literary figure. In early March 1938, he had written to Maxwell Perkins about his 'next venture':

> Meanwhile, I am filling a notebook with stuff that will be of more immediate interest to you, but please don't mention me ever as having any plans. "Tender is the Night" hung over too long, and my next venture will be presented to you without preparation or fanfare. (FP, 242)

And a few months later, in October, Beatrice Dance was told that a new Gatsby-like novel was at least taking shape in his mind:

> I have a grand novel up my sleeve and I'd love to go to France and write it this summer. It would be short like "Gatsby" but the same in that it will have the transcendental approach, an attempt to show a man's life through some passionately regarded segment of it. (C, 517)

Perkins, encouraged perhaps by Fitzgerald's reference to a future novel, mentioned in his reply a 'secret hope' of his own of one day publishing an omnibus volume of Fitzgerald's three novels *This Side of Paradise, The Great Gatsby*, and *Tender is the Night*, while at the same time making it clear that this would only be possible 'after a big success with a new novel' (FP, 243). Fitzgerald, increasingly obsessed with the idea that he was a forgotten man, and having just learned from Scribners that *This Side of Paradise* was now out of print, inevitably jumped at Perkins's long-term proposal:

> I note in your letter a suggestion of publishing an omnibus book with "Paradise," "Gatsby" and "Tender." How remote is that idea, and why must we forget it? If I am to be out here for two years longer, as seems probable, it certainly isn't advisable to let my name slip so out of sight as it did between "Gatsby" and "Tender", especially as I now will not be writing even the Saturday Evening Post stories.

What he himself has in mind, he tells Perkins, is to return 'to the idea of expanding the stories about Phillipe, the Dark Ages knight ...' (FP, 245). Perkins responds with enthusiasm to this proposal:

> You know I wish you would get back to the Phillippe. – When you were working on that you were worn out, and I thought could not do it justice. – But if you could get at it now it would be different, and you could make a fine historical novel of that time, and the basic idea was excellent and would be appreciated and understood now better than when you were writing it. (FP, 246)

This last idea is one that Perkins appears particularly attached to: in December, once again urging Fitzgerald to solve the problem of keeping his name before the public by publishing the Phillippe material as a book, he argued that 'that historical sort of book is fitted better to these days than to those in which you wrote it' (FP, 252). Presumably what Perkins has in mind is the Spanish Civil War and Europe's reversion into a world of war and violence. If so, he had the wrong Scribners author in his mind: it was Hemingway's fiction, not Fitzgerald's, which would gain new relevance and meaning from Europe's descent into the conflict of the Second World War.

A book based on the Phillippe material was not Fitzgerald's only suggestion to Perkins. Other 1938 proposals included the idea of a new version of *Tender is the Night*, with its chronology rearranged, and a big new collection of stories that would include the Phillippe novella plus the Basil and Josephine material and some Jazz Age stories. Yet another scheme was a reissue of *This Side of Paradise* – now that it was out of print at Scribners – in a cheap American Mercury edition. In a January 1939 letter to Perkins, Fitzgerald argues that anything is better than the book being 'not in print at all' (FP, 253). What lies behind all these proposals is Fitzgerald's fear that he is disappearing from the contemporary literary scene. He is encouraged by learning from the borrowings in the Los Angeles public libraries that he still has readers, but he is desperate to make the wider reading-public recognize that he is still around and still writing. In the January letter to Perkins in which he urges the desirability of keeping *This Side of Paradise* in print in any form, he also says that he has decided against the Phillippe idea because it would require too much work: 'I would much rather do a modern novel' (FP, 254). The 'modern novel' he has in mind clearly has to be linked to the notebook he had been filling with material ever since his arrival in Hollywood, and to the grand novel he told Beatrice Dance he had 'up his sleeve'. But actual work on what would become *The Last Tycoon* was to be deferred for some months longer.

In February 1939, Fitzgerald told Perkins how wonderful it was 'to be writing again instead of patching' (FP, 255). What he was writing, however, brought him little more in the way of success than his film work had done. Deprived of his regular MGM salary, Fitzgerald tried initially to break back into the lucrative short fiction market represented by *Saturday Evening Post* and *Collier's* magazine. *Collier's* finally accepted the much-revised Civil War story originally called 'Thumbs Up' but published (in June 1940) as 'The End of Hate'. But neither the *Post* nor *Collier's* accepted anything else and Fitzgerald was forced to admit that he could no longer meet the demands of the mass-circulation market. In June 1940, he conceded to Scottie that whether he would 'ever be able to recover the art of the popular short story is doubtful' (L, 97). About the same time he told Zelda that changes in editorial policy at the *Post* had made it impossible for him to write for it; and that anyway he had never been able to write purely formulaic fiction: 'As soon as I feel I am writing to a cheap specification my pen freezes and my talent vanishes over the hill ...' (L, 136). Earlier, in the summer of 1939, Fitzgerald told Kenneth Littauer, editor of *Collier's*, that he could not go on writing stories about such subjects as young love: 'I would either be a miracle man or a hack if I could go on turning out an identical product for three decades' (L, 609). His difficulty was in finding a new topic that would appeal as widely as the old love-theme had done.

Since almost the beginning of Fitzgerald's career, Harold Ober had been the loyal agent through whom he had established his commanding position in the short fiction market. Even when the going began to get tougher, and Fitzgerald was finding it more diffi-cult to go on producing marketable stories, no one remained more positive and supportive than Ober. Having become a close friend, a virtual banker, and substitute father for Fitzgerald's daughter, he also became a critical booster of his client's declining morale. As late as the first half of 1937, Ober was still working hard to sell Fitzgerald's stories, offering him advice and constant reassurance. Praising the revised version of a football story called 'Athletic Interview' (subsequently rejected by *Collier's*, the *Saturday Evening Post, American Magazine, Cosmopolitan*, and *Red Book*, and never published), he wrote, 'I am sure you are back in your stride' (FO, 311). However, in the middle of 1939, Ober suddenly departed from what had become standard practice, and refused to advance Fitzgerald cash for a still unplaced story. A day or two earlier he had actually written a letter to Fitzgerald explaining that he could not go on with the established arrangement because of financial prob-lems of his own – but had not sent it. Thus Fitzgerald was surprised and angered by the sudden change of policy. He immediately wired Perkins: 'Ober has decided not to back me though I paid back every penny and eight thousand commission' (FO, 397). Two weeks later he was still communicating his surprise and dismay to Ober: on 12 July 1939 he wired, 'Still flabbergasted at your abrupt change in policy after 20 years' (FO, 400). A long letter followed a week later in which Fitzgerald fondly thanked Ober for all his past support and help and in particular for his 'care and cherishing of Scottie during the intervals between school and camp in those awful sick years of

'35 and '36'. He says he is writing with 'no touch of unpleasantness' but nevertheless goes on to imply that Ober's 'sudden change of policy' had cost him money because he had turned down several picture offers while unwell, on the assumption that an advance from Ober would tide him over until he was feeling better. Now without a 'partner' able or willing to help him, Fitzgerald feels 'he must find his own way out – and quickly' (FO, 402–3). On the same day, 19 July 1939, Fitzgerald also wrote to Maxwell Perkins announcing that he had broken with Ober. This letter too is long and measured; Fitzgerald insists he will be 'forever grateful' to Harold 'for his part of the help in backing me through that long illness' but he believes 'his attitude has changed' to 'a sort of general disapproval and a vague sense that I am through'. Interestingly, Fitzgerald goes on to say that Ober has developed 'a new fashion of discussing my stories as if he was a rather dissatisfied and cranky editor ...' which might suggest that even though he never complained at the time Fitzgerald had actually resented Ober's attempts to suggest improvements in the stories he had been trying to place in the previous few years. Fitzgerald insists to Perkins that he has 'no moral compunction' over his decision to leave Ober and deal personally with editors – 'This is a matter of survival' – but he does beg his editor not to discuss the situation with Ober:

> Above all things I wish you wouldn't discuss this with him. I have not, nor ever will say, nor *could* say anything against him either personally or professionally, but even the fact that I have discussed the matter with you might upset him ... (C, 536–7)

Perkins did not respond immediately to Fitzgerald's letter, but he was clearly deeply upset by this turn of events. After further letters from Fitzgerald mentioning the break-up, Perkins finally wrote on 26 July 1939, urging Fitzgerald to stay with Ober whom he described as 'one of the very best and most loyal friends you have in the world'. 'I hope to God you will stand by him,' he added (FP, 257). Fitzgerald, however, had no intention of changing his mind. He had already written to Kenneth Littauer at *Collier's* both explaining and justifying the new situation. On 2 August he wrote another long letter to Ober basically arguing that his agent had let him down badly: 'I have been and still am somewhat shocked by your sudden and most determined reversal of form.' He insists he has been working hard – even when ill; Ober has been slower than in the past in dealing with the material sent to him; the change of policy over advances had come without warning; he has been 'all too hauntingly aware during these months of what [Ober] did from 1934 to 1937 to keep my head above water' – 'But you have made me sting none the less.' And the letter concludes with Fitzgerald insisting he hasn't had a drink for two months – 'but if I was full of champagne I couldn't be more confused about you than I am now' (FO, 407–8). That last phrase may just have been meant to indicate that the break between them was not final – but if so it did not produce a result. Next day Fitzgerald replied to Perkins's letter, which had urged him to remain with Ober, in terms which made any reconciliation sound highly unlikely: Ober's function, writes Fitzgerald, 'is to encourage me rather than play the disapproving schoolmaster' (FO, 409). After the sundering of the relationship with Ober, Fitzgerald acted as his own literary agent. Nonetheless the Obers continued from time to time to provide a home for Scottie; and after her father's death, Ober, along with Maxwell Perkins, saw to it that she was able to complete her studies at Vassar College.

III

By the time of the break with Harold Ober, Fitzgerald had decided that his 'next venture' as he described it to Perkins – meaning his next venture in the writing of serious literature – would indeed be a modern novel set in Hollywood. At the end of May 1939, he had written to Ober explaining exactly how he was planning to proceed:

> I *have* blocked out my novel completely with a rough sketch of every episode and event and character so that under proper circumstances I could begin writing it tomorrow. It is a short novel about fifty thousand words long and should take me three to four months. (FO, 389)

From the first though Fitzgerald appears almost paranoid in his insistence on the need to keep the Hollywood subject-matter secret. Frances Kroll recalls that when he interviewed her for the job as his secretary he was concerned over possible contacts she might have with the film studios: 'In a confidential voice, he told me that he was planning to start a new novel about the motion picture industry and wanted no word of it to leak out.'[2] Perhaps what was in question was his memory of the trouble he had had in publishing 'Crazy Sunday' because of the covert hostility towards the story of the Hollywood establishment. The concern had originally appeared a little earlier in May when Fitzgerald had written to Perkins expressing alarm at a letter he had received from Charles Scribner which had assumed his new novel was about Hollywood: 'It is distinctly *not* about Hollywood', he told Perkins, before suggesting it was 'progressing nicely'. He went on to say he was blocking out the novel 'so that, unlike "Tender", I may be able to put it aside for a month and pick it up again at the exact spot factually and emotionally where I left off' (FP, 256). Perkins replied by return, assuring Fitzgerald that there was no danger that news about a Hollywood novel would get out, and saying that he was 'mighty glad' Fitzgerald had been able to get going on a novel (FP, 257). In reality the major issue for Fitzgerald was not whether news of his next novel would leak out, but whether he could create a financial situation which would allow him time to write it: these would be the 'proper circumstances' he had mentioned in his letter to Ober. No longer on a salary from a studio, he knew perfectly well he would soon once again find himself facing financial problems. He was right. His actual earnings for 1939 would amount to $21,466.67 from film work and stories, but in September he nonetheless found it necessary to borrow $360 from Gerald Murphy to help pay Scottie's tuition fees for her second year at Vassar.

'Blocking out' what would be *The Last Tycoon* in the manner he described to both Ober and Perkins makes it clear that Fitzgerald's plan was to write the novel in between freelance assignments in film work. When such assignments proved to be elusive in the second half of 1939, he decided that the way forward was to set up a deal on the serial rights of the novel which would provide him with enough advanced money to support him while he wrote it. He had already tried to interest Kenneth Littauer at *Collier's* in his new novel; in the middle of July he had suggested that in return for an advance of $750 Littauer could have first look at the novel plus a specified number of short stories. Littauer did not respond, so at the end of September 1939, he sent both Perkins and Littauer a long and detailed synopsis of the entire novel hoping that this would be good enough to persuade the *Collier's* editor to come to an agreement at this stage over serial rights. Fitzgerald was now of course acting as his own agent – Ober was to have no part in these negotiations and Fitzgerald even told Perkins he didn't want him 'to know *anything about the subject of the novel*' (FP, 258). This time Littauer was interested but still cautious; he was unwilling to agree to an advance on the basis of the outline alone. His suggestion was that Fitzgerald send him the opening section – or about fifteen thousand words; assuming he was satisfied with what he read he would advance Fitzgerald $5000 with another $5000 to come on submission of the next twenty thousand words. Fitzgerald calculated that Littauer wanted to acquire the serial rights for $15,000 in total. He told Perkins that this was just not enough:

> But (without taking such steps as reneging on my income tax, letting go my life insurance for its surrender value, taking Scottie from college and putting Zelda in a public asylum) I couldn't last four months on that. (FP, 258)

He felt that *Collier's* should have been prepared to pay at least $20,000 for such a serial. On 2 November Littauer agreed to make a final decision on the basis of the six thousand word opening section. Fitzgerald then sent both Perkins and Littauer the opening chapter; Littauer found it 'pretty cryptic' and decided against making an advance. Fitzgerald's reaction was a wire reading: 'No hard feelings. There has never been an editor with pants on since George Lorimer' (C, 561–2). Perkins, on the other hand, was enthusiastic; his wire, on 29 November, read: 'A beautiful start. Stirring and new' (FP, 259). His follow-up letter the next day was in much the same vein:

> I thought the book had the magic that you can put into things. The whole transcontinental business, which is so strong and new to people like me, and to most people, was marvellously suggested.... It was all admirable, or else I am no judge any more ... I can believe that you may really get at the heart of Hollywood, and of what there is wonderful in it as well as all the rest. (FP, 259)

Even more to the point, Perkins was willing to back his judgement with his own money; he was prepared to send Fitzgerald a thousand dollars – from a small bequest he had received – to allow him to get on with the novel. Fitzgerald replied that this loan 'was the kindest thing I have ever heard of' (FP, 260).

Maxwell Perkins's highly positive response to the opening of *The Last Tycoon* gave Fitzgerald an enormous psychological boost. He could still be a winner. Frances Kroll records that he was a man transformed: 'The contrast was extraordinary – like watching an athlete who had let himself go to fat decide that he was going to make a comeback.'[3] But even with the unexpected bonus of Perkins's thousand dollars, Fitzgerald was finding it difficult to finance the writing of *The Last Tycoon*. With the failure of the hoped-for serialization in *Collier's*, Fitzgerald asked Perkins to approach the *Saturday Evening Post*. Its response too was negative – the material was too strong for its readership. Fitzgerald's next thought was to approach a Hollywood agent who might be able to persuade a studio to finance the writing of what would become a picture; but this idea too got nowhere. At this point, towards the end of 1939, Fitzgerald was forced to recognize that his only remaining source of income was what he described to Perkins as 'this unprofitable hacking for Esquire' (FP, 260). Arnold Gingrich was still prepared to use almost everything Fitzgerald sent him, but his price remained a mere $250 per item. 'Design in Plaster', subsequently published in *The Best Short Stories 1940* volume, drawing on Fitzgerald's experience of wearing a cast on his shoulder in North Carolina in 1936, appeared in the November 1939 issue, and 'The Lost Decade' in the December one. At this point, however, Fitzgerald finally did what he had attempted but failed to do several times since the success of the Basil Lee and Josephine stories years earlier: he created a character who could become the protagonist of a series of stories. In January 1940, *Esquire* published 'Pat Hobby's Christmas Wish', the first of what would be seventeen Pat Hobby stories appearing in *Esquire* throughout 1940 and continuing, after Fitzgerald's death, into the first half of 1941.

The Pat Hobby stories are short and often seemingly inconsequential. And no doubt it is possible to exaggerate their importance. But Fitzgerald himself approached them with professional seriousness, and wrote regularly to Arnold Gingrich on matters related to their publication. He was much concerned about the order in which the series should appear, and frequently sent Gingrich lists of revisions and corrections. He was pleased when an actor suggested that some kind of theatrical performance could be made out of the material, and he allowed Frances Kroll's brother to attempt to dramatize the stories. What is of greatest significance, however, is the kind of character he created in Pat Hobby. Fitzgerald's attitude towards both his film and literary career in the final Hollywood years is, I believe, not wholly unrelated to the 'writer only' figure he proclaimed he had become at the end of the 'Crack-Up' articles. Despite the occasional drunken binges, he was in these years on the whole more purposeful, better organized, and generally more professional. On the other hand, unlike the projected 'Crack-Up' writer, he did not cease to be a man who was 'kind, just or generous'. Had he done so, presumably he would have had no hesitation in removing Scottie from Vassar and sending Zelda to a public asylum. What he did do was, as it were, to siphon off the impulse towards the coldly professional, dehumanized artist figure, signalled with whatever protective layer of bitterness and cynicism at the end of the *The Crack-Up*, into the darkly comic figure of Pat Hobby. The Hobby stories are sardonic, cynical, and mordantly amusing. Pat Hobby himself, who once in the 1920s owned a house in Hollywood with a swimming-pool, is a failed screenwriter, a has-been, a loser. He is seedy, broke, ready and willing to exploit any situation or any person in his struggle for survival; he has no scruples and no morals. Through his protagonist's encounters with producers, directors, screenwriters and actors, Fitzgerald is able to evoke a Hollywood utterly devoid of glamour and beauty. This is a Hollywood that does not appear in *The Last Tycoon* – though Fitzgerald's notion of perhaps having a failed actor mistakenly invited to be a pall-bearer at Monroe Stahr's funeral at the novel's end – and having his career resurrected as a result – does have a touch of the Pat Hobby about it. Hobby himself experiences no such resurrection, and such reader sympathy as he evokes largely depends on the sense that none of his scheming is going to succeed. Fitzgerald was perfectly clear about the kind of character he had created in these brief stories. Commenting to Gingrich on 'Pat Hobby's Christmas Wish' he wrote:

it characterizes him in a rather less sympathetic way than most of the others. Of course, he's a complete rat but it seems to make him a little sinister which he essentially is not. (C, 568)

Fitzgerald is right: Pat Hobby does not have enough weight to be sinister. When Frances Kroll's brother was attempting to dramatize the Hobby series, Fitzgerald again indicated the limits of Hobby's nastiness:

> … the series is characterized by a really bitter humor and only the explosive situations and the fact that Pat is a figure almost incapable of real tragedy or damage saves it from downright unpleasantness. (C, 595)

On the other hand, Pat Hobby is unquestionably a man for whom the notion of being 'kind, just or generous' has no reality whatsoever; a totally amoral self-interest has replaced any kind of concern for others. Perhaps the creation of such an unappealing figure did much more for Fitzgerald than earn him the money to allow him to write *The Last Tycoon*: only by successfully imagining what it would be like to cease to be a man of kindness, justness and generosity could Fitzgerald fully recover from his crack-up and return in *The Last Tycoon* to the world of the generous and compassionate imagination.

IV

Fitzgerald approached the writing of *The Last Tycoon* in a frame of mind not unlike that in which he had undertaken the writing of *The Great Gatsby*. Then he had been determined to prove that those patronizing critics who had regarded him as no more than a popular, lightweight entertainer were wrong: he would show that he was a serious artist, the leading figure in a new generation of American writers. Now he would restore a lost reputation; his new novel would make it impossible for him to be written off, and he would regain his position in the forefront of American letters. As he wrote in his Notebook:

> I want to write scenes that are frightening and inimitable. I don't

want to be as intelligible to my contemporaries as Ernest who as Gertrude Stein said, is bound for the Museums. I am sure that I am far enough ahead to have some small immortality if I can keep well.[4]

To confirm or even enlarge that claim to 'some small immortality' was his aim in the writing of *The Last Tycoon*.

As has already been noted, Fitzgerald in this period was obsessed with the idea that he was a forgotten man. In a melancholy letter to Perkins in May 1940, he regrets the loss both of friends – Hemingway, John Peale Bishop, Ober – and of his literary reputation. A little earlier he had told Zelda that *The Great Gatsby* had had to be taken out of the Modern Library series because it didn't sell. Now he again asks Perkins about the possibility of a cheap edition of the novel:

> Would a popular reissue in that series [he means the American Mercury twenty-five cent editions] with a preface *not* by me but by one of its admirers – I can maybe pick one – make it a favorite with classrooms, profs, lovers of English prose – anybody.

The irony of this – given what would happen to *Gatsby* within a few years of its author's death – is overwhelming. But writing this letter, Fitzgerald could only anticipate a very different fate for himself and his work:

> But to die, so completely and unjustly after having given so much. Even now there is little published in American fiction that doesn't slightly bear my stamp – in a *small* way I was an original.

Nevertheless, the deep despondency present here was not really characteristic of Fitzgerald in 1940, and at bottom he recognized that the answer to the problem of his lost reputation lay not in the reissue of his earlier books but in the production of a major new novel. That was exactly what he intended *The Last Tycoon* to be, and however depressed he felt, he insisted to Perkins: 'people will *buy* my new book ...' (FP, 261).

As early as October 1939, Fitzgerald had written to Scottie expressing his confidence in his new project:

I have begun to write something that is maybe great, and I'm going to be absorbed in it four or six months. It may not *make* us a cent but it will pay expenses and it is the first labor of love I've undertaken since the first part of *Infidelity*. (L, 77)

Strangely, in his many subsequent letters to Scottie, Fitzgerald never mentions progress on *The Last Tycoon*: given his obsession with keeping the subject of his new novel secret, he may have felt that any information passed on to her would soon be made known to others. Better then to tell her nothing. To Zelda, on the other hand, he was much more forthcoming.

Even in 1940, however, not all of Fitzgerald's energies were devoted to writing *The Last Tycoon*. In the first half of the year he wrote Pat Hobby stories, worked on the screenplay of 'Babylon Revisited,' wrote 'Last Kiss', a Hollywood story declined by *Collier's* and *Cosmopolitan*, 'Director's Special' (unpublished), and 'Dearly Beloved', a short sketch declined by *Esquire*. But in the second half of 1940 almost all of Fitzgerald's creative energies went into *The Last Tycoon*.

Five outline plans of *The Last Tycoon* survive in Fitzgerald's papers. All indicate that Fitzgerald's intention was to write a 'selective', 'dramatic' *Gatsby*-style and length novel, divided, like *Gatsby*, into nine chapters. The last surviving draft consists of some 44,000 words taking the story as far as the opening of Chapter Six. In terms of his plot outline, however, Fitzgerald was little more than halfway through the story, so it is improbable that *The Last Tycoon* could in the end have rivalled *Gatsby's* 50,000 word economy. Matthew Bruccoli is certainly also right to insist that none of the chapters is finished in the sense that they might not have undergone further revision by Fitzgerald. The account of these final months provided by Frances Kroll clarifies what Fitzgerald meant by 'blocking out' the novel; he started simply with series of notes; the notes were then sorted out into chapters; brief biographies of the characters were added; then the chapter notes were expanded into chapter outlines, and finally into drafts of roughly written chapters.[5] Using this method of composition Fitzgerald's progress was not determined by simple narrative chronology. Writing to Zelda in October 1940, Fitzgerald told her he was working hard on the novel, hoping to finish it by the middle of December: 'I think of nothing else' he wrote, and described his room as covered with charts as it used to be for *Tender is the Night*, telling the different movements of the characters and their histories. However, this one is to be short, as I originally planned it two years ago, and more on the order of *Gatsby*. (L, 145)

A few days later he reported 'I am deep in the novel, living in it, and it makes me happy'. Once again the comparison is made with *Gatsby*:

It is a *constructed* novel like *Gatsby*, with passages of poetic prose when it fits the action, but no ruminations or side-shows like *Tender*. Everything must contribute to the dramatic movement ... Two thousand words today and all good. (L, 146)

But Zelda was not the only recipient of news about the novel. A little earlier, in September, Fitzgerald had reported progress to Gerald Murphy: 'I have a novel pretty well on the road.' And he goes on to suggest something of its quality: 'I think it will baffle and in some ways irritate what readers I have left. But it is as detached from me as *Gatsby* was, in intent anyhow' (L, 450). What this comment implies is that Fitzgerald had recognized that part at least of the reason for the interminable delays over finishing *Tender is the Night* was his own over-involvement in the material he was writing about. To get away from such damaging personal over-engagement with his subjects was of course Fitzgerald's declared aim at the end of the 'Crack-Up' articles. In *The Last Tycoon* the change is signalled in formal terms by the return of a *Gatsby*-style narrator – Cecilia Brady is both inside and outside the story she is telling – as well as by the objective emotional honesty with which the relationships between the characters are presented and analysed.

Progress with the novel was not always as straightforward as the October letters to Zelda suggest. At the beginning of November Fitzgerald reported to her:

The novel is hard as pulling teeth but that is because it is in its character-planting phase. I feel people so less intently than I did once that this is harder. It means welding together hundreds of stray impressions and incidents to form the fabric of entire personalities. But later it should go faster. (L, 147)

(The hint here of how Fitzgerald used his extensive notes as a way into the creation of individual characters is worth noting.) A letter written a week later indicates steady progress at least: 'I'm still absorbed in the novel which is growing under my hand – not as deft a hand as I'd like – but growing' (L, 148). Then on 23 November, Fitzgerald graphically described for Zelda the kind of novel he was writing:

> It will, at any rate, be nothing like anything else as I'm digging it out of myself like uranium – one ounce to the cubic ton of rejected ideas. It is a novel *à la Flaubert* without 'ideas' but only people moved singly and in mass through what I hope are authentic moods.
>
> The resemblance is rather to *Gatsby* than to anything else I've written. (L, 149)

The reference to Flaubert suggests a focus on stylistic accuracy and precision, while the rejection of 'ideas' in an abstract sense, as opposed to the exploration of mood and emotion, shows how well Fitzgerald now understood where his strengths as an imaginative writer lay. There will be no sententious philosophizing in *The Last Tycoon* – only the authenticities of feeling. For one more time Fitzgerald seems to be subscribing wholeheartedly to the Conradian aesthetic of *The Nigger of the Narcissus* Preface. In October he had written to Edmund Wilson expressing admiration for *To The Finland Station*, objecting to hostile reviews by Clifton Fadiman and Malcolm Cowley, and adding as a postscript: 'Am somewhere in a novel' (L, 369). A day or two after the Flaubert letter to Zelda, he wrote to Wilson again, this time being less cryptic about his novel, and repeating the point about his commitment to a heightened degree of emotional honesty:

> I think my novel is good. I've written it with difficulty. It is completely upstream in mood and will get a certain amount of abuse but is first hand and I am trying a little harder than I ever have to be exact and honest emotionally. (L, 369)

At the end of November 1940, Fitzgerald suffered his first heart attack and was ordered to rest in bed. What concerned him most was the possible impact on his writing. On 6 December, he wrote to Zelda: 'No news except that the novel progresses and I am angry that this little illness has slowed me up' (L, 149). But even in bed he continued to write. Zelda was given a progress report on 13 December: 'The novel is about three-quarters through and I think I can go on till January 12 without doing any stories or going back to the studio' (L, 150). That same day he wrote to Maxwell Perkins confirming that he now intended to go ahead and complete a first draft:

> The novel progresses – in fact progresses fast. I'm not going to stop now till I finish a first draft which will be some time after the 15th of January. (FP, 268)

Next day, 14 December, Fitzgerald prepared a schedule, with a 15 January deadline for completing that first draft, which involved a daily output of 1750 words. On 20 December he worked on episode seventeen in Chapter Six of the novel – the meeting between Monroe Stahr and Brimmer, the trade union organizer. However the following day, 21 December 1940, Fitzgerald suffered his second and fatal heart attack. He was forty-four years old.

Fitzgerald's earnings in 1940 were $14,570 from film-work and stories. At the time of his death his debts amounted to just under $12,000: almost five and a half thousand to Scribners, just over four thousand to Highland Hospital, Asheville, North Carolina, where Zelda was being treated, around fifteen hundred to Perkins, and just under a thousand to Ober. These debts were met out of his life insurance.

In addition to his life insurance, and a small sum in his bank account, Fitzgerald's assets included his copyrights and manuscripts. His book royalties having declined to almost nothing, his copyrights were treated as of little value, but the State of California valued his remaining manuscripts at $6000. From the first Zelda was sure that the unfinished *Last Tycoon* should be published: 'Scott cared so deeply about his work,' she wrote to Perkins, 'and would so have liked to reach his public again ...'[6] Having received a typed copy of the original of the incomplete novel from Sheilah Graham, Perkins quickly agreed that the material should be published in some form. His first thought was to have the novel completed by another writer working from the plot outlines Fitzgerald had produced. Two of the younger writers Fitzgerald had got to know well in the Hollywood years were approached – but both John O'Hara and Budd Schulberg declined the task. Apparently Perkins even entertained the idea of approaching Hemingway, but Zelda unsurprisingly vetoed any such notion; she suggested Gilbert Seldes who had always been an admirer of Fitzgerald's work.

By the end of January 1941, however, Perkins had decided that the best thing to do was to publish *The Last Tycoon* in its unfinished state. The more carefully he read the text, clearly the more impressed he became. Telling Sheilah Graham he still had not made up his mind about the best format for its publication, he went on:

> All I know is that it promised to be the most completely mature, and rich, and in a deep sense the most brilliant book he ever did. I think Stahr, though incomplete, is his best character.... It would break a man's heart to see what this book would have been, and that it wasn't finished.[7]

After further consultations with Gilbert Seldes, who had also read the unfinished novel, Perkins wrote to John Biggs, Fitzgerald's legal executor, telling him that they were agreed that the incomplete *Last Tycoon* should be published:

> The unfinished book is most interesting. It is a tragedy it is unfinished. It was a clear step forward. I don't say that it was better in actual writing itself, or even that it would have been than *The Great Gatsby*. But it has the same old magic that Scott got into a sentence, or a paragraph, or a phrase. It has a kind of wisdom in it, and nobody ever penetrated beneath the surface of the movie world to any such degree. It was to have been a very remarkable book.... it ought somehow to be published for the sake of Scott's name.[8]

Soon Edmund Wilson agreed to edit *The Last Tycoon* but his initial proposal was that the new Fitzgerald volume should include the 'Crack-Up' articles and the Pat Hobby stories as well as the incomplete novel. This time it was Maxwell Perkins who disagreed. As a result, what Scribners finally published on 27 October 1941, was a volume comprising *The Great Gatsby*, five of Fitzgerald's best stories – 'May Day', 'The Diamond as Big as the Ritz', 'The Rich Boy', 'Absolution', and 'Crazy Sunday' – and *The Last Tycoon*. The book received favourable reviews and sold slowly but steadily; it was reprinted in 1941, 1945, 1947 and 1948. Within a year or two, the literary revival that would restore his reputation to a level beyond Fitzgerald's most fabulous dreams was well under way. In 1981 Matthew Bruccoli calculated that Scribners' total sales of Fitzgerald's work amounted to some eight million copies. Twenty years on, the total number of books sold by Fitzgerald's publishers worldwide must amount to double that number.

V

After all the problems and difficulties, the emotional and psycho-logical struggles, the loss of confidence and sense of failure of the 'Crack-Up' years, Fitzgerald's final period of at least relative calm and security in Hollywood often gave him the opportunity to reflect with some degree of objectivity on his past life and experi-ence, including his literary career and what he had learned from it. Something of what he had learned went into his relationship with Sheilah Graham and in particular into his plans for her instruction and education detailed in her memoir *College of One*. Fitzgerald drew up what amounted to a two-year college degree course in the arts and humanities to compensate for Sheilah's lack of formal education. The lengthy booklists and tutorial-style discussions indi-cate the seriousness with which Fitzgerald undertook this task. But it was to his daughter Scottie, now a young woman of college age, that he passed on most of his hard-earned understanding of the nature of life and experience and the role of art and literature within them. Fitzgerald's letters to Scottie, that is, sometimes read like a running commentary on his own literary life. Scottie was beginning to develop an interest in writing herself and as a result her father's letters often contain advice on literary style, on what she should read, and how she should avoid repeating his mistakes.[9] In July 1940, for example, Fitzgerald told her: 'A good style simply doesn't form unless you absorb half a dozen top-flight authors every year' (L, 102). A letter written a month later contained a long para-graph about Keats's brilliance as a poet: works such as the Grecian

Urn and Nightingale odes, St. Agnes Eve, and the sonnet 'Bright Star' were recommended as poetic touchstones (L, 104).

Even more revealing are letters in which Fitzgerald touches on themes that had clearly come to preoccupy him from at least the period of the finishing of *Tender is the Night*, including the theme of his own career as a writer. A letter of April 1939, glosses the decade-old idea of emotional bankruptcy:

> Our danger is imagining that we have resources – material and moral – which we haven't got. One of the reasons I find myself so consistently in valleys of depression is that every few years I seem to be climbing uphill to recover from some bankruptcy. Do you know what bankruptcy exactly means? It means drawing on resources which one does not possess. (L, 70)

Almost exactly a year later, when the writing of *The Last Tycoon* was about to get under way, Fitzgerald returned to the idea that writing involves a using up of the self: 'Often I think writing is a sheer paring away of oneself leaving always something thinner, barer, more meager' (L, 86). When Scottie became the co-author of a musical show at Vassar, Fitzgerald, recalling his own work for the Triangle Club at Princeton, reminisced interestingly on his own reasons for not pursuing a career in the musical theatre:

> Again let me repeat that if you start any kind of a career follow-ing the footsteps of Cole Porter and Rodgers and Hart, it might be an excellent try. Sometimes I wish I had gone along with that gang, but I guess I am too much a moralist at heart and really want to preach at people in some acceptable form rather than to entertain them. (L, 78–9)

A recurring theme in these letters is the emphasis Fitzgerald places on the discipline of work. He takes the closest interest in Scottie's progress at Vassar, writing about what courses she should – or should not – take, complaining about her grades, and returning endlessly to the absolute necessity of her making whatever effort or commitment is required. Scottie is to be a deserving beneficiary of her father's youthful mistakes. It is in this context of Scottie's studies that Fitzgerald made the statement, already referred to, about how his own accomplishments had come only from 'the most laborious and uphill work', and about how much he regretted having failed in his duty to make the necessary commitment to his writing after the success of *Gatsby*. Still more crucial is the July 1938 letter – also already referred to – in which Fitzgerald explained to Scottie that the reason for his failure to do the work demanded of him was his marriage to her mother. After his marriage he says he became a man divided, and there is no question that the division he is pointing to is that between his life as a writer and his life as a husband and lover. Married to Zelda, writes Fitzgerald, 'I was a man divided – she wanted me to work too much for *her* and not enough for my dream.' By the time that Zelda herself realized that work was dignity – the only dignity – it was too late: she 'tried to atone for it by working herself, but it was too late and she broke and is broken forever'. Furthermore:

> It was too late also for me to recoup the damage – I had spent most of my resources, spiritual and material, on her, but I struggled on for five years till my health collapsed, and all I cared about was drink and forgetting.
> The mistake I made was in marrying her. (L, 47)

This letter may readily be seen as containing the fullest account Fitzgerald ever provided of his own view of the course of his literary career. One may only speculate on what Scottie must have felt when she read that her father should never have married her mother – and where that left her. And it is certainly true that Fitzgerald here is collapsing history, failing to acknowledge the seriousness of his drinking problem – and its damaging impact on his marriage – in the years well before Zelda's initial breakdown. Nor is there here even a hint of guilt over his harsh treatment of Zelda and her writing in the months before the completion of *Tender is the Night*. But even if there is an element of self-pity in Fitzgerald's account, a blaming of Zelda for his own weaknesses and failures, and a refusing of responsibility for the choices he made, at bottom the outline of Fitzgerald's literary life provided by this letter is an accurate one. Fitzgerald was in truth a divided man. His life as a writer and his life as a man did pull in opposite directions. As it happens this division within Fitzgerald's art and life was recognized by some of his earliest commentators and biographers. Thus Malcolm Cowley returned regularly to the idea that Fitzgerald was possessed of what he chose to call 'double vision': simultaneously observer and participant, both deeply immersed in life and detached from it. In *The Far Side of Paradise* Arthur Mizener identified the same division by describing Fitzgerald as at once 'the romantic young man' and 'the spoiled priest'; the romantic young man 'wanted to participate in life and took delight in spending himself and his money without counting the cost ...' but the spoiled priest 'shocked by debt and fearing the spiritual exhaustion Fitzgerald was later to call "Emotional Bankruptcy," wanted to stand aside and study life.'[10]

It is my view that in the early part of his literary career Fitzgerald more or less succeeded in combining his total personal involvement in life with the detachment of the artist-observer. But as the years passed, this juggling act became increasingly difficult to perform. By the end of the 1920s the plates are falling off their sticks, and as a result Fitzgerald's literary career is going nowhere. During the crack-up years of the mid-1930s he is compelled to admit that he no longer has the resources even to try to get in on the old act – hence the inevitability of the decision to begin over as a 'writer only'.

In the Hollywood years, with their changed circumstances, Fitzgerald was able to regain at least a measure of stability and as a result, carefully husbanding his resources, *The Last Tycoon* could begin to be written. But the writer of *The Last Tycoon* was in no danger of forgetting the lessons of the immediately preceding years. Few people, he reminds Scottie, have the time to form what he calls 'the wise and tragic sense of life'. The sense, that is

> that life is essentially a cheat and its conditions are those of defeat, and that the redeeming things are not 'happiness and pleasure' but the deeper satisfactions that come out of struggle. (L, 112)

Fitzgerald's literary life, from its early promise and quick success through to its sombre conclusion, was characterized much more by struggle than by happiness and pleasure. Happiness and pleasure, however intense, proved fleeting; struggle remained an enduring reality. Nevertheless, from time to time Fitzgerald did find the deeper satisfaction of creative success: certainly with *The Great Gatsby*, probably with the completion of *Tender is the Night*, and perhaps with the progress made with *The Last Tycoon*. Among Fitzgerald's notes for *The Last Tycoon* is this meditation on the meaning of America and its history:

> I look out at it – and I think it is the most beautiful history in the world. It is the history of me and of my people. And if I came here yesterday like Sheilah I should still think so. It is the history of all aspiration – not just the American dream but the human dream and if I came at the end of it that too is a place in the line of pioneers.[11]

What is most moving here is the elegiac sense of beginnings and endings, echoing the mood of the unforgettable closing sentences of *The Great Gatsby*, and inevitably reinforced by one's knowledge of just how close the end of Fitzgerald's own life was looming. But for all the many ironies and struggles of his life, including his literary life, in his art Fitzgerald achieved more than enough to guarantee him 'some small immortality' at least.

Notes

1 Becoming a Writer

1. F. Scott Fitzgerald, *Afternoon of an Author*, New York, 1957, pp. 135–6.
2. See M. J. Bruccoli, *Some Sort of Epic Grandeur, the Life of F. Scott Fitzgerald*, New York and London, 1981, p. 140.
3. *Afternoon of an Author*, p. 132. 'His antennae were already out, feeling over this new world' is a sentence from a 1929 story 'The Rough Crossing' describing the male protagonist's reaction to meeting a group of young people aboard a transatlantic liner. To me it seems admirably descriptive of the sources of Fitzgerald's writing method.
4. See 'Mrs Oscar Kalman remembers the Fitzgeralds' in M. J. Bruccoli (ed.), *Fitzgerald/Hemingway Annual*, 1976, 117–23.
5. See Bruccoli, *Some Sort of Epic Grandeur*, p. 22.
6. 'Mrs Oscar Kalman remembers the Fitzgeralds', p. 118.
7. See Bruccoli, *Some Sort of Epic Grandeur*, p. 25.
8. Edmund Wilson (ed.), *The Crack-Up*, New York, 1956, p. 76.
9. Jackson R. Bryer, John Kuehl (eds), *The Basil and Josephine Stories by F. Scott Fitzgerald*, New York, 1973, p. 75.
10. Ibid., p. 78.
11. Ibid., p. 147.
12. Ibid., p. 19.
13. Ibid., p. 85.
14. See Bruccoli, *Some Sort of Epic Grandeur*, p. 29.
15. *The Basil and Josephine Stories*, p. 119.
16. *The Crack-Up*, p. 76.
17. *Afternoon of an Author*, p. 83.
18. Ibid., pp. 185–6.
19. *The Crack-Up*, pp. 69–70.

2 Succeeding with *This Side of Paradise*

1. See Bruccoli, *Some Sort of Epic Grandeur*, New York, 1957, p. 86.
2. *Afternoon of an Author*, pp. 84–5.
3. See A. Scott Berg, 'The Man Who Discovered Fitzgerald', *Princeton Alumni Weekly*, 23 October 1978.
4. See Nancy Milford, *Zelda Fitzgerald*, Harmondsworth, 1974, p. 52.
5. *The Crack-Up*, p. 26.
6. A. Scott Berg, 'The Man Who Discovered Fitzgerald'.
7. *The Crack-Up*, p. 86.
8. See Bruccoli, *Some Sort of Epic Grandeur*, p. 120.

9. Ibid., p. 120.
10. F. Scott Fitzgerald, *This Side of Paradise*, Harmondsworth, 1963, p. 178.
11. Ibid., p. 195.
12. Ibid., p. 244.

3 Locating *The Beautiful and Damned*

1. See Bruccoli, *Some Sort of Epic Grandeur*, p. 122.
2. See D. B. Good, '"A Romance and a Reading List": The Literary References in *This Side of Paradise'*, *Fitzgerald/Hemingway Annual*, 1976, 35–64.
3. The best exploration of Fitzgerald's Irish-Catholic background remains Owen Dudley Edwards's 'The Lost Teigueen: F. Scott Fitzgerald's Ethics and Ethnicity' in A. Robert Lee (ed.), *Scott Fitzgerald: The Promises of Life*, London and New York, 1989, pp. 181–214.
4. See Bruccoli, *Some Sort of Epic Grandeur*, pp. 165–6.
5. Ibid., pp. 163–4.
6. Edmund Wilson's article is reprinted in Arthur Mizener (ed.), *F. Scott Fitzgerald: A Collection of Critical Essays*, Englewood Cliffs, New Jersey, 1963, pp. 80–5.

4 Writing *The Great Gatsby*

1. In fact Fitzgerald seems to have been changing his mind by the middle of 1923. Reviewing Thomas Boyd's World War I novel *Through the Wheat* in May of that year, he wrote: 'No one has a greater contempt than I have for the recent hysteria about the Nordic theory...' (See M. J. Bruccoli, ed., *F. Scott Fitzgerald on Authorship*, Columbia, 1996, p. 88.) And certainly by the 1930s his views on race had come full circle. According to Tony Buttitta, who knew Fitzgerald in North Carolina in the summer of 1935, his reaction on hearing Buttitta's name was: 'Sounds Italian. I hated Italians once. Jews too. Most foreigners. Mostly my fault like everything else. Now I only hate myself.' (See Tony Buttitta, *After the Good Gay Times*, New York, 1974, p. 5.)
2. See Bruccoli, *Some Sort of Epic Grandeur*, p. 169.
3. See Fitzgerald, *Afternoon of an Author*, p. 93.
4. See Bruccoli, *Some Sort of Epic Grandeur*, p. 162.
5. *Afternoon of an Author*, p. 91.
6. Ibid, p. 95.
7. See Bruccoli, *Some Sort of Epic Grandeur*, p. 178.
8. See Bruccoli, *F. Scott Fitzgerald on Authorship*, p. 87.
9. See Bruccoli, *Some Sort of Epic Grandeur*, p. 170.
10. Ibid., p. 392.
11. Ibid., p. 199.
12. See *The Crack-Up*, p. 176.
13. However, the Scottish colourist J. D. Fergusson and his wife, the dancer

Margaret Morris, also contributed to this change in fashionable life-style.

5 Trailing *Tender is the Night*

1. Bruccoli, *Some Sort of Epic Grandeur*, p. 227.
2. *The Crack-Up*, p. 47.
3. See Bruccoli, *Some Sort of Epic Grandeur*, p. 263.
4. Carlos Baker (ed.), *Ernest Hemingway Selected Letters 1917–1961*, London, 1981, pp. 306–7.
5. *The Crack-Up*, p. 51.
6. See Bruccoli, *Some Sort of Epic Grandeur*, pp. 335–7.
7. Ibid., p. 341.
8. *Afternoon of an Author*, p. 132.
9. See Bruccoli, *Some Sort of Epic Grandeur*, p. 370.
10. Ibid., p. 378.
11. *Hemingway Selected Letters*, p. 483.
12. On December 31, 1935, after the unexpected death of his son Baoth, and knowing that Patrick, his other son, was fatally ill with tuberculosis, Gerald Murphy wrote to Fitzgerald: 'Sara's courage and the unbelievable job she is doing for Patrick make unbearably poignant the tragedy of what has happened – what life has tried to do to her. I know now that what you said in "Tender is the Night" was true. Only the invented part of our life, – the unreal part – has had any scheme any beauty. Life itself has stepped in now and blundered, scarred and destroyed.' (See Amanda Vaill, *Everybody Was So Young, Gerald and Sara Murphy – A Lost Generation Love Story*, New York, 1998, p. 270.)
13. F. Scott Fitzgerald, *Tender is the Night*, Harmondsworth, 1985, p. 207.

6 Experiencing *The Crack-Up*

1. See Buttitta, *After the Good Gay Times*, p. 80.
2. André le Vot, *F. Scott Fitzgerald: A Biography*, New York, 1983, p. 269.
3. *Afternoon of an Author*, p. 182.
4. See Bruccoli, *Some Sort of Epic Grandeur*, p. 405.
5. Ernest Hemingway, *True at First Light*, New York, 1999, pp. 171–3.
6. *The Crack-Up*, p. 67.
7. Most of this draft letter is cited by Bruccoli in *Some Sort of Epic Grandeur*, pp. 346–7. The original is in the F. Scott Fitzgerald Papers in the Manuscripts Division, Department of Rare Books and Special Collections, Princeton University Library.
8. Ibid, pp. 348–53. However, the extracts quoted by Bruccoli do not include all the passages I have cited. The complete transcript is contained in the Craig House Records in the Manuscripts Division, Department of Rare Books and Special Collections, Princeton University Library.

9. *The Crack-Up*, pp. 81–3.
10. See Peter D. Kramer, 'How Crazy was Zelda?', *New York Times Magazine*, 1 December 1996, p. 108.
11. See Eleanor Lanahan, *Scottie: The Daughter of . . . The Life of Frances Scott Fitzgerald*, New York, 1995, pp. 64–5.
12. *Afternoon of an Author*, p. 188.
13. See Bruccoli, *Some Sort of Epic Grandeur*, pp. 353–5.
14. *Afternoon of an Author*, pp. 140–1.
15. Ibid., p. 132.
16. Ibid., p. 131.

7 Leaving *The Last Tycoon*

1. Frances Kroll Ring, *Against the Current: As I Remember F. Scott Fitzgerald*, Berkeley, 1987, p. 99.
2. Ibid., p. 23.
3. Ibid., p. 47.
4. See Bruccoli, *Some Sort of Epic Grandeur*, p. 488.
5. Frances Kroll Ring, *Against the Current*, pp. 47–8.
6. See A. Scott Berg, *Max Perkins, Editor of Genius*, New York, 1978, pp. 389–90.
7. Ibid., p. 393.
8. Ibid., p. 394.
9. However, as T. P. Roche has pointed out, on at least one occasion Fitzgerald came close to repeating a past mistake. When Scottie published an article on modern youth in *Mademoiselle* Fitzgerald chastised her in terms inevitably reminiscent of the old dispute over Zelda's writing. See Thomas P. Roche, Jr., 'The Children of Legend, A Reading of *Scottie: The Daughter of. . .*', *Princeton University Library Chronicle*, LVII (Winter 1996), 270.
10. Arthur Mizener, *The Far Side of Paradise*, Boston, 1951, p. 60.
11. See Bruccoli, *Some Sort of Epic Grandeur*, p. 493.

Index